THE

Spanish

Adventures

OF
WASHINGTON
IRVING

BOOKS BY CLAUDE G. BOWERS

WASHINGTON IRVING
Bust by Daniel Chester French

THE *Spanish Adventures* OF WASHINGTON IRVING

CLAUDE G. BOWERS

19 40

ILLUSTRATED

HOUGHTON MIFFLIN COMPANY · BOSTON

The Riverside Press Cambridge

The Riverside Press
CAMBRIDGE · MASSACHUSETTS
PRINTED IN THE U.S.A.

CONTENTS

Wilkie to a bullfight — By diligence to the Escorial with Wilkie and Dolgorouki — Queen in residence — Viewing Escorial by moonlight — Sees Queen at her devotions — Freedom of the palace — El Greco ignored — A journey to Toledo — The palace and gardens at Aranjuez — Cloistered quiet — Moonlight rambles in narrow streets — Tinkling guitars on screened balconies — The Cathedral — The Alcazar — Views paintings — Driving mules through the rain.

Chapter III: ANDALUSIAN JOURNEY   49

Irving pursued by malice — Overwork — Nervous trouble — Discovers writing history not easy — Trouble with copyists — Finishes the 'Columbus' — Three thousand guineas — Work on 'Conquest of Granada' — Starts on Andalusian journey — The interest of Antoinette — A diligence to Cordoba — La Mancha evokes no thrills — Posada at Manzanares — Uninterested in Valdepeñas — Sinister repute of the Sierra Morena Mountains — Rugged beauty and danger — La Carolina — Oranges, aloes, and myrtle — A night at Andujar — Where Andalusia begins — Moonlight river ramble — Cordoba — Granada — Irving's thrills — Spring beauty — Fascination of the Alhambra — Meditations in Court of the Lions — A letter to Antoinette — Irving discovers the gate of Boabdil — The search — Chats with the beggars of the Alhambra — Idea of the 'Tales' born — Adventurous mountain journey to Malaga — Sinister muleteers — Meals in the open air — A suspicious acquaintance — Roadside crosses marked site of murders — Village of Cadiar — Spanish hospitality — Armed guards through the mountains — The charms of Malaga — The mountain road to Gibraltar — Dinner with Sprague, American Consul — The mountain road to Cadiz — Nightingales and flowers — Beauty of Cadiz — Meets Burton, the American Consul — Beauty of the women — Irving forgets his passport — A long-lost request of the Consul — A river journey to Seville.

Chapter IV: ANDALUSIAN DAYS   67

Irving's forgotten Sevillian days — Delighted with the city — Wilkie's hotel — With Wilkie in pursuit of Murillos and Zurbarans — The Williams collection — Palace of Medinaceli — Wilkie sketches Irving — Bravo's collection — Church of La Caridad — Walks with Wilkie — Dinner with 'Widow Merry' — Her American background — Irving's lodging in Santa Cruz section — Wilkie departs — Russian friends arrive — Bullfights — The fair at Mayrena — The dusty journey — Country scenes — Watching the procession pass — Work on 'Conquest of Granada' — The Cathedral library — Work in the Archives of the Indies — The building — Irving's workroom — More bullfights — Tertulias at Williams's — Climbing Giralda Tower — Irving's favorite promenade — The Alameda of Hercules, then and now — The Delicias Gardens — The cigar factory of 'Carmen' — Irving fascinated with the Cathedral — Views it by night and day — Advice to Antoinette — San Fernando's Day — A king in his coffin — Corpus Christi — Dancing on the high

Contents

altar — Another bullfight — Why do beautiful Sevillian women hide? — Marquesa del Arco Hermoso — The English colony — Sunday picnics — At Alcala de la Guadaira — After a century — The picnic baskets — At San Juan de Alfarache, then and now — A country house — John Nalden Hall — Irving seeks country release from heat — Joins Hall at Casa Cera — Its walled-in garden — Sebastian, the bad servant — Bad companions — Country rambles — Visit to Palos and Monastery of La Rabida — The living Pinzons — A patriarchal household — A wayside debate on bulls — Irving and Hall go to Port of Saint Mary's — Lodge in a saddler's house — Take 'Caracol,' a country house — A gorgeous view — Dispossessed by fever epidemic — Move to 'Cerillo' — Work on the 'Conquest' — Irving's nerves bad — Hall ill — Irving returns to Seville — Opera — Rambles — 'The Enchanted Soldier' — At palace of Medina Sidonia — Ramon Gelien — Death of Hall — Irving's experiment with ghosts — Prince Dolgorouki arrives.

Granada at sunset — Dangerous journey — Viewing ruins — A night at Arahal — Suspicious strangers — Lure of a cigar— A gasconading veteran — The landlord's daughter — Night at Osuna — A perilous mountain — Night at Antiquera — A Moorish ruin — A beggar cavalier — At Loxa — An Andalusian widow — A horseman bold — A guitar serenade — Victims of robbers — Another Gascon: his tales of blood — Irving aroused by a charivari — Day-dreaming in the Alhambra — Proffered quarters there — Tia Antonia, landlady — Irving joins her social circle — Dolores, Irving's gentle maid — 'Angel of the Alhambra' — Regal breakfasts — Mateo, 'my valet de chambre' — 'Son of the Alhambra' — Soaked in lore of the palace — 'The loquacity of a village barber' — A patriarch of the Alhambra — Irving joins the gossips — La Reina Coquina — A mine of palace lore — An impecunious scion of a hero — 'Poor as a rat, proud as he is ragged' — Irving's daily routine — Discovers Queen Elizabeth's chambers — Takes possession — Ghosts — Bats in the darkness — Irving's fright — 'Delicious abode' — Garden of Lindaraxa — A Moor's rhapsody — A gallery lookout — Irving completes the 'Conquest' — Works on 'Tales of the Alhambra' — Joins in fête of Corpus Christi — A rival appears — Count of Luque — Divides the kingdom — The daughter, Carmen — Duke of Gor — Meets him in the Alhambra — The Gor palace — The Jesuit library of the university— Irving entertains ducal family in Court of the Lions — Visits Count of Teba and bounces a future Empress on his knee — Happy days.

Irving is made Secretary of Legation in London at instance of Van Buren — Irving loath to leave Spain — Begins journey sadly — A sorry vehicle — A tough guide and guard — Sadness at the Alhambra — Dolores in tears — A silent farewell — A melancholy procession — A

night in a country castle — The dreadful roads — Skulls of robbers —
Two soldiers for protection — Sleeping on the floor — Poverty of peasants — At Barcelona — Guest of Conde de España — A picturesque
character — A wicked reputation — He treats with bishops — A dramatic scene — A cruel joke — Days in England — 'Sunnybank' — John
Tyler appoints Irving Minister to Spain — The lure of Spain — A relic
of Mateo.

ILLUSTRATIONS

Nothing interested me more than Irving's chivalric and paternal partiality for the child Queen, Isabella. History has been unkind to her, as were her people in her time, and we are prone to think of her as reactionary in her politics and as a bit careless in her morals. Irving was presented to this twelve-year-old Queen in the Porcelain Room of the palace in the presence of her nurse, and thereafter he followed her perils with an almost fatherly solicitude. Through his letters and dispatches it is possible to present a new and more appealing Isabella whose treatment by the old roués of dynastic politics goes far to explain, if not to justify, the conduct of her maturity.

I set out to follow the Spanish meanderings of Irving for my own pleasure, but in the end it was my intention to tell the story for the Spaniards only. Tragic events have intervened. I therefore give it to publication, without pretensions, in the hope that the friends of Irving in the United States may find some interest in a story that interested me so much.

CLAUDE G. BOWERS

SAN JEAN DE LUZ
May 14, 1939

Chapter 1: IRVING GOES TO MADRID

In FEBRUARY, 1826, a middle-aged man of distinguished mien was struggling by slow stages from the Spanish border at Irun to Madrid. Thrilled by the scenery, astonished by the strange customs of the people, he was especially enchanted with the beauty of the Basque women. Delighted, he wandered through the magical cathedral at Burgos, admiring Vigarni's superb carvings and annoyed by the cough of the ancient verger which resounded dismally through the church. At Lerma he spent the night in a hotel and sat with fellow wayfarers on a bench around a raised brick platform in the center of the room where a fire was burning, the scene illuminated by a huge lamp 'hitched to a cord.' Three others shared the room, in which he found some repose until midnight, when he rose to resume his journey, and at daybreak he rode into the historic village of Aranda de Duero. Despite some inconveniences, he was charmed with the country, so different from his native America and the English countryside he knew, or the flat lands of France.

At length he entered the gate of Madrid, weary but alert for his adventure, and found lodgings at the Fonda del Angel in the Calle Montéro. Having made his toilet, he fared forth to call upon his friend the American Minister, who lived modestly on the Carrera de Geronimo and had promised to make him an honorary attaché of his legation, with the suggestion that he translate Navarrete's 'Voyages of Columbus,' soon to appear in the bookstalls. But the Minister was not at home and Washington Irving, the traveler, returned to his cheerless room at the Fonda del Angel, where he spent the remainder of the day in his room hovering over a brazier of glowing coals.

A man of moods, given to moments of self-criticism and depression, he was not entirely happy with his fate, though life had been kind to him and he was even then the first American writer to win European recognition. He had wooed and won fame with little effort, and his whimsical sketches had been written more as a diversion than in grave earnest. He had been living in London, where he had been surrounded by a host of clever friends, poets, novelists, painters, and wits, and at Abbotsford he had been royally entertained by Sir Walter Scott on terms of equality. And then he had gone to Paris for many happy, carefree days in the company of Tom Moore. And now he had turned his back on this glamorous, easy-going existence to seek new opportunities for literary achievement in a strange land, far from his familiar companions.

But in Alexander Everett, the American Minister, he had a friend on whose partiality he could depend. The diplomat, though overshadowed by his more brilliant brother, a premier American orator of the academic school, possessed abundant merits of his own. At Harvard he had distinguished himself; when he was a student in the law office of John Quincy Adams his mentor was made Minister to Russia, and the nineteen-year-old student had accompanied him to St. Petersburg in the rôle of secretary. Thence he had passed to a secretarial position with the Legation at The Hague, and here he was Chargé d'Affaires when Adams reached the Presidency of the Republic, and appointed him Minister to Spain.

But for this appointment it is probable that the 'Tales of the Alhambra,' the 'Life of Columbus,' and 'The Conquest of Granada' never would have been written.

Everett's work in Madrid justified his selection, for though charged with the most delicate missions he so managed them that he soon possessed the confidence of both governments. It was after his return to America and the publication of his two volumes on 'America' and 'Europe,' and their translation into several languages, that he succeeded Jared Sparks in the editorial chair of the foremost American magazine. Strangely enough, in the enumeration of the literary men who have served the United States in Madrid he is seldom, if ever, mentioned. He was a man of ability and much charm of manner, but his desertion of the Whigs, in sheer disgust at their instability, brought him under the frown of those who, in his day, presumed to assign men their historic stations.

Some time before Irving's arrival in Madrid, he had approached Everett with the suggestion that he might visit Spain on a literary pilgrimage if he could be given an honorary position at the Legation to facilitate his work. The diplomat had given the assurance, and now Irving was in the Spanish capital, hovering and shivering over the brazier of a drab hotel room and entirely at sea as to his immediate future.

The next morning, Everett accompanied him to the home of Obadiah Rich, an American, named Consul at Valencia, who lived now in Madrid, where, between serving at intervals in the Legation, he pottered about through dusty book-

shops and in garrets in search of old volumes and manuscripts dealing with the Americas. On the way to the house
of the bibliographer, Irving was introduced to the Marquesa de la Casa Yrujo and her pretty daughter, Narcissa.
He knew the lady by reputation, since she was the daughter
of Governor McKean of Pennsylvania, and had been one of
the belles of Philadelphia when she married the Marques de
la Casa Yrujo, the Spanish Minister in the United States.
After all, Spain did not seem so remote. And Narcissa was
charming.

Irving was pleased with Rich and his household, and excited by his literary and historic treasures. That first day he
was permitted to see an unpublished play of Lope de Vega in
his own handwriting, and a letter of Cortez. Within a few
days he had taken a room at the home of Rich for five dollars
a week.

The next few days found him threading his way with
Everett through the narrow streets, making his calls of
courtesy on members of the diplomatic corps. The Russian
Minister was out, but in the garden of the Legation on the
Calle de Alcala he found his lady walking and reading as her
charming children played. Her 'pale but very pleasing
countenance' attracted him, and when she introduced her
niece, 'a charming young person' who 'reads English,' his
spirits rose. The relations of Irving with this niece have remained an intriguing mystery to this day. The Russian
Legation was to become his second home.

The Nuncio, the Bishop of Tyre, 'a tall, thin, pleasant
man,' delighted him with his informality and liberality.
Did he not frequent the parties of the Duchess of Benavente
and play cards on Sundays?

Within four days of his arrival in Madrid, Everett had
taken him to the interesting home of this clever woman, who,

contrary to the custom of the Spanish aristocracy, liked to
surround herself with the diplomatic corps. She lived in
luxury and had no patience with parsimony. When at a
party at the French Ambassador's the champagne ceased to
be served before the evening was over, she found a unique
way of rebuking the host. A few days later, when the Ambassador with a numerous retinue called upon her at her palace,
he was astonished on entering the court to find servants in
livery solemnly waiting to offer the horses champagne out of
large pails.[1] On another occasion at the Duchess's palace
the Ambassador held up a card game while looking for a
small coin he had dropped on the floor. In impatience and
disgust the Duchess seized a handful of large notes from the
table, and, lighting them with a match, nonchalantly
assisted in the feverish search for the peseta.[2] In the drawing-
rooms of the Duchess, Irving was ever to be a welcome guest.
Thus, within a few days he was to form the social ties that
were to bind him in Madrid during his first sojourn.

BUT he was in serious mood,
eager to get to work on something he hoped might live.
The home of Rich, bulging with rare books and manuscripts, proved an inspiration to him, as it did to Prescott,
the historian.

Even to Americans, Obadiah Rich is scarcely more than
a name, and one known only to bibliographers and students

[1] *The Attaché in Madrid*, p. 12.   [2] *Ibid.*

of Irving's life. There is no biography; and even the sketches, laboriously compiled, have failed to throw light on his personality and character. In Madrid it is as though he never had been. It seemed for a time a hopeless task to find a portrait or even a description of his appearance. And the house in which he lived in the old section near the Prado and the Alcala cannot be definitely determined, though Prescott and Irving passed hours and days within its walls, excitedly turning the yellow pages of old manuscripts and thumbing rare and precious volumes. We know that the house of Rich was large and rambling, and surrounded on three sides by a garden into which one entered from the house through windows reaching to the floor. Irving wrote that 'We have the stillness of a cloister with now and then the bell of a neighboring convent to help the illusion.' In the archives of the American Embassy in Madrid I have found some interesting revelations of Rich's life and character, and by mere chance I found his grandson, who opened two chests of family papers that contribute more.

He was born in Massachusetts of an excellent family. In early manhood he abandoned his first love, botany, for a new one, bibliography, and in his new field he attained some local distinction. It was his appointment as Consul at Valencia that changed the course of his life. Keenly interested in old manuscripts and books pertaining to the early history of the Americas, he found these could easily be obtained by a little scouting in the Spanish literary byways. Soon he was scouring the bookshops and finding much treasure. When he was summoned to Madrid to serve first as Consul and then temporarily as a Secretary of the Legation, he established a home which was a combination of residence and museum. His dispatches to Washington — and there are a number in the archives of the American Embassy today addressed to Henry

Clay — indicate no mean capacity in diplomacy. In the interval between the departure of the preceding Minister and the arrival of Everett, he was Chargé d'Affaires, and Everett appreciated the skill with which Rich inducted him into his office. 'I think it proper,' he wrote Clay, 'to mention upon this occasion that I have been quite satisfied with the manner in which Mr. Rich has performed the duties of the office of Chargé d'Affaires, and that I consider him a valuable public servant as well as an upright, industrious, and intelligent man. Should the Government ever establish at this place such employment as Consul General or agent for claims with a salary . . . Mr. Rich is the person who should by every account be invested with it.' [1]

This was written when Irving had been for two months a member of the Rich household, and it is not improbable that the author may have suggested the recommendation to his friend.

On the retirement of Everett, the bibliographer retired to his combined library, museum, and home and intensified his activities as a collector. Harmless as the pursuit now seems, it was not the most serene in those days of Ferdinand VII, when books were looked upon as potential, if not actual, enemies of Church and King. Thus Rich had not a few adventures. The customs officers along the frontier found something sinister in the passing of these mysterious volumes back and forth across the border, and Rich constantly was sending books to London and bringing them in from England. More than once this dangerous habit of his was to call for exchanges of diplomatic notes.

In the autumn of 1825 Rich was returning to Madrid from London and Paris bearing dispatches from the Ministers of the United States in England and France, and a few books.

[1] MS. Archives of the United States Embassy at Madrid, April 9, 1826.

When he reached the border village of Miranda del Ebro he was detained for three hours by the customs officers, and despite his possession of the legal attestation of his character as courtier, his dispatches were taken from him and one of them was opened. These finally were returned to him, but the books were confiscated as subversive. This, thought Everett, was 'an outrageous act.' [1] With not unnatural indignation, he made a vigorous protest to Gonzales Salmon, the Foreign Minister, declaring that the books had been 'purchased at my request and for my use.' Six days later Salmon returned the books and promised an investigation. [2] However, thought the Minister of State, the activities of Obadiah Rich were not above suspicion. Had Everett heard of the incident of two years before? 'It should be remembered,' wrote Salmon, 'that toward the middle of the year 1824 a considerable quantity of prohibited books and of illegal circulation belonging to said Mr. Rich were detained at the same place on their way from Madrid to Bilbao.'

But this did not close the incident. Everett replied with much spirit and some heat, denouncing the breaking open of the sealed dispatch, and declaring, on his own responsibility, that Rich was 'an honorable and upright citizen who has been employed in the public service of the United States.' With this reply was enclosed Obadiah Rich's own version of the affair of 1824:

> In the year 1824 I delivered to a waggoner ten cases of old books to be taken to Bilbao in order to be embarked at that place for England. These cases had been packed some months previously, and it appears that the persons employed to pack them had, unknown to me, made use of a portion of papers printed at the time of the Cortes to fill up the vacancies and to protect the bindings of the books from injury. On the arrival of the waggoners at Miranda, the boxes were

[1] MS. Archives, October 25, 1826.   [2] *Ibid.*, October 31, 1826.

OBADIAH RICH

examined, and, as I was informed at the time, a number of books in unintelligible characters, supposed to be Jewish or Masonic, were found among them, which the officer declared, as I have heard on the authority of persons present, to be deserving of being burned, together with the wagon, mules, and drivers. The work, so highly obnoxious in the eyes of this zealous officer, I found to be a Polyglot Bible. This circumstance will appear the less singular to you after what I related to you respecting the beautiful collection of prints from the statues of Canova now in your possession, which the very same officer pronounced to be scandalous in the highest degree.[1]

These books also had finally been returned, but Everett persisted in his protest until the officers offending had been severely reprimanded.[2]

Being a man of spirit and courage, not without a sense of humor, Rich did not permit his occasional brushes with the authorities to interfere with his work. From all quarters of Spain, richer than all the world beside with source material on the history of the Americas, he continued to draw precious volumes and valuable manuscripts into his house in Madrid, crowded with books and documents craved by the historians. No one writing on the early history of America or on Columbus appeared in Madrid who did not spend hours and days with the Obadiah Rich collection. In time, even the most zealous of the minor officials came to look upon him as a harmless eccentric, and one lost nothing in respectability if seen entering or leaving his house.

Rich was to continue in Spain, retaining his post as Consul, until the spring of 1828, when he abandoned his position and removed to London to open his once famous rare-book shop and to broaden his reputation as a bibliographer on the

[1] MS. Archives, February 9, 1827.
[2] Gonzales Salmon to Everett, April 7, 1828.

Americas. In 1849 he lived at 12 Red Lion Square in London. There he was by no means obscure. Among his papers long hidden away in a storage-house in New York City one finds letters from not a few famous literary figures of his time.

In 1847, during the Irish famine, the children of Boston, acting through William D. Ticknor of Ticknor and Fields, the publishers, sent articles of food and clothing for the starving children of Edgeworthstown, and for some reason Maria Edgeworth asked Rich to undertake the transmission to the Boston Samaritans of some remembrances from her to them. 'Miss Edgeworth wishes to know,' she wrote, 'whether the Mr. Rich to whom she is now writing is the gentleman mentioned by Mr. Prescott in his "History of Peru" as the great bibliographer to whom he is much indebted.' He appears to have acknowledged the identity and to have found the little stickers in the shape of hearts which she wished him to paste on each remembrance to the children. She had left him in no doubt as to what she required, for she had drawn a heart with her pen to indicate the dimensions. To show her 'appreciation and deep respect' she sent him a copy of one of her books for children:

> Aware of his high standing in antiquarian lore and historic literature from the honorable mention of him in Prescott's 'History,' she nevertheless has the audacity to send him a little story for children, her last, in the hope that he will generously accept it as a Christmas souvenir from her and as an acknowledgment of his obliging services.

Edward Everett, then American Minister to the Court of Saint James's, saw Rich frequently and freely borrowed his books, as Rich's papers show, and while wishing he 'could take advantage' of Rich's collection 'to replenish [his] library,' he could not afford it.[1]

---

[1] Letters in the possession of the Reverend Lawrence Rich.

Later Rich was to serve for a time at Port Mahon in the Balearic Islands in charge of naval stores for the American Navy, and while there he dwelt in an old deserted convent with the bones of long-dead monks in the cellar. The invitation to the marriage of his daughter Julia to Commodore Morgan, once Commander of the Navy Yard in Washington, is still in the family.

SUCH was the man who turned Irving's mind to the writing of his Spanish books. The Rich ménage when Irving first took lodgings with him was in the Calle San Fernando in the old part of the town, and there the idea of writing the 'Life of Columbus' had its inception. Nine months later, apparently on the suggestion of Irving, better quarters were sought, and a house was found near the outskirts of the town close by the wall and near the Puerta Santa Barbara. Here Irving remained throughout the remainder of his first sojourn in Madrid. After a century this quarter is in the heart of the city, much of the fashionable section extending now into what was the country then. But it is impossible to locate the house, or the site if it has been torn down to make way for a more modern structure.

That it was a pleasant place, one must conclude from the Irving journals. Rich himself was a genial host. His library and his manuscripts were at the service of his interesting guest. Mrs. Anna Rich, the hostess, while busy with her children, was gay and pleasant, and night after night friends, including the Marquesa de la Casa Yrujo and Narcissa, called for conversation, and Irving joined the group. The few letters extant of Mrs. Rich show character and decision. She had none of the qualities of the clinging vine, though when she first appeared in Madrid as a bride her husband annoyed her not a little by forcing her to appear veiled in public.

With the conclusion of his visits of courtesy, Irving settled down to a study of Navarrete's 'Voyages of Columbus.' Immediately he pushed aside any thought of its translation as impossible for his purpose. A source book, yes; but Irving's genius for creative and original writing would have none of its translation. It was while browsing among Rich's books and papers that the desire took root in Irving's mind to write a 'Life of Columbus.' Soon he was busy at his task. His previous work had permitted a leisurely and even a lazy life, and he had now reached middle age. He had turned to his 'Sketches' in moments of inspiration, and there had been little interference with the social life he loved. Now he was confronted with the grueling work of the serious historian, with endless hours of meticulous research unrelieved for days by the joys of composition. But the delights of discovery had their recompense, and through the spring and hot summer he literally slaved at his work. Sternly he bent above his desk, frequently writing from four and five in the morning throughout the day until evening, and often midnight found him unrelieved.

That was the summer that his nephew and biographer came upon him at the home of Rich, finding him 'in the midst of books and manuscripts, full of the subject on which he was engaged and in excellent spirits.' As he pursued his studies, he became fascinated with what he found of the moving drama of the Christian conquest of Granada, and for a moment he was miserable with uncertainty. Abandon the 'Life of Columbus'? That was impossible. But to turn from the lure of the conquest of Granada when he was aflame with enthusiasm was impossible as well. A few months later and the fever and the fervor might not be recaptured. Thus, early in August, while still living in the Calle San Fernando, he temporarily laid aside his work on Columbus, and for three months, writing in a fever, he sketched the rough draft of the book that would be known as 'The Conquest of Granada.' Then only did he return to his manuscript on the Discoverer.

The American colony was much too meager to divert him from his work. Indeed, a year later the only members of the North American colony were Everett and his wife, Obadiah Rich and his family, Smith, the Secretary of the Legation, and Lieutenant Slidell of the Navy, who, like Irving, was to fall under the magic spell of Spain and to write entertainingly of its witchery. Irving saw much of them all, for they were as members of one family: occasionally an evening of literary chat with the Minister and Mrs. Everett, an attractive, motherly woman, who received him cordially with none of the chill and stiffness of the official manner; many evenings with Rich, who, despite his dry pursuits, had a lively sense of humor. When Longfellow, the poet, was in Madrid he found Irving the center and soul of these unconventional gatherings of his fellow countrymen. 'He makes no ceremony at all with one and of course is a very fine man in society,' wrote the promising youth, 'all mirth and good humor.' In a friendly spirit he observed, what an English rival commented upon in ill humor, that he had 'some halting and hesitating in his conversation, but said very pleasant agreeable things in a husky, weak, peculiar voice.' [1] The very

---

[1] Samuel Longfellow, *Life of Henry Wadsworth Longfellow*, I, 108, 109.

young poet soon was sharing his more illustrious compatriot's enthusiasms for the Spanish people. Living in the home of a Spanish family he found that 'the whole house is goodness from the mistress down to the domestics.' But Longfellow's sensibilities had been touched by the daughter of the household — 'a young lady of sweet sixteen with the romantic name of Florence.' He observed 'a much more frank and sincere feeling of kindness' than he had found in France, and concluded that, while 'the outside of the Spanish character is proud, there is a warm current of noble sentiment flowing around the heart.' [1] He found a receptive listener in Irving as they promenaded the Prado together in the night. With the passing of his timidity, the young poet saw Irving as frequently as possible, and he was enormously impressed with Irving's concentration on his biography of Columbus. Always he found his older friend working at the home of Rich, but invariably his host would say, 'Sit down — I will talk to you in a minute but I must finish this sentence.' One morning at six the poet, passing the house of Rich, was astonished to find Irving's study window wide open to the morning breeze. 'Yes,' said Irving when Longfellow remarked upon it, 'I am always at work as early as that.' [1]

But in the Madrid of those days Irving found much charm, and wandering aimlessly through the streets, he lost nothing of its life and its fiestas. Let us meander a bit in the Madrid that Irving first knew.

[1] *Life of Longfellow*, I, 118.

It WAS the Madrid of the days of
Ferdinand VII. The street scenes were colorful and picturesque. Except through the siesta hours, the streets were
thronged, and with a predominance of women who differed
from their sisters of Seville in the soberness of their dark
dresses, and in the absence of bonnets and gay ribbons. But
with their combs, their mantillas, and their inevitable fans,
through which, so subtly, they expressed themselves, they
played as cleverly on the sensibilities of the male as their
more colorfully garbed sisters of the South.

The men, however, offered a greater diversity. Here one
met the peasant with his crimson sash and his turned-up hat;
there was the humblest of all the tradesmen, the water-
carriers with their short green jackets, bare legs and sandals.
Mingling with these of the lower classes were many military
men in the dashing costumes of their order, and the friars
and priests in theirs. Before one in the afternoon, the narrow
streets were thronged, the water-carriers crying shrilly,
'Agua fresca!' the peasants wide-eyed in wonder, the soldiers
jauntily sauntering arm in arm, with keen eyes for the ladies.
The old streets sang of life. But between one and four there
was almost solitude. The busy men of the morning were
enjoying their siesta behind closed shutters. The shops were
closed or curtains were drawn across the door. Over their
wares on the sidewalk the shopkeepers had spread cloths.
Here and there in the shade, the laborer or idler was stretched
in blissful slumber. In the Puerta del Sol one would find here

and there a man leaning indolently against a building, scarcely mustering the energy to fleck the ashes from his cigar.

Then, after the siesta, the city stretched itself and yawned, and passed out into the streets again.

Not only was the stranger pleased with the color of the town — there were odors in the air that pleased him; for before each chocolate shop men stood beating cinnamon in large mortars, and the fragrance mingled with that of the melons and the fruit piled on the sidewalks whichever way one turned.

Strolling through the streets, the stranger could but be impressed with the importance of the part played by the comb in the lives of the women, for every tenth shop had its display of the ornament. But even more numerous were the bookstalls, through which Obadiah Rich constantly was passing like a shadow, picking up rare bargains for the enrichment of his library and the edification of historians; gold- and silver-embroidery shops, drapers' and silk mercers' shops, shops for stockings and jewelry, and wine and chocolate — for the spirit of frivolity was in possession of Madrid.

But one waited for the evening to see Madrid in festive mood, when the greater part of the population poured in a solid stream down the Calle de Alcala to the Prado for the nightly promenade. The Prado was the town's delight and pride, and some years later, when Irving returned as Minister from the United States, it was quite as much so. It was two miles in length, reaching then, as now, from the present site of the post-office to the Atocha Station, but the promenaders seldom used more than a mile. A handsome *paseo* it was, and is, of from two to three hundred yards in width, with a quadruple row of trees, and with fountains here and there. One part was reserved for the walkers, while another was sacred to royalty, the nobility and aristocracy in their handsome carriages. Dragoons constantly moved up and down regulating traffic.

Soon the Prado was packed from one end to the other and from side to side, the pedestrians so close together they could not see beyond their immediate neighbors. There one might note the most distinguished leaders of fashion and politics, and among these, in the gaily decorated coaches, one caught flitting glimpses of Ferdinand and his Queen, so soon to die, and not infrequently of Don Carlos, whose cultivation of the crowd was much too evident for the King's pleasure. As royalty passed by, the other carriages stopped, the pedestrians paused and uncovered, and since the carriages drove back and forth slowly, not a few of the diplomatic corps discontinued their promenade at the fashionable hour to save themselves much bother. Irving liked to mingle with the crowd at times to catch the color and the exhilaration, but he more often took his walks at a later hour when only occasional lovers slyly disturbed the solitude after ten o'clock.

To the stranger surveying the animated scene there was nothing suggestive of poverty in the lowliest of the promenaders, for the ill-dressed man or woman was rare, but the knowing knew that not a few who appeared in attractive clothes and with elaborate and costly combs and eloquent fans went home to garrets to dine on bread and grapes. Seldom did the stranger fail to comment on the incomparably graceful walk of the Spanish women. 'No other woman knows how to walk,' wrote one who made his observations in the days of Irving's sojourn. 'The elegant, light, and yet firm step of the small and well-attired foot and ankle ... the graceful bearing of the head and neck ... the elegant disposition of the arms, never to be seen hanging downward, but one hand holding the folds of the mantilla just below the waist, the other inclining upward, wielding with an effect the most miraculous that mysterious instrument, the fan.' [1] And the gallants on adventure bent never failed to read the language of the fan. For the lady, conscious of the observation of an admirer, fanned herself slowly if no longer maid, and rapidly if not attached, and the cavalier thus knew without a word his prospects or his dangers.

At ten, the throng rapidly dispersed, though here and there a couple lingered, and if the stranger wished, he might have recourse to a café. At this time the Café de Santa Catalina was the finest in the town, thought by many unapproached in Paris. [2] One entered through a beautiful, brilliantly lighted room, passing the tables of those who preferred the illumination into an open court with the star-studded sky for a canopy. Here in the twilight of the stars others were grouped about tables, partaking of the refreshments suited to the season. In the court there was more of mystery and romance, but in the illuminated room there was gaiety enough. The women who had seemed so demure during the promenade now unbent and gave their tongues free rein in wit and cajolery. Fans fluttered their messages to inquiring eyes. The gallant paid his compliments without restraint.

Irving was to be drawn to the Prado, especially on Sundays, by the color and animation of the scene, when a goodly portion of the population promenaded under the trees and beside the fountains. But in pensive mood — and he was moody — he preferred to walk alone in the Retiro. Once the property of the kings, it had been given to the people as a park, and now, more than a century after Irving walked beneath its shade, it is one of the most beautiful parks in any European capital. But in the eighteen-twenties little

[1] Henry David Inglis, *Spain in 1830*, I, 91.   [2] Inglis, I, 91.

had been done to improve the grounds. One who sometimes sought its shade in the days of Irving's sojourn has described it as 'a vast and ill-laid-out garden and shrubbery, three or four miles in circumference,' possessing 'no particular attraction except its fresh air, and freedom from dust.' [1] Irving was to find amusement and delight in sauntering in the Prado, lounging in the Retiro, mingling with the throng on the Alcala, and in wandering aimlessly through the picturesque narrow streets of the old section. Like a native he loved to stroll in the Puerta del Sol, observing its interesting figures in the popular center associated with the festivities and fights of the populace; and to re-create in his imagination the gay and tragic scenes in the Plaza Mayor, where so long ago the gay young heir apparent of James I, and the gayer Buckingham, looked down from the balcony of the still familiar 'Bakehouse' upon the fiesta so elaborately arranged by the subtle Olivares for their delectation and deception; and to stroll about the then unfinished palace, within whose walls Ferdinand was taking his siesta daily in the library on the cool ground floor.

And then the theaters — for the Madrileños were lovers of the stage and of the opera — offered Irving relaxation and amusement too. The fine new theater in the neighborhood of the palace, then still in course of construction, and now, after more than a century, undergoing a restoration, he was not to visit. But the Teatro del Principe was crowded daily, though it held but fifteen hundred people. Here he saw La Torre, the premier Spanish actor of the day. Done in white and gold and with busts of the Spanish dramatists, novelists, and poets around the ceiling, the theater was not unattractive, and Irving knew it well. He was drawn thither no more by the play itself than by the bolero after

[1] Inglis, I, 98.

the conclusion, danced by two persons in Andalusian dress. Some natives thought the dance indecorous, though foreigners were mystified by the epithet.

But the Teatro de la Cruz, where Italian opera was being presented twice a week, drew him more frequently, and there he was happy listening to the artists and observing the ladies with their flashing eyes. Signora Tosi was the prime favorite of the hour with the people of Madrid, and the music-lovers fought for tickets to hear the artist, who was then receiving twelve hundred pounds for three performances a week.

But of society in general, Irving, during his first sojourn, was to see but little outside his small coterie of friends. There was no court society at all. Ferdinand was deep in political intrigues, now battling with rebellious subjec*t* in Catalonia, and now watching with catlike alertness the movements of his ambitious brother, Carlos, and of the Infante Francisco's conniving Sicilian wife, Louise Charlotte. There was little time or heart for festivity at court. 'The Sicilian Ambassador, Prince Casaro, who takes a great deal of interest in the subject of the Americas,' reported Everett to Henry Clay, 'told me the other day as a great secret that his wife had been informed by the Infanta Doña Louise Charlotte that the other brother and heir apparent, Don Carlos, is the great obstacle in the way of pacification, and that he had declared in the Council of State, where he presided in the King's absence, with great violence against any such proceedings.' [1] These political conflicts that consumed the time of Ferdinand scarcely interested Irving at all, though among his diplomatic friends, and at the board of Everett, he must have heard all the gossip of those uninspiring days. The King did not love Madrid, preferring to spend much of his time at

[1] MS. Archives, February 24, 1826.

the Escorial, the palace of Pardo, or at San Ildefonso. The palace in Madrid was dull.

And there was a corresponding social lethargy among the aristocrats of the time. Once a week, true, the Duchess of Benavente opened her great house on Sundays to the members of the diplomatic corps, but the foreign diplomats were made uncomfortable by the pointed manner in which the members of the nobility took their departure on the entrance of a diplomat. The prejudice in this circle was then so powerful against the foreigner that the diplomats attending the *tertulia* of the wife of Manuel Gonzales Salmon were made to feel that they were looked upon as little better than spies, and most of them discontinued their attendance. A few great houses received them graciously, but in general the diplomatic corps was dependent on itself for entertainment.

But Irving was content. He had other fish to fry.

Chapter 2: MADRID DAYS AND IRVING'S CIRCLE

FROM the moment Irving began on his biography of Columbus, he was to work more intensively and continuously than ever before in his life. Almost every day found him at his task in his room at Rich's. Frequently he rose at four or five o'clock to begin the daily grind, which continued until seven or eight o'clock at night. Often he persisted at his desk until far after midnight. Unhappily, because of the impossibility of finding the house of Rich, if it still is standing, it is not possible to visualize Irving at his work. We only know that the room had French windows that looked out on a garden.

This intense application exacted its toll of the none too robust health of the writer, and frequently he noted in his meager diary that brain fag at times stayed his pen. When he thus spurred his mind beyond all reason, and relaxation was forced upon him, he found his way to the shade of the Retiro, where he walked by the hour, or lay prostrate on the cool grass looking at the blue sky or reading a favorite author. He came to love the Retiro, and scarcely a day passed that he did not spend a little time in its refreshing shade.

It was when his mind refused to go on, rebelling against its punishment, that he frequently found his way to the bullfights, and it is impossible to conclude that he found these exhibitions shocking. There is evidence enough that he enjoyed them, and he came to know the names and methods of the matadors, but the people attending interested him quite as much.

> I did not know what a bloodthirsty man I was till I saw them [bullfights] at Madrid on my first visit. The first was very spirited, the second dull, the third spirited again, and afterward I hardly ever missed. 'But the poor horses,' someone interposed. 'Oh, well, they were very old and worn out, and it was only a question whether they should die a triumphant death or be battered a few years longer.' [1]

One day he went to the *toros* with a 'little round-bellied Spanish marquis, as round as a pumpkin yet pale and withered in the face,' and was amused by the old roué's routine for a day of ideal pleasure. He went to the bullfight in the morning, dined at a *fonda*, returned to the bullfight in the evening, and then went to the theater, after which he topped off a perfect day with 'a girl for the night.' [2] And the theater found Irving rather regular in attendance. He knew the actors and actresses and he had a deep admiration for the opera singers, all Italians. Often at the opera he was the guest of the French Ambassador in his box.

But nothing pleased him more than his aimless wanderings through the narrow streets of the old section, and once, on such a jaunt, his sense of chivalry was stirred and he narrowly escaped a brawl. His attention was attracted to a number of muleteers who were teasing two girls, chasing them and pelting them with stones. When one of the rowdies overtook and caught one of the girls and was pulling her about roughly, a young soldier, suspected by Irving of being her

[1] Pierre W. Irving, *Life and Letters of Washington Irving*, III, 359, 360.

[2] W. P. Trent and G. S. Hellman, editors, *The Journal of Washington Irving*, III, 30.

lover, interposed and dealt the muleteer a heavy blow on the head with his saber. On removing his cap and finding blood on his hand, the muleteer set up a ferocious howl, and his comrades, infuriated by the soldier's interruption of the sport, were furious and bent on murder, but when a soldier on duty approached with musket and bayonet the defender of the girl made a neat escape. Angered by the loss of their prey, one of the muleteers attacked the other girl, when Irving interposed and pushed him back. The thwarted rowdy immediately prepared to give battle to the stranger, when one of the soldiers rushed to his defense. With simulated nonchalance Irving continued his walk, clearly pleased with the episode.[1]

Occasionally Everett offered a diversion by taking him to the palace, where he met Ferdinand and his excellent Queen, Don Carlos, and Don Francisco; and he walked to King Philip's seat, the stone on the mountain-side whence the great monarch watched the rising of the amazing edifice of the Escorial, the 'eighth wonder of the world.' More than once he witnessed the court ceremony when the King washed the feet of the lowly, and the Queen washed the hands of poor women and gave them food and drink. But if he found anything to admire in Ferdinand he left no record. He had been given free access to the King's library on the ground floor of the palace in Madrid, and many days he spent in the cool retreat among the priceless volumes and manuscripts, waited upon by attendants in brilliant uniforms and with swords dangling by their sides.

Toward the last of August of his first year he accompanied Everett to San Ildefonso, where the King was in residence. With a merry little party he set forth at six in the morning and, after five and a half hours of riding, drew up before a

[1] Trent and Hellman, III, 16, 17.

little inn in the Guadarrama Mountains for lunch. There he learned that the servants of the British Minister had been robbed in the mountains; but he found the drive through the great pine forests, with the charming vistas from the heights over the valley, a delight, and at twilight the party arrived safely in La Granja and found lodgings at the Fleur de Lis. It had required fourteen hours of hard driving over rough mountain roads to make the journey that, little more than a century later, one would make in two hours and a half by motor over roads as perfect as may be found in Europe. Long before, the first of the Bourbon kings, chilled by the cold austerity and solemn dignity of the Escorial and by the simplicity of the Pardo, conceived the idea of making a bit of Versailles in Spain. Near La Granja, in the village of San Ildefonso, he built himself a palace, and converted the extensive surrounding grounds into a garden similar to that of the French kings — a green spot in a desert. Through the great wooded space he built formal walks; flowers were planted everywhere; fountains were constructed, and one threw the highest jet in Europe. On a little lake he launched the ornate pleasure boat which one may see today, and so dearly did he love the spot that, rebelling against the rule that the Spanish kings should lie together in the ornate crypt at the Escorial, he provided for his own burial at San Ildefonso.

Before breakfast the morning after their arrival, Irving, with his brother Peter, walked about the village and past the palace, where soldiers stood guard and a band played. After breakfast he promenaded with the Everetts through the beautiful gardens, where they were found by a messenger of Ferdinand with an invitation to the Queen's apartments in the palace and for a walk in the gardens with the court at five. That evening the fountains all were playing.

The next day, Irving drove on to Segovia, little different then from what it is today, with its beautiful cathedral, its impressive alcazar, its fine Roman aqueduct, its charming narrow streets. Everett, who was along, had some trouble with a priest because the ladies of the party were uncovered, and Irving was amused at his friend's embarrassment. He was impressed with the church and with the throne room of the alcazar, but he saw but little of a town drenched in history since the days of the Romans.

That same day he returned to La Granja, and in the afternoon again walked in the gardens with Mrs. Everett and her daughter, delighted with the fountains, and vastly interested by the mingling of the court and populace under the trees.

And so, working himself to exhaustion and into a state of nerves, he found restoration in the Retiro, parading the Prado at night, meandering in the streets, attending bullfights and the opera. But in the evenings, as a rule, he found his way to the homes of some of his friends. Biographers have given us their names only. We must know them better.

AT THE home of the Everetts he came and went at will, always welcomed by the wife of the Minister. In the home of Rich he was as one of the family, sharing their visitors. At both houses he met no one more often than the Marquesa de la Casa Yrujo, and at her home he attended many parties and had many dinners and teas. In the dying days of the eighteenth century she had been one of the most charming and beautiful of the belles of Philadelphia, clever, sprightly, and charming in her gracious manner. The dashing young Spanish diplomat wooed and married her, and for some years, both in Philadelphia and Washington, she was the most popular woman of diplomatic society. Hers was the finest coach that splashed through the puddles of Washington's muddy streets. A favorite of Thomas Jefferson, she and her husband frequently were guests at Monticello. Unhappily, in the misunderstanding over the purchase of Louisiana and the boundaries of the Floridas, the Marquis momentarily lost his head, and he was caught red-handed using money to influence the press against the policy of the American Government. With genuine sorrow, Jefferson was forced to ask for his recall. Madrid agreed, but requested that he be permitted to return to Spain on leave after the dangerous season on the sea had passed. The request was granted, but Yrujo lingered on and on, and finally informed the Government in Washington that he could not be ordered out of any country by anyone save his King. It was an unhappy episode, encouraged by the party opposition in the United States.

Thus ended the American phase, and the American girl was not to see her native land again. She had gone with her husband to Brazil and then to Spain, where Yrujo became Minister of Foreign Affairs and a personage of importance. Through the partiality of the King he had been given a monopoly on the grinding of grain by modern methods in Cadiz and thus had enhanced his fortune.

Now he was dead, and his widow, no longer young but not without the charms of youth, was living in Madrid with her daughter Narcissa. Irving had met them the first day he ventured forth after his arrival with Everett, and throughout this first sojourn they were to be of his most intimate

circle of friends. He loved to see Narcissa in the Spanish
dances at the small parties in the homes of Rich and Everett.

I̲T WAS at a soirée in the home of
the Marquesa de la Casa Yrujo soon after reaching Madrid
that Irving first met Isabella O'Shea, but recently the bride
of a Madrid banker, who was to become one of his closest
friends during his first sojourn, and to share with another
during the second the description of 'my favorite.' Only a
little while before Irving reached Spain, John O'Shea arrived
from Ireland, and after a brief pause at Malaga he took up
his residence in Madrid, where he founded the very prosperous banking house of John O'Shea and Company. He had
not gone to a land of utter strangers with none of the ties of
consanguinity, for in the middle of the seventeenth century
some of the O'Sheas from Limerick and the County of Kerry
had migrated to Spain after the rebellion of 1641. Soon after
founding the banking house, O'Shea married a beautiful
and lively Spanish girl, Señora Doña Isabel Hurtado de
Corcuera, and when Irving first knew her as a bride, she
was living in an immense house which he described in his
diary as the 'Donatz palace.' The description is confusing,
since there never has been a Donatz palace in Madrid. But
the O'Sheas did live in 'an immense building' and 'a chapel,
etc.,' as Irving wrote; and within its walls he was to pass
many cheerful evenings. Whether this house was on the
Calle de las Infantas, where Irving found them some years

later when, as Minister of the United States, he was their
neighbor, it is impossible to determine.

Mrs. O'Shea belonged to the little coterie with which
Irving was most intimate during his first sojourn. Many
nights she was found at the home of the Riches, where Irving
lived, and he was meeting her constantly in the home of the
Marquesa de la Casa Yrujo, or in the drawing-room of the
Everetts. Though a young woman of Spanish beauty, with
large dark eyes, her charm to Irving was in her intellectual
keenness, and in her sprightly talk. He found, to his delight,
that he could exchange views and impressions with her in
sustained conversation; and years later, when as a diplomat
he often found himself at large social functions, frothy, frivolous, with magpie chattering of inanities and no real talk, and
felt alone and lonesome, isolated from the spirit of the throng,
Mrs. O'Shea was one of the two women he invariably sought
out to draw aside from the crowd for companionship. She
was a knowing woman, with a kindly manner that inspired
confidence and real friendship.

John O'Shea, the husband, was a typical Irishman, with
curly brown hair and the bluest of Irish blue eyes, and Irving
was warmed by his radiant smile and delighted with his ready
Irish wit. Occasionally Irving accompanied him on little
excursions about Madrid, going with him once to the Royal
Chapel to hear the 'Miserere,' but in the evenings at the
home of the Riches O'Shea seldom was found with his wife,
for he could not resist the lure of the card table. Indeed, he
was an inveterate gambler, and his constant playing for
high stakes was a source of annoyance to his wife and family,
though he was a most skillful player and usually won.

It was almost twenty years after Irving last saw Mrs.
O'Shea that the fascinating and disturbing young wife of
her husband's relative arrived in Madrid for a year's resi-

dence, and found her still beautiful, though now old and stout, and still kindly in her manner. This lady from Ireland was destined for a romantic and rather tragic rôle, for she was the Kitty O'Shea whose love affair with Charles Stewart Parnell, ending in a divorce and marriage, was to wreck the political career of the 'uncrowned king of Ireland' and send him heart-broken to his grave.

In no house in Madrid was Irving to dart in and out with more frequency and gaiety during the three years he was engaged on his literary labors; in none but one — the home of the Russian Minister.

B UT Irving found real magic in the home of the Russian Minister, Pierre D'Oubril. That personage, as we have seen, was not at home on the occasion of Irving's call of courtesy, but he had found Madame, pale, distinguished, pretty, in the garden reading, while her children played about her. And he had met Antoinette Bolviller, the niece of Madame, and found her charming. To no one throughout his life was he to write such letters as he wrote to her.

The Russian Legation at the time stood at the corner of the Alcala and the Calle del Turco, probably on the site of the Beaux Arts Club of today. It was a large house with a garden, and it was to become Irving's second home.

Pierre D'Oubril was an interesting personality with a colorful career that was not without its shadows, though history

MRS. JOHN O'SHEA

gives him scarcely a line. The Russia of today prefers to know nothing of pre-Soviet days, and but for the papers in the archives of the Foreign Office in Madrid it would have been impossible to paint even the shadow of a portrait. Had not the Spanish Ambassador in Paris been stationed once in Russia and been familiar with D'Oubril's antecedents and career, it would have been exceedingly difficult to find any record of his character or past. But the Ambassador, learning of D'Oubril's appointment to Spain, thought it well to furnish the Foreign Office with a skeleton biography and his own impressions of the character of the diplomat. From some of Everett's dispatches we get the impression that he was a clever and a rather pugnacious champion of autocracy, and not unnaturally an inveterate enemy of revolutions, for he was most insistent that Ferdinand should not recognize the independence of the South American republics, when Everett, on instructions from Washington, was offering to act as mediator in the recognition of an established fact.

D'Oubril was of French blood. That woman of uncanny wisdom, the great Catherine, had discovered his father, who was a Frenchman, and had attached him to her service and put him in charge of one of the divisions in the Foreign Office. Pierre, the son, was sent to France for his education and was enrolled at Strassburg. Under royal favor, he entered the foreign service of Russia at an early age, and after but meager training in St. Petersburg he was made Chargé d'Affaires in Paris in 1804. It was a dangerous post and position for an inexperienced youth who must cope with Napoleon and Talleyrand. And Pierre was to find his path not one of roses.

Certainly it was not an easy instruction that reached him from his Emperor, to call on the Minister of the Conqueror with a stern protest from the Czar against the killing of the Duc d'Enghien, which implied that there had been an assassination. That was on the twelfth of May. Four days later he was summoned to the French Minister's and presented with a reply to D'Oubril's royal master which was brusque, if not brutally insulting, and the young diplomat was so indiscreet as to accept the note and send it to his court. The Emperor did not condescend to accept the note with gracious favor, but made it quite clear to his young servant that he was to call at the Foreign Office in Paris and just as bluntly express his disapproval of the tone of the note.

After that, there was nothing for D'Oubril to do but to return to St. Petersburg, where he was to be retained for two years more of training.

However, the court clearly had great expectations, and Nesselrode, the wily fox of Russian diplomacy, sent D'Oubril to Vienna, where he came under the spell of the genius of Metternich, who smiled upon him and quite won his heart.

But scarcely had he become settled in Vienna when again he was sent on a dangerous mission to Paris, commissioned with full powers to adjust the difficulties between his nation and the French. He was described by the Emperor as 'our Councillor of State, and Knight of the Order of Saint Woladimic and of Saint John of Jerusalem.'

Napoleon commissioned General Clarke to negotiate, and in July, 1806, a treaty was concluded. This agreement, which gave King Ferdinand of Naples the Balearic Islands in exchange for Sicily, so much coveted by Napoleon, to France, rather irked Alexander, who was unable to see just what Russia had gained by the exchange of islands. Thus, when young D'Oubril, flushed with the triumph of having affixed his signature to a treaty, returned to his capital he was left in no doubt as to the coolness of his reception. The Czar refused to ratify the treaty, and implied that instead of following his instructions the young diplomat had acted in direct contravention of them.

Thus, like so many servants of autocratic rulers, he passed through a period of disgrace. He was banished from the drawing-rooms of the capital, and for some years he lived in gloomy retirement on his estate in the interior of the empire. Because his father was French, and he himself was a Frenchman by education and in all but citizenship, it was darkly suspected that he had permitted his blood to influence his actions, and so long as Napoleon remained in power he rusticated in the country, remote from the gay circles of the court.

Napoleon's Waterloo thus turned out to be D'Oubril's resurrection, and in 1815 he was summoned back to the capital and reinstated in the Foreign Office as Chief of Protocol. After a while he was made Minister to Naples, and thence he was sent to Madrid.

Franco de Lea Cermudez, the Spanish Ambassador in Paris, who painted D'Oubril's portrait for the Foreign Office in Madrid, clearly was not an ardent friend. He wrote of him:

> As for his character, I can say only that I consider him astute and tactful and frank in his bearing and manner. More shrewd in his conduct than capable and well informed, and not a little distrustful. And a little bit backward about taking on himself the slightest thing, no matter how just it may be, but quite arrogant when he knows he is well backed in the matter. When I was in Russia he was considered by some to be a little Anglomaniac in his political leanings, and a favorite with the Prince Metternich, which I believe has some base. I must tell you that I found him most difficult and a usually poor supporter of the interests of Spain, more so than Nesselrode. Perhaps now it may be different, and I will be very happy if it is so, but I must tell you his past life and add that D'Oubril, as I understand it, is subordinate to the Ambassador of Russia in Paris, as was his predecessor.[1]

[1] MS. Archives, Ministry of Foreign Affairs, Madrid.

It was enough for Irving that he was 'astute and tactful and frank in his bearing and manner,' for the American then was neither a diplomat nor a politician. He found the Russian charming, and his household a fountain in the desert. The palace on the Alcala was perhaps the most luxurious among the homes of the diplomats in Madrid. D'Oubril's entertainments were lively, while remaining stately. His wines were the choicest, and from the list he brought with him to his new post, we may assume they were abundant. That he liked the Spanish Valdepeñas may be suspected from the fact that he had twenty small barrels at one time. His cellar was always stocked with a superabundance of champagne, Burgundy, Bordeaux, and whiskey. His table was that of an epicure.

No doubt Irving sampled his wines at many a luncheon and dinner, but quite as attractive to him were the excellent library, the bronzes, the paintings, the large number of fine Chinese prints, and the Chinese lacquer work. And there was excellent music, and always animated conversation. Irving found the Russian an interesting *raconteur* and could sit for hours listening to his reminiscences of Napoleon and the Paris of his day, of Metternich and his Vienna, and of Nesselrode and his St. Petersburg, related with the light cynicism of a man of the great world, who kept digging into an elegant box for pinches of snuff, 'very fine, a coffee color and with a strong rose-like odor.' He had had an interesting experience in Spain when he was held up by brigands and was made to lie on his back on the ground, while his captors playfully waved a sinister-looking knife above his throat in an effort to make him disclose the treasures he had left at home. But he had made no complaint to the Government, merely informing it of the occurrence.

He maintained three carriages, and often Irving rode forth

with him and his interesting wife and charming niece in his coach and four with ornate trappings. But he found his greatest pleasure in the house, overrun with children. He was devoted to them, and they to him, for he would sit for long periods spinning fascinating yarns from his fancy, and sometimes, when he was tired and discouraged about his work, he would refresh his spirit by romping with them on the floor.

BUT it was Mademoiselle Antoinette Bolviller, the niece of Madame D'Oubril, a charming member of the household, who gave to the ménage a touch of romance. She was young, with the enthusiasm of youth, sprightly, interested in books and music, and Irving found her a charming conversationalist. He learned that he could talk to her of his delvings into Spanish history and legends and find an intelligent and sympathetic response. Biographers have been curious about their relations because of the brilliant and lengthy letters to the young girl during his Andalusian journey — the best he ever wrote. But Irving was middle-aged and she was a young woman of great charm and sweetness, and there is nothing of record to indicate anything more than a mutually attractive friendship. Her relations with Irving alone have preserved her name for the general public, for after Irving left Madrid it has been impossible to trace her life's journey. We catch a tantalizing glimpse of her many years later. Inside the book cover of one of Irving's unpublished diaries his nephew and biographer recorded a trace of her in 1858. She had left Rome soon after the death of her mother. In April of that year she was living in Florence, detained there by the illness of a servant, but a little later she was living again in Rome in apartments at 32 Via Bocca de Leone. Thirty years had passed since her intimate friendship with Irving, and she was unmarried. A casual observer seeing her in the streets and galleries might have taken her for a nun, for while not of the sisterhood then, she invariably dressed in black like one. D'Oubril was dead, and probably Madame too, and the children of the once happy household in Madrid were scattered, and Mademoiselle Antoinette, an amateur painter, spent much of her time in the galleries studying the masterpieces and copying for pleasure.

Some have suggested a romance, her love for Irving that came to nothing, but this is mere conjecture. More probable it is that they merely were good friends and enjoyed one another's companionship. But the fact remains that she was to Irving one of the bright and beautiful spots of his first Madrid sojourn.

I T WAS through his relations with the household of the D'Oubrils that Irving found himself in the midst of a Russian coterie of intimate friends. Foremost among these was Prince Dimitri Ivanovitch Dolgorouki, for a time Secretary of the Russian Legation. An aristocrat both

by blood and brain, Irving found in their common interests
and enthusiasms a bond that held, and together they were
to make many explorations into far places remote from travelers' highways, and not without their perils from the brigands.
Irving was delighted. There were so few with whom one
could talk with the utmost freedom without the fear of being
misunderstood. And Dolgorouki was as gentle and sympathetic as he was brilliant and cultured. It was with him, as
we shall see, that Irving made his mad, wild journey through
the mountains from Seville to Granada, and for a brief time
the Prince was to share the Governor's apartments at the
Alhambra with him. But the friends had lost touch for
the moment at the time of the publication of the 'Tales
of the Alhambra,' and in his preface Irving referred to their
friendship:

> Accident had thrown us together from distant regions of
> the globe, and a similarity of taste led us to wander together
> among the romantic mountains of Andalusia. Should these
> pages meet his eye, wherever thrown by the duties of his
> station, whether mingling with the pageantry of courts, or
> meditating on the true glories of Nature, may they recall the
> scenes of our adventurous companionship, and with them
> the recollections of one, in whom neither time nor distance
> will obliterate the remembrance of his gentleness and worth.

At that time the Prince was the Russian Minister in Persia,
and some years later when Irving was Minister in Madrid
they were corresponding. Included in the Russian coterie
were Stoffregen, a Secretary at the Legation, and Gessler,
the Russian Consul-General. An intimate friendship soon
developed between them, and it was with them, as sole
companions, that Irving made his first Andalusian journey
from Madrid, braving the hardships and the perils of the
mountains, all the more romantic because of the danger of

bandits springing upon them from the rocks. Sharing Irving's enthusiasm for points of historic interest, they were quite content to linger with him on the way as he sought the ancient highways and castles associated with the final war against the Moors.

Such was the Russian coterie with whom Irving passed so many happy evenings and afternoons at the palace of D'Oubril on the Alcala. 'You promised to write me the news of the gay world at Madrid,' he was to write Mademoiselle Antoinette later from Seville. 'I shall be delighted to receive it from you, but you need not go out of the walls of your own house to find subjects full of interest to me. Let me have all the news you can of your domestic circle; you have a world within yourselves; at least it was all the world to me when in Madrid.' [1]

ASIDE from the Russians, Irving's closest friendships during his first sojourn were with the English. One of the sons of Lord Stanhope was an attaché at the British Legation, and with him Irving lounged and broke bread; and at this time he had a prolonged visit from his brother, Philip Henry Stanhope, better known as Viscount Mahon, the historian. Irving was pleased both by their presence in and partiality for Spain, because their great ancestor had suffered a humiliating defeat at the hands of the Spaniards at a point not remote from Madrid. He found

[1] Irving, *Life*, II, 107.

the brothers interesting as human beings, cultured, intellectual, and as tireless as himself in seeking out points of historic and artistic interest. It was natural that the grandnephews of Lady Hester Stanhope and of Chatham, at whose table and over whose drawing-room she had presided with so much brilliance, if sometimes with too much irony, should be pleasant conversationalists.

Of the two, the favorite with Irving was Viscount Mahon, though he was much younger than the American, being only twenty-three and fresh from Oxford. The congeniality grew out of their common interest in Spain historically, and, about the time of the publication of the 'Conquest of Granada,' Mahon was to publish his 'History of the War of Succession in Spain,' based largely on the personal papers of his ancestor. Thus, as the English youth and his older friend explored the country, each was in search of 'copy.' Mahon was to return to England, and within two years to be a member of the House of Commons, and within seven years Minister of Foreign Affairs; but, like Irving, his permanent fame was to rest on the products of his pen.

B<small>UT</small> a more interesting companion to Irving than the Stanhopes was Sir David Wilkie, the English painter, who was to enter intimately into Irving's Spanish life. He had known the painter in his London days when he moved familiarly in the literary and artistic circles of the city. Beginning his career in 1803, he was a noted artist when Irving first met him, and by 1819 he had painted two of his most famous pictures, 'Sir Walter Scott and His Family' and the 'Death of Sir Philip Sidney.' Overwork, and the futility of physicians, had driven him to try the climate of other countries and the healing properties of a change of scene, and thus he appeared in Spain in search of health. Strangely enough, no other English painter had ever visited the land of Velasquez, Murillo, and El Greco, of Goya and Zurbaran, though some of the English portrait-painters had been influenced from afar by the art of the first two. The knowledge that his friend Irving was in Madrid, and also Mahon, made his anticipations all the brighter. But Irving knew nothing of his coming until one day in the home of Obadiah Rich he met him, to his infinite delight. It was the day of Wilkie's arrival.

Irving instantly took him in tow, and throughout the months of his sojourn was to be his most intimate companion. Soon Wilkie was writing to England that he was getting along very well in Madrid. 'Here there are few Englishmen,' he wrote, 'and no cockney travelers, and having little inter-course with the natives, our chief society is among the corps diplomatic. The English, French, Russian, Neapolitan, and American houses of legation have shown me marked atten-tion, and it is there I find my chief society. I owe very much of this to Irving, who has been most zealous and hearty in his efforts to serve me.' [1] So much was Irving bent on making his friend's visit pleasant that when Sir Robert Peel wrote the artist, and he wished to send a copy of the letter to a friend, it was Irving who found time to act as copyist.

And it was Irving who insisted that Wilkie set up his easel and thus leave some lasting mementoes of his Spanish visit. On his arrival in Madrid the artist, in search of lodgings, had

[1] Allan Cunningham, *Life of Sir David Wilkie*, II, 476.

found rooms in the Puerta del Sol in the house of Doña Maria
Puertis y Reymat, and this for the moment was to serve as
his studio. But the more he reflected on the beauty of the
landlady, 'too handsome and too fine a lady,' the more he
was persuaded that it was no place for him. And then, aside
from the charms of the lady, 'she had no chimney and a very
bad stair.' Hearing the misgivings of the artist, Irving, who
visited him in these quarters almost daily, was of the opinion
that he might do better. Of course, the aristocracy and
nobility would wish to visit his studio, and it really was too
bad to have no chimney and a bad stair. Thus, the two
friends in their strolls through the picturesque streets of the
city looked for better quarters, and at length, within a month,
lodgings were found on the Calle de Majaderites, where
Wilkie could boast 'a chimney and three good rooms,' where
'the entrance is good enough to induce ladies of rank to call
... which was before impossible.'

Soon Irving was shooing the diplomats and the nobles
toward the studio with all the zest of a promoter. When
Sir Thomas Lawrence congratulated the painter on having
Irving with him, he wrote: 'You are right in supposing the
satisfaction I should feel in being here with such a man and
such a friend as Washington Irving. He has been much
gratified by your mention of him; we have often talked
about you.'

And so it came about that, under the approving eye of
Irving, Wilkie was soon at work at his easel. Daily Irving
found his way to the studio, which became his club, and he
spread the news of the artist's presence until soon the studio
was thronged with the grandees of Spain and the ladies of
fashion. The American was jubilant in finding in his friend's
rooms when he called the Duke de Infantado, the Duke and
Duchess of Alba, the gay Duke of Osuna, the Duke of Vil-

hermoso, the Marques and Marquesa de Santa Cruz, the Duchess of Benavente, the Marquesa de Villanueva, and the entire diplomatic corps. They called, like Irving, to see Wilkie working on his Spanish paintings. It was in this little studio, with Irving watching the daily progress, that Wilkie painted his 'Defense of Saragossa,' his 'Council of War,' and 'The Guerrilla Taking Leave of His Confessor,' all of which were to be purchased by George IV; and his 'Spanish Señorita.' Wilkie was delighted with the enthusiasm of the Spanish critics, and with the applause of Don Lopez, the King's painter, over his 'Defense of Saragossa.' Irving may well have growled disdainfully over any opinion of Lopez, since he did not like him. But, since the King's painter agreed with him, 'Irving, who encouraged me much to begin it, has seen it on almost every day of its progress,' wrote Wilkie.

Thus, Irving was not only to fire the imagination of the English-speaking world with his 'Conquest of Granada' and of all the world with his 'Tales of the Alhambra,' but to inspire the painting of some of the famous historic canvases on Spain.

And so the days went by, with Wilkie painting in his studio, and Irving writing at his desk, exchanging visits even in work hours now and then; but in the evenings the two joined their friends at the D'Oubrils' or at the British Legation. Wilkie's health and spirits returned, and he, too, was happy. Irving, who had arranged to go to Seville in the autumn, put his plans aside to remain with Wilkie until the spring, and soon, as we shall see, the two friends had a reunion on the banks of the Andalusian river.

ONE October day — and what day so lovely as an October day in Spain? — Irving took Wilkie to see his first bullfight in Madrid. The artist wrote that he had seen six bulls fought and killed, two men severely wounded, and six horses killed — for this was generations before pads were ordered for the better protection of the horses. Neither foreigner confessed to a partiality for this form of entertainment, but neither made it their last fight. Irving enjoyed the pageantry, the color of an ancient drama, the animation of the vast throng, but he was a little apologetic about the bloodiness of the contest, while admitting that he himself caught something of the spirit of the crowd. After the fight, the friends went from the ring to Wilkie's apartment for the evening, but there is nothing of record concerning their observations on the 'tragedy' of the afternoon.

Three days later, Irving, Viscount Mahon, and Stanhope clambered into a dizzy diligence at seven in the morning for a visit to the Escorial. The journey, easily made today in a motor-car over perfect roads in a little more than an hour, required four and a half hours in 1827. The roads then, while infinitely better than in the days of the great Philip, whose journey in a chair, because of his gouty leg, required a week, were none too good, but the travelers took the jolting in high glee. They were quite ready for their lunch when they alighted at the Fleur de Lis, where they found Wilkie, who had preceded them. A little later in the day, Prince Dol-

gorouki joined them, he having missed the diligence and
followed in a *calesin.*

Ferdinand was not in residence, being with his soldiers
who were struggling with rebellious subjects in the North,
but the Queen, then ailing, whose death-knell Irving was to
hear soon afterward in Granada, was living in the palace at
the time. This very pious woman appeared daily for her
devotions in the chapel of the convent. For six days the
friends lingered in, and within the shadow of, the most imposing and impressive, and certainly the most austere, structure in the world. The Fleur de Lis offered comfortable
accommodations, but the friends spent the greater part of
the day in the Escorial, and at night they enjoyed the awe-
inspiring spectacle of the enormous pile of granite in the
silence and solitude of the moonlight.

They were there on the anniversary of the death of Queen
Margaret, and in the center of the chapel they saw the coffin
of the dead woman with its crown and pall. The Reverend
Padre Buendia graciously acted as their guide, and, like all
who visited the Escorial in those days, they were delighted
with their cicerone, while feeling that he made too much of a
god of Philip. Irving found him 'a fat, pleasant-faced man.'
For the pageantry of royalty they could scarcely have chosen
a better time, for in addition to the Queen at her devotions,
and the casket of the former Queen, the Infanta, wife of Don
Carlos, who so soon would tear the land with civil war, was
there throughout their sojourn. Every evening the Infanta
descended to the brilliantly illuminated pantheon.

The foreigners were impressed by this marvelous mausoleum
of the monarchs from the days of the great Charles. That
which they saw may be seen today, unchanged in any detail,
for the shelves were filled with their marble caskets, many
then empty, and the eternal couches of Ferdinand, Maria

Christina, Isabella, Francisco, and Alfonso XII were patiently waiting for their tenants.

Padre Buendia gave permission for Wilkie and his friends to wander about the Escorial at all times and at will. Wilkie shared in Irving's enthusiasm over the great library, with its priceless manuscripts and ancient tomes, and Irving reverently went with Wilkie to see the paintings of the masters. The painter was immensely pleased with Velasquez and Murillo, then the fashionable reaction, but if either the author or the painter found anything worth noting in the 'Legion of Saint Mauritius,' one of the masterpieces of El Greco, it is not recorded by either. That supreme artist had long suffered an eclipse in fashion, and it was not until many years later that El Greco again was to have his day, when the masterful work of Cossio was to reinstate him in critical appreciation among the greatest of the masters, and when Julius Meier-Graefe, in his 'Spanish Journey,' was to challenge the supremacy of Velasquez and give the palm to the wandering Greek. Not once during his eight years in Spain did Irving so much as mention El Greco in his letters, and Wilkie returned to London without having discovered him at all. Nor did either discover Goya, who had just died, leaving immortal canvases and cartoons behind him, to which the world was to pay homage a century later.

A few days after his return from the Escorial, Irving, with Wilkie, Lord Mahon, and his brother Peter, fared forth for a four-day sojourn in Toledo with its innumerable treasures. Irving had just sent his publisher corrections of his manuscript on 'Columbus' and was in need of more relaxation and recreation. They went by way of Aranjuez.

It was not until two years after Irving had made this journey that a diligence was for the first time put in service between Madrid and the ancient capital of Spain. At seven

o'clock one October morning the friends merrily entered a
coach drawn by six mules and started on their journey. The
road was miserable, unpaved, and full of treacherous ruts,
despite the fact that royalty constantly was passing back
and forth from Madrid to the royal palace in Aranjuez. It
was after seven hours of jolting that their driver whipped his
six mules into the favorite hamlet of the monarchs. It had
required that long to cover seven leagues. In the *posada* of
Andalusia they found comfortable lodgings, and after lunch
they visited the palace and its gardens. Whatever any of
them thought of the palace with its porcelain room is not
recorded, but they were entranced with the gardens, which
have lost none of their charm and beauty after more than a
hundred years.

In Aranjuez they stayed the night, and at seven the next
morning the mule-drawn coach lumbered out of the town
on its way to Toledo, another seven leagues, and it was two
o'clock when they pulled into one of the treasure cities of
the world. The Toledo that once had boasted a population
of two hundred thousand had dwindled to about seventeen
thousand, though no buildings were tenantless, and the
streets were crowded to capacity on occasions; and being
the ecclesiastical center of the kingdom, there was no public
entertainment for tourists — only the time-honored *tertulias*
of the citizens. The theater that once had thrived had been
suppressed by royal order on the request of the Canon of the
University, and even the bullfight was prohibited. But for
religious processions and fiestas the ancient city would have
drowsed interminably. The accommodations for strangers
then were rather meager, and the *posada* where the four
friends stopped, though clean and comfortable, offered no
luxuries.

But to Irving and Wilkie the town was a treasure house.

The very narrow winding streets with their balconies, through which several civilizations had marched through the centuries, entranced them with the glamour of romance.

That night the four friends sallied into the streets that were bathed in moonlight, delighted with the tinkling of guitars from the balconies that were so mysterious. By day they visited the cathedral, the Alcazar, once the royal residence and now, after a century, a military school; they marveled at the ancient gates and the time-stained city walls that had played such a colorful part in history, and they enjoyed the Tagus, almost circling the town. Irving, primarily interested in history, sought the spot in the river where once stood the summer residence of the last of the Visigoth kings, in which, according to tradition, the unhappy Roderic had seduced the daughter of a general, who took his revenge by leading the Moors into the realm. Later, Irving was to record not a few of the legends of Toledo, including the tragedy of Roderic, in one of his most entertaining books.

To Wilkie, Toledo was interesting because of its paintings. Thus the party spent hours viewing the canvases in the great cathedral. And again both the painter and the author passed by the work of El Greco without a word. They visited the little church of San Tomas, dominated wholly by the greatest of El Greco's masterpieces, 'The Burial of Count Orgaz' — to which so many thousands make reverential pilgrimages today — without so much as recording its existence. But Wilkie had not gone to Spain with an open mind. The English artists had followed the lines of Velasquez and Murillo, and consequently they had merit. None other had. And Wilkie was to leave Spain with the dogmatic assertion to Sir Thomas Lawrence that 'the only Spanish pictures which will do in England are those of Murillo and Velasquez.' He had been wholly oblivious to both El Greco and Goya. For the inspection of the paintings they had visited the church and convent of the Capuchins, where Wilkie was struck by the spectacle of a young monk confessing to an old one.[1]

Much of interest, now available to visitors, was not then accessible, but the friends were charmed with their experience, and they found life pleasant as they rumbled down the hill behind the six mules to the plain on their way back to Madrid. But never were they to forget that journey in a dismal rain. Even two years later there was no perfectly defined road covering the entire distance between the town on the Tagus and the capital. They were within ten miles of Madrid before they found a road worthy of the name, and part of the way they passed over trackless sands and meadows. The way was hub-deep in mud and the going heavy, the rain relentless, but they passed without a glance Illescas, where they might profitably have rested near the old hospital and its church with another El Greco masterpiece. To increase their troubles, darkness came on prematurely, and they were forced to spend the night 'in a miserable cottage, all four in a room.' [2] The next morning the earth was flooded with a warm and brilliant sunshine as they rode into Madrid.

Thus passed the winter that Irving had Wilkie as a companion. Jaunts here and there, days at the art museum, evenings at the D'Oubrils' or at the British Legation with the Stanhopes, visits to Wilkie's studio, and early mornings at his writing table made the days pass rapidly. On the last day of the year Irving recorded in his diary that it had been 'a year of labor, but much more comfortable than most I have passed in Europe, and leaves me in a state of moderate hope as to the future.' [3]

[1] Cunningham, II, 82.   [2] Cunningham, II, 467.
[3] Cunningham, II, 83.

Chapter 3: ANDALUSIAN JOURNEY

NEVER had Irving worked so intensely and continuously as during the year 1826. The fever of creation possessed him as he surveyed the richness of material for colorful history spread before him. Like most men of worth-while achievement, he was the object of envy and malice, and the only cloud upon him during this and the succeeding year came from the action of some secret enemy in his own country, who kept sending him all sorts of disagreeable comments and clippings. Supremely sensitive, and not conscious of having done anything to invite such cowardly malignity, he was deeply hurt, and one evening, walking in the Prado with his brother, he spoke with feeling of the persistency of his unknown foe.[1]

But shut up in his apartment at Rich's, or surrounded with rare volumes and manuscripts in the King's library, he usually was in a cheerful mood. The intensity of his application had an effect on his health. He was very nervous at times and had difficulty in sleeping, and at other times, because of overwork and nervous exhaustion, he felt too sleepy and heavy to work. But only once during the summer did he permit himself a change, when he went with Everett on the

[1] Irving, *Life*, II, 66, 68.

journey to La Granja and Segovia; he found refreshment in riding slowly through the great pine forests of the Guadarrama Mountains, with their beautiful vistas over the plains, and he found Segovia a feast for the soul. But in a few days he was back at his desk in the house of Rich.

His researches on Columbus disclosed so much pertaining to the Homeric struggle for the redemption of Granada that in August, when the Madrid sun is most pitiless, he paused to write with feverish haste the rough draft of his 'Conquest of Granada.' But he was happy — happier than he ever had been before. On the last day of the year he wrote on his biography until too weary to go on and then took a stroll through the Madrid streets, that always fascinated him, and then, too sleepy to resume his work, went to bed.[1]

Meanwhile, Murray, his English publisher, after the manner of publishers, was impatiently pressing him for the Columbus manuscript, and Irving was finding that the writing of authentic history required meticulous work, and that the research was never over. 'There are points continually rising to be inquired into and discussed which cause delay,' he wrote in January.[2] He had hoped to have the greater part of the manuscript in Murray's hands by February, but he had suffered disappointment. He had been forced to wait for the inspection of important manuscripts, and a view of the documents had compelled revisions. 'I find the finishing off of a work of the kind involving so many points foreign to my usual course of reading and pursuits, requires time and care.'[3] Most annoying was his difficulty in getting copyists of the manuscripts, and once he was four or five months in finding one; and, having at length found one, he was disheartened to find that at the end of five weeks but

[1] Irving, *Life*, II, 69.   [2] Irving, *Life*, II, 70.
[3] Irving, *Life*, II, 71.

twenty pages had been copied. And no sooner had he re-written to include new material than something else of real importance was discovered and he had to rewrite again. It had all seemed so simple when he began, but constantly he was meeting perplexing controversies as to facts in sources seemingly of equal authority. 'I had no idea,' he wrote in a moment of depression, 'of what a complete labyrinth I had entangled myself in when I took hold of the work.' [1]

It was not until the last of July that he was able to write Murray that the manuscript was ready, and he was fairly pleased with the result. He thought the latter part of the work 'full of incident and interest,' since he had woven into it 'many curious particulars not hitherto known.' He wrote the publisher that he had 'labored hard to make the work complete and accurate,' and had sought 'to execute it in such manner as would render it agreeable to the average reader.' Because of the magnitude of his toil he did not want to part with the copyright for less than three thousand guineas. Murray accepted the terms, and for a time Columbus was off Irving's mind.

But now he turned zealously to the 'Conquest of Granada.' Day by day, when not bent above his writing table, Irving might have been seen hurrying through the old part of the town to the King's library, where he copied manuscripts of Fernando Gonzales and others of the gallant figures of the Conquest, and often through August and September mid-night found him at his task in his apartment. For recreation he would occasionally spend an evening with Everett at the American Legation, but more frequently he found his way to the D'Oubrils', where he could chat with the cynical snuff-taking Minister, or better still with the charming Antoinette; or still better, if suffering from brain fag, he could romp with the children on the floor.

[1] Irving, *Life*, II, 72.

In August young Henry Wadsworth Longfellow came, and Irving introduced him to his friends and advised him on his travels, loaded him down with letters of introduction, took him to the palace of the Duchess of Benavente. And then in October Wilkie appeared, and Irving, while not abandoning his desk, was no little diverted until the artist went on to Seville.

The year dropped from the calendar, and in March Irving was ready for his Andalusian journey. The lure was not alone in the delights of that region of fertility and romance, for he went forth in search of color for his 'Conquest of Granada' to visit the scenes of high emprise of that gallant adventure. He went less as a tourist than as an author.

No ONE sympathized more with his purpose than Antoinette Bolviller, whose keen intelligence in conversation and whose sympathetic response to his enthusiasms had delighted him. To her, for she was young and romantic, nothing could have seemed more entrancing and daring than the journey he planned to make. For not only would it take him to the scenes of valor and more tender scenes of gallantry, but through the perils of the mountains infested then with bandits. As they talked it over, she exacted his promise to write her of his progress, and to this we are indebted for some of the most charming and brilliant letters he ever wrote.

For companionship, Irving had Stoffregen, Secretary of

the Russian Legation, and Gessler, the Russian Consul-General. He had hoped to take his brother Peter with him, but the more he discovered of the real hardships and exposure of the journey, the more he was persuaded that the frail health of the brother could not bear the strain.

The first day of March found the Irving party rolling out of Madrid in a diligence for Cordoba. Irving was familiar with the country as far as Aranjuez, but beyond he was in a new country. For a time thereafter he was to find the countryside barren and uninteresting, though the little towns of La Guardia and Tembleque had much to offer, then as now, in the picturesqueness of old age. Even La Mancha somehow failed to arouse his enthusiasm, and that is strange. For near the town of Puerto Lapiche he found the windmills that Don Quixote charged — windmills that one sees today. The fact that, aside from the occasional olive plantations, the soil seemed sterile and unproductive appears to have dampened even his enthusiasm for Cervantes. Had his enthusiasm been keener, he might have delighted in the flocks of sheep in the neighborhood where Don Quixote saw them when he cried out to Sancho: 'This, oh Sancho, is the day that shall manifest the great things which fortune hath in store for me — seest thou that cloud of dust before us, the whole of it raised by a vast army composed of various and innumerable nations that are marching that way?'

At the *posada* at Manzanares, presided over then by an old man of seventy, they found excellent food and wine, and after a century the *parador* there offers unexcelled hospitality to the traveler. But Irving was still cool. Despite the twenty barrels of Valdepeñas wine in the cellars in the home of the uncle of Antoinette, it did not occur to Irving to tell her of the town of Valdepeñas, 'Valley of Stones.' And though he passed the Venta de Cardenas, a solitary and lonesome house at the edge of the mountains, where Cervantes fixes the adventure with the galley slaves, he makes no mention of it. Soon after Irving passed, this famous house, now a ruin, was a sort of tavern whose proprietor was said to have an understanding with the bandits who roamed the roads nearby. Certainly these gay robbers of the highway were not remote when Irving passed. There is nothing even now to indicate the house's history — merely the front wall bearing the name — and Irving and his companions had no guide. All he had to write to Antoinette of this La Mancha journey was that 'we passed through the scenes of some of the exploits of Don Quixote.'

But, despite their sinister reputation, the Sierra Morena Mountains impressed and pleased him. Previous to the reign of Charles III, these mountains were abandoned to the bandits, who roamed at will, and many a hapless traveler who had entered their defiles on one side never emerged upon the other. This was true to a less degree even in Irving's time. But it was the beauty of the mountains primarily that moved him then. The light of the full moon fell upon the rugged scenery. He thought the scene 'wonderfully wild and romantic, especially after passing the summit of the Sierra.'

The dawn was breaking when they entered 'the stern and savage defiles of the Despeñaperros.' Then, as now, the traveler wound his way along the brink of precipices, 'overhung with cragged and fantastic rocks.' The vistas were breath-taking in their beauty, and not a little terrifying in their possibilities. Even today, with the most perfect roads protected by abutments, it is not a journey for the timid, and when Irving rode the heavy, rolling, jolting diligence that turned the sharp curves on the edge of the precipice, it was far from pleasant.

Soon, however, the perils passed; they 'descended to Carolina' and found themselves 'in another climate.' Orange trees and aloes and myrtle now began to speak softly of Andalusia. The air was sweet and balmy. The little town of La Carolina, which Irving neglects to mention, was neat and clean in those days.[1] The country between it and Bailen, a wide, undulating plain, was rich in corn and oil, but Irving seemingly was ignorant of the significance of Bailen, where Spanish valor had rebuked the arrogance of Napoleon's men not so long before. He passed it without a mention, but in a few years the hero of that engagement would command his admiration at the court of Isabella.

It was not until he reached the town of Andujar that his enthusiasm for towns revived. He was 'delighted with the neatness and cleanness of the houses, the patios planted with orange and citron trees and refreshed by fountains.' It was a town of twenty thousand, and others, passing that way within three years after Irving saw it, found the people more prosperous-looking with fewer ragged than in the small towns of the Castilian plains.[2] It stands at the head of a great plain watered by the Guadalquivir, whose banks were green with vines and olives. It was here that Irving and his companions passed the night, charmed with their introduction to the Andalusia of song and story. Together that night they walked the banks of the river, exalted by the balmy air and the fragrance of growing things, 'and rejoicing certainty that [they] were at length in the land of promise.'

And so, in time, they drove over a road bordered by hedges of aloes, with leaves twelve inches long and stalks from twenty-four to thirty feet high, and entered Cordoba, the ancient capital of the Moors. The book on the 'Conquest of Granada' was now uppermost in Irving's mind.

[1] Inglis, II, 31.   [2] Inglis, II, 34.

THE once populous and glorious capital of the Moors had dwindled in Irving's time until it contained but twenty-two thousand people. Aside from the mosque, it had few attractions at that period. The three friends visited the mosque and explored the streets of the older section, but the most interesting palaces were then closed to strangers. Mounting horses, Irving and his companions rode out to the heights of the Sierra Morena behind the city. Familiar with his old books and manuscripts, Irving was in search of the scenes associated with the conflict of the Moors and the Christians. 'Every mountain summit in this country spreads before you a mass of history, filled with places renowned for some wild and heroic achievement,' he wrote Mademoiselle Antoinette. One day they rode to the famous convent of San Geronimo. Over the mountain-side he found aromatic shrubs and flowers that in other countries came only from the hothouses. 'From these heights,' he wrote, 'the eye revels over a delicious landscape; a broad green valley fertilized by the shining Guadalquivir and bounded by low lines of mountains famous in the hardy predatory wars of the Moors and Christians.'

From Cordoba he rode on to Granada.

'The evening sun shone gloriously upon its red towers,' he wrote his fair friend, 'as we approached it, and gave a mellow tone to the rich scenery of the *vega*. It was like the magic glow which poetry and romance have shed over this enchanting place.'

In the Fonda del Comercio they took up their abode, but

the noise and dirt could not break the spell of being in the town of the Alhambra, with its rare beauty and thrilling associations. For several days the three friends explored the town and its environs. The weather was ideal. It was spring in Granada, and what more wonderful! 'There is an intoxication of heart and soul in looking over such scenery at this genial season. All nature is just teeming with new life and putting on the first delicate verdure and bloom of spring. The almond trees are in blossom, the fig trees are beginning to sprout, everything is in tender bud, the young leaf or the half-open flower' — so ran Irving's rhapsody.

As he wandered wonderingly through the gorgeous gardens of the Generalife, and the marble halls and courts of the Alhambra, he little dreamed that quite soon he would be living in the old quarters of the French Queen in that magic palace, and that the ragged loiterers who dwelt as vagabonds in its hidden corners would soon be his familiar neighbors.

One day he sat in the Court of the Lions, where, a little later, he would have his breakfasts, writing to Antoinette. With the water from the fountain he had diluted his ink. Within view was the fountain which, according to tradition, was the scene of a tragic massacre. It seemed almost strange to Irving, his imagination heated by the scenes about him, that he should be writing a gossiping letter to a lady of the world of fashion 'on the place which has been the scene of an atrocious massacre.' But he found that the sheer beauty of the palace, even in its decay and neglect, so enveloped him as to put his historic imagination in a drowse. The living present was much too vivid — the utter tranquillity, the bright sunshine on the towers, the mellow light on the colonnades, and the marble halls. He tried to recapture the vision of the unfortunate Boabdil, last of the Moorish kings, but an Andalusian peasant was chattering near-by as he set out rosebushes, and a pretty Andalusian girl, who one day would be his most faithful servant, was chanting a romance which Irving had no doubt had been handed down from generation to generation from the time of the Moors; and it was no use to dream.

One day, leaving his friends behind, Irving went alone to the Alhambra. He was eager to locate the gate through which the unhappy monarch had left the palace grounds to descend to the *vega* and surrender to Isabella and Ferdinand. This gate had long fascinated Irving as he read about it, for just as it was the gate of tribulations, it was the gate of triumph; for through it, after Boabdil had passed out, the Grand Cardinal of Spain, surrounded by the cream of the cavaliers, had passed in to take possession. The defeated Moorish king had asked for just one boon from the Catholic monarchs — that no one ever again should be permitted to pass through the gate, which to him was one of tragedy. The boon was granted and the gate was sealed. All this Irving had read in an old chronicle, but to his disappointment he found no one in Granada who knew the story or so much as suspected the location of the gate.

Refusing to be thwarted, Irving determined on a systematic search. Finding a 'poor devil' at work who lived in a hole in the palace, he engaged him to make the search around the walls. Before beginning the search without a chart, the workman inquired of some old residents of the Alhambra's out-of-the-way places. One of these, who was more than eighty years old and had lived all his life on the grounds, indicated the spot. As a child he had heard his parents speak of the walled-up gate and its pathetic story. And so the gate was found, to the delight of Irving. Thoroughly excited by the discovery, he followed the route the Moorish king must have taken from the gate to the *vega* until he reached the small chapel of San Sebastian, which formerly had been a mosque. And there he found an inscription on the wall proclaiming this the spot where Boabdil had surrendered to Isabella and Ferdinand.

Encouraged by his success with the old man of the Alhambra, Irving had many talks with these humble folk who had dwelt there for so many years. With the garrulity of age they were flattered to be asked to talk, and thus one day in March, in the bright sunshine of a Granada spring, Irving listened to the old legends of the palace that had been handed down by word of mouth from generation to generation — the old superstitions that time had accumulated about the chambers of the palace and its crumbling towers. These were stories of the Moors, of buried or hidden treasures, of the uneasy spirits of the dead that stalked the silent courts and corridors in the night. Irving was charmed, and made notes of these old legends and got the promise of more to follow. Thus was born the idea of the 'Tales of the Alhambra,' some of which would be written a little later within the palace walls.

But the journey was not over, and one day the travelers with reluctance turned from Granada and started on their way. From the height, like Boabdil, they paused for a last look on the Alhambra, with its red towers surrounded by its green groves.

THEY were going to Malaga. Even now with its splendid paved roads it is an adventure to cross the mountains, but when Irving ascended the foothills it was a grim peril to make the crossing. No one seeing them riding out of Granada would have suspected that they were merely faring forth for a fashionable outing in the neighboring country. Their equipment was as rough and crude as their journey was to be. Irving thought the muleteers they had engaged carried the badge of brigandage on their faces, and he had little doubt that occasionally they did 'indulge in the profession, as a gentleman occasionally lays by his humanity and indulges in the pleasures of the chase.' As they struggled through the mountain passes and skirted the edges of precipices on constantly winding roads, they spread no linen for their repasts and did not bother about silver. Sometimes they dined among the rocks beside a brook on the roadside, and sometimes on the sands of the sea by the shore in the shade of a crude fisherman's hut. Now and then they ate on the brow of a mountain. But never had Irving's appetite been keener. 'You cannot conceive the luxury of these repasts in the open air in wild and picturesque places, and how charmingly the magic leather bottle of Gessler diffuses an enchantment over the scene,' he wrote Antoinette.

Despite the ill-repute of these mountains, the travelers made merry over the possibility of bandits, while keeping a keen eye out for suspicious characters. Just as they were driving out of the village of Lanjaron, which Irving thought beautiful, they fell in with a stranger whose aspect, manner, and discourse puzzled them not a bit. He seemed waiting for them at the bottom of a wild and solitary pass, and his manner, all agreed, was that of a 'predatory rover who hovers like a hawk among the Spanish mountains to pounce upon the traveler.' Were there companions in crime hiding near-by behind a rock? They wondered as they approached. The mule he rode was young and active, and they noted that it 'bounded among the rocks like a goat.' His hat and jacket were flauntingly Andalusian, and silver lace bordered his pantaloons. Over his shoulder was thrown a cartridge-belt of crimson velvet. Indeed, he was a small arsenal. Two carbines were slung behind his saddle, pistols he had in front, and by his side hung a cutlass. In the pocket of his vest was a long Spanish knife that had a sinister shimmer. Irving, while wondering, could but regret that Wilkie could not have had him as a model for one of his Spanish pictures.

The friends approached; the mysterious creature saluted gaily, and, having received a cordial greeting, deliberately joined them as they rode along. All through the morning the stranger rode by their side through some of the wildest and most isolated sections of the mountains. Were they being personally conducted to their massacre? The travelers wondered. None of the Three Musketeers in their most eloquent moments of gasconading could have surpassed him in the boasting of his prowess. But at noon the mysterious companion with guns and knives waved them a cordial farewell and disappeared into the forest.

They breathed more freely, for constantly they were being reminded of the fate of travelers in these savage defiles. At frequent intervals a cross by the roadside seemed to Irving 'an inexpressible touch of horror.' These crosses generally loomed with their threatening message just around the bend of a road where the assassin had found a convenient hiding-place for his surprise attack.

It was just as the sun was going down on the evening of their morning ride with the stranger that they reached the village of Cadiar. All about the village were olive groves. They dare not brave the dangers of the night now, and so they found lodgings in a village *posada* which Irving was to remember as 'the most wretched' he had seen in Spain. To offset this inconvenience of travel, they met with another

illustration of true Spanish hospitality. The richest man in
the town, who had a large and well-furnished mansion, invited them to his house and urged them to stay the night as
his guests. But preferring their independence to the formali-
ties of hospitality, they returned to their miserable beds in
the rather dirty inn.

Now they were confronted with the most difficult and
dangerous part of their journey. The master of the solitary
mansion assigned them a guide to direct them through the
intricacies of the mountains, and the sergeant of a company
of *douaniers* went with them with his trusty gun. Never was
Irving to forget the solemnity, sublimity, and savagery of
the scenery of that day, as they wound their way through
dangerous passes, on dizzy heights that shook their nerves,
for notoriously along this route the bandits often lay in
wait for their prey. The muleteer and the soldier led warily,
taking no chances against a surprise attack.

At length they emerged from the mountains into the fertile
region that reaches to Malaga. This charming and voluptuous city, so delightful now after many generations, was
famous for its beauty and the liveliness of its population
when Irving and his Russian friends rode into it in April,
1828. It was the perfect season. The air was soft and warm,
and the blue sea was spread out in ripples at their feet.
'We have had beautiful moonlight nights,' he wrote Antoinette, 'and you have no idea of the charming appearance of
one of these Mediterranean ports by moonlight.' The town
was noted for the charm and sprightliness of its women, and
travelers at the time were amazed to find to what extremes
the women carried their love of dress. It was not well for
susceptible youth to attend the Italian opera and subject
themselves to the lure of gorgeously beautiful women with
dark, sparkling eyes, in gowns that would have been in keep-

ing with a gala occasion in the court at Madrid. There was less aloofness toward strangers, for somehow Malaga had early divested itself of the Moorish influence. As the three friends walked about the streets, thronged with merry idlers in Andalusian costumes, and promenaded in the evening in the Alameda, or sipped their Malaga wine in the shops, they soon were aware that gallantry held sway, and that flirtations were not frowned upon.

But the Malaga that Irving saw had more than its fair share of men with no ostensible means of support, who, rumor said, plied their lawless trade by night. But, on the whole, Irving fell in love with the town, and the three friends lingered on for several days. Again Irving wished for Wilkie as they sauntered through the market-place and observed the picturesque characters seated on mats, Moorish-wise, upon the ground, or on low stools. Here and there a lounger seated on the ground, with his back against a wall of a house or a convent, drowsed in the sun, or, with gusto, devoured a luscious melon.

It was there Irving met Kirkpatrick, the American Consul, whose beautiful daughter was to become the mother of the Empress of the French. But notwithstanding the entertainment offered by the Americans and English, Irving had other things to do. At the edge of the town and reaching up to the summit of an eastern hill were the ruins of the castle and of the old Moorish fortifications. His mind obsessed with his 'Conquest of Granada,' he prowled about the ruins, trying to recapture the past.

At length, with real regret, they resumed their journey to Gibraltar.

THEY might have followed the sea along the route of the present fine macadam road, with its marvelous panorama of scenic beauty, with the bluest of blue seas on one side lapping the shore murmurously, and with the mountains on the other side reaching down almost to the water. But when Irving made the journey the road by the sea was all but impassable — a strip of mud and little more. Instead he preferred the more roundabout route through the mountains of Ronda. The mountaineers delighted him, and he thought them the finest he had seen. Even the contrabandists among them he described as 'the knight-errants of the Spanish vulgar.' But they had no adventures through the Ronda Mountains — only the adventure of beauty on every side.

Soon the travelers reached Gibraltar, and as Irving walked the changeless narrow streets he was happy in the thought that he had touched a bit of England: the English names of the streets, the English names on the shop windows, the English garb of the pedestrians, all very much as today. Then, as now, the Moors, the Indians, the Chinese — the same medley of races and nationalities.

On the night of their arrival, they dined at the home of the founder of the 'Sprague Dynasty,' as the American Consulate was called in the American diplomatic service for more than a hundred years. The Sprague with whom Irving dined was to be succeeded after many years by his son, and he by his, and more than a century after the grandfather

entertained Irving at dinner I had luncheon with the last
of the line, within a year of his death and the end of the
dynasty. Irving and his Russian friends found the first of
the Spragues a congenial soul, and in the midst of jollity they
lingered at the table until past midnight. But Irving passed
a sleepless night. Four days he lingered, climbing the rock,
walking the main street, and pleasing his fancy with the
conglomerate races.

And then he started on to Cadiz.

Today he would have crossed to Algeciras, lunched perhaps in one of the most charming hotels in Europe, and then,
over roads that are a paradise for motorists, he would have
reached his destination in a little while. For some reason he
only skirted Algeciras, not then famous as the site of the conference that saved the world from war, and, going by way of
San Roque, again entered the mountains. He was in happy
mood. The country seemed 'sweet and fragrant,' the flowers
were in a riot of blossoming, and the nightingales were singing. By noon he was four leagues from San Roque, and at
a *venta* in the hills he made a meal on eggs and sausage. And
there he was entertained by the appearance of a contrabandist in romantic costume, with his wife, or, as Irving suspected
from his manner, his mistress. It was night when he skirted
the heights of Fagina. Perfume of flowers, songs of the nightingales, the hum of the sea insects, lights, and the voices of
herdsmen from the darkness — it was idyllic. But the next
day he hired a coach and four mules and hurried on to Cadiz.

At six o'clock on the evening of the second day his mules
drew up in front of the Hôtel Anglais. He did not know at
the time that a little later he would return to Cadiz and pass
over to the Port of Saint Mary and take a cottage in the
country to escape the heat and facilitate his writing. He
found Cadiz on his first visit pleasant, with its clean streets

and fine houses; and with Burton, the American Consul, he liked to ramble on the promenade beside the ramparts, to watch the pageantry of the sea with its fishing smacks, its ferryboats, and larger merchant vessels, the fishermen on the rocks, the sea gulls swooping about. He walked the Alameda under its palm trees, and at night went to the theater, where, as it happened, he saw a 'miserable play,' but found compensation in the beauty of the women in the audience; for Cadiz also was famed for the charm of its women.

But he was not to leave Cadiz without causing the Consul some trouble because of a last-moment thought of his passport and his neglect to familiarize himself with the dates of all the fiestas. He had taken passage on the steamboat *Betis* to proceed to Seville on the Guadalquivir, and on the day he was to sail he went to the passport office for his visa, only to find it closed because of the fiesta. In desperation he appealed to his friend Burton. And among the archives of the Cadiz Consulate, now in Seville, one may read today the appeal of Burton to the Chief of Police under date of April 13, 1828:

> Necessary Mr. Washington Irving, Attaché to the American Embassy, to pass today without fail to Seville, and the passport office is closed today due to the festivity of the day. I should like you to take the trouble to order his visa, asking you to excuse this trouble. God keep you for many years.[1]

The police chief 'took the trouble' and Irving boarded the *Betis*. He found it a real adventure, for from the deck he could see the mountains of Ronda, looking 'like a blue haze,' and the great herds of cattle on the banks, and the fruit of the fertile fields.

Thus he reached Seville, where he was to linger more than a year engaged again in intensive literary work.

[1] MS. Archives, United States Consulate, Seville.

Chapter 4: ANDALUSIAN DAYS

NOT long ago a house in Seville was opened for the accommodation of North American students and called the 'Washington Irving House.' An inscription was prepared for a tablet on the house, but one of the committee objected to the wording on the ground that one might presume from the language that Irving actually had lived in the house. 'And,' he added, 'he probably never was in Seville.' This was before the portrait of Irving, painted in Seville by Sir David Wilkie, had been presented to the City Hall. And yet few Sevillians today know that Irving passed almost a year profitably and with pleasure in the charming city of Andalusia.

The Seville in which he arrived the middle of April, 1828, was a city of ineffable charm, not greatly different from that of a century later. Then, as now, it was the romantic center of Spain, the city which more than any other symbolizes the Spain that foreigners envision — a city of romance, of mystery, of infinite beauty. Irving was to find a never-ending delight in wandering through its narrow streets with their overhanging balconies and barred windows, their clean white houses with enticing glimpses into the patios with their fountains and trees heavily hung with golden oranges, with the fragrance of flowers titillating the nostrils of the curious passer-by.

Driving to the Fonda de la Reyna, Irving found comfortable quarters and hastily unpacked and washed away the stains of dusty travel. Then he hurried away to the Fonda del Sol, which stood where it stands today on a charming little plaza where Wilkie was staying. It was a substantial brick building with iron balconies at all the windows opening on the plaza, and if it accepted the sun that poured into the open space by day, it caught more of the breezes at night than houses shut in by the narrow streets.

There Irving and Wilkie had their reunion, and during the next ten days the writer devoted himself exclusively to his friend. The latter had been in hot pursuit of the paintings of Murillo and Zurbaran, and was eager to share his pleasures with Irving. Living in Seville was Mr. Julian Williams, a rich British merchant, who possessed one of the finest private collections in Seville, and Irving was hurried to the house, where Wilkie was a welcome visitor. There, among the paintings of Murillo, was the artist's portrait of himself, the 'Christ on the Cross,' painted at first on the lid of a relic box, and, most precious of all, his 'Christ Crowned With Thorns.' But Irving was strangely unilluminating in his observations. 'Some fine Murillos,' he wrote in his diary.

Thence Wilkie hurried him to the beautiful old palace of the Duke of Medinaceli, built in imitation of Pilate's house, which visitors may view today. It is difficult after three centuries to find in the whole of Spain a palace so vividly illustrative of the pomp, luxury, and magnificence of the high nobility of the seventeenth century. The main patio, with its exquisitely carved balconies, its busts of the Roman emperors and orators, its incomparable tiles with the shimmer that came from an art long lost to the tilemakers of our

time, could not have been different in the days when the
two travelers stood in awe before its beauty. Irving was to
revisit the palace later and to meet a strange character.

That night they dined at the home of Mrs. Stalker, an
English woman who was to be closely identified with Irving's
life in Seville; but immediately after dining the enthusiastic
Wilkie led his friend to a convent to see the Murillos in the
chapel. The 'Conquest of Granada' could wait. The corrections on the 'Columbus' could be postponed. Irving was
entitled to a vacation from his desk, and, aside from the
sketch of Irving, Wilkie was to stretch no canvas in Seville.
Murray, the London publisher of Irving's books, had commissioned the artist to make a portrait of the author as a
frontispiece for one of his volumes, and one April day a book-
lover, browsing in a library, might have seen a handsome
man seated quietly at a window while another rapidly
sketched his likeness. But in two days that was over.

Most of the time was spent in feverish pilgrimages to galleries and private houses. One day a young Spanish painter
took them to see the collection of Bravo, a shopkeeper, where
Irving laconically found 'some superb Murillos,' and Wilkie
was fascinated by the portrait of the painter with black,
flowing hair. Others who visited the same collection at this
time wrote that 'among a great many indifferent pictures in
this collection there is an excellent "Magdalen," ' which
apparently made no impression on Irving.[1] Nor did this
visitor's admiration for the 'Saint Anthony Preaching to the
Fishes' find a reflection in the comments of either Irving or
Wilkie.

That evening the two friends dined alone at the Fonda del
Sol, and Irving returned to the Fonda de la Reyna for a
siesta in preparation for an evening of light comedy at the
theater.

[1] Inglis, II, 78.

A visitor in Seville today is apt to overlook the little Church of La Caridad, connected with the hospital of that name. But those who are well advised and find it, entering the church through the patio, will retrace the steps of Irving and feast their eyes on the same artistic treasures. The 'noble painting of Moses striking the rocks' impressed him most. Thence the two adventurers in beauty hurried to the Church of San Tomas to see Zurbaran's painting of the saint, which Wilkie admired. And from San Tomas they went to the chapter house of the cathedral to see 'the beautiful portrait of San Justa by Murillo'; and thence to the library of the cathedral, a few steps, and for the first time Irving entered the solemn and impressive rooms in which he was to pass so many laborious days a little later.

But the day was not done; and that afternoon the two friends strolled along the Alameda of Hercules, which soon was to become Irving's favorite promenade when he could force himself from his desk; and a little later he walked with Wilkie to the top of the Giralda Tower. To Irving this masterpiece of architectural beauty, handed down from the Moors to the cathedral, was to be a source of constant delight so long as he was to remain in Seville. Though the ascent is not by steps, but by an easy winding walk, the top of the tower is three hundred and fifty feet high, and it is by no means a mean walk to its summit. But when, on the same day, Irving's Russian friends, Stoffregen and Gessler, arrived in Seville, Irving made the ascent the second time, eager to show them the city from the heights. The next day Irving ascended again to see the town in a different light.

It was toward the close of Wilkie's sojourn that the two friends, with the Russians, dined at 'Widow Merry's.' She was the widow of an English diplomat who had been accredited to Spain, and then to the United States during

Jefferson's administration, and she was known personally to Wilkie, and at least by reputation to Irving. Washington had found her a pronounced bluestocking, with a mind more masculine than her husband's. Though by no means frail or dainty, being a lady of imposing presence and more impressive manner, men of intellect had found her interesting as a hostess. But the crudities of Washington, then five years old, had disgusted her, and she kept no secrets from her public. Running afoul of Jefferson's code of etiquette, she had preferred to think herself insulted at a White House dinner, and the party enemies of Jefferson had sympathized with her grievance and fanned the flames of her resentment until the petty incident became the subject of diplomatic correspondence between Washington and London. En route to America she had met Tom Moore, the Irish poet, who later was to share the pleasures of Paris with Irving, and when he visited her in Washington she enlisted him in her battles. Out of this had come Moore's famous poetic satire on the young capital of the States. With all this Irving must have been acquainted. Now, her husband dead, Mrs. Merry was living in Seville. No doubt there was much chat concerning Moore among his friends, and perhaps the hostess recalled with feeling her experiences with the democratic court in Washington.

But the guests could not linger through the afternoon, for there was a bullfight that evening, and the artist, the American, and the two Russians witnessed the pageantry and the drama from the box of the Captain General of Seville. It would have been interesting to hear the impressions of Irving and Wilkie as they slowly paced the Alameda under the trees that night.

But these pleasant days with Wilkie were now ending, for the artist was responding to the call from home. Irving, who

found his friend's health vastly improved by the Spanish
sunshine, sought to hold him yet a little longer, but without
success. And one morning Irving and a group of friends
waved Wilkie farewell as his diligence swept out of Seville in
a cloud of dust.

A few days later Irving left the Fonda de la Reyna and took
lodgings in the home of Mrs. Stalker. A few days more and
his Russian friends were gone, and Irving turned with all the
more zest from his pleasures to his literary work — for there
was much to do.

N O ONE knows positively where
Irving lived in Seville. The boarding-house of Mrs. Stalker
was in the Santa Cruz section near the alcazar at 4 Plazuela
de la Constitucion. After more than a century it remains the
most charming section of the city, with its very narrow
streets, its pretty little plaza, its picturesque houses, its atmosphere of serenity, mystery, and romance. Here was the house
of Murillo, and of other celebrities of the arts. After the
Alhambra, it may well be doubted if Irving ever found a
dwelling-place so appealing to his poetic imagination. The
traveler wandering through the delightful little passages of
Santa Cruz today sees little that did not meet the eye of
Irving.

Wilkie now was gone and there was work to do, but the
remaining week in April Irving set aside for pleasure. One
day found him with his Russian friends at a bullfight; and

BARRIO SANTA CRUZ WHERE IRVING LIVED IN SEVILLE

one early morning found him in a carriage behind four mules bound for the famous fair at Mayrena, about seven leagues away. He had come to love all Spanish pageantry, fiestas and customs and legends. The day was clear, the sky never bluer, and the sun never more brilliant. They had drawn out of Seville at five in the morning, but it was not until seven in the evening that they drew up at the *posada* at Mayrena. Here they found a small room on the ground floor, and then prepared to join in the festive spirit of the day. With the son of the Marquis of Amarillas they went out to see the horses, to get the 'feel' of the crowd and the occasion.

Spread before Irving was a great rich plain, with the ruins of an old Moorish castle in the near ground and with the pleasant mountains of Ronda on the horizon. The scene before him reminded him of 'an Arab or Moorish encampment after a foray.' Droves of horses, of sheep and cattle, rude tents, and dashing horsemen on fine horses in the picturesque Andalusian garb went thundering here and there. Here a group of men stood gossiping; there some were drowsing in the shade, and yonder a group was copiously drinking the fine wine of the region and singing gypsy songs. The landscape seemed 'trembling with the heat of the sun.' So delighted was Irving with the picture that he sketched it in a fragmentary diary: 'Hedges of aloes, fields of olives, clouds of dust; distant mountains confused in sultry mist — tinkling of bells; oxen standing patient and immovable — horses prancing and neighing . . . groups of gypsies.'

Irving was finding the soul of Andalusia and finding it good.

On the return journey, Irving and his friends drew up at a white tower by the roadside, a relic of the Moors, and threw themselves on the grass to see the pageantry of the cavalcade of horsemen and carts moving through the dusty mist toward Seville. Many were walking. And then Irving's party joined the procession. Near the village of Portalazza one of the wheels of their carriage came off, but without injury to their pride.

May Day found Irving shut up at Mrs. Stalker's writing 'a little on the history of Granada.' Henceforth we shall find him hard at work, almost every day, and yet finding time to drain the cup of Sevillian pleasure.

THROUGHOUT the month of May he shut himself up in his rooms and wrote almost daily on his 'Conquest of Granada,' varying his labors now and then by writing corrections in his 'Life of Columbus.' His researches in Seville were confined to the library of the great cathedral and the Archives of the Indies.

Of the two rooms in the cathedral library, then open to students engaged in research, it is probable that he used the one that looks out on the street where the very Columbus books that he used are now displayed in cases. In his diary he mentions the very notations in these volumes that may be seen today behind their glass protection. Many days found him in this long, narrow room, cool and silent, poring over the volumes that had intrigued Columbus, but a search by the librarian fails to disclose any relic of his study there. Books have been shifted in the intervening century, the volumes associated with Columbus being now in cases, but the room is much the same — eternal and unchanging as the superb cathedral.

When Irving was in Seville it was not a simple matter to consult the invaluable manuscripts in the Archives of the Indies, as now when Americans flock to that fount of information in large numbers. The fine stone structure was the same then as now, and Irving must have found its history interesting. In the days of Philip II it had been built by the architect of the Escorial. For generations the traders and shippers of Seville had called their wares and bartered on the steps of the cathedral, until complaint was made that the noisy trading disturbed the worshipers within. To furnish the traders with a stock market of their own the present edifice of the Archives was conceived and built, but the barterers resented the interference with an ancient custom and could not easily be persuaded to leave the cathedral steps. In the latter part of the eighteenth century the splendid edifice was made the repository of books and documents relating to the two Americas. But to secure access to this valuable collection in the days of Irving a permit from Madrid, signed by the Minister, was required. Many days were lost before Everett forwarded the permission. Armed with the ministerial letter, Irving presented himself to Higuera y Lara, the director, in mid-April, and thereafter as long as he was in Seville he frequented the Archives building. It could not have been the most refreshing spot in Seville in midsummer. When the summer heat falls on Seville today those engaged in research work on the ground floor, but in Irving's day they were confined to the second floor, closer to the sun.

Fourteen years before, it was there that a large manuscript book in the nature of an index setting forth all the material on Columbus had been prepared, and this, in perfect condition, is in use today. This was the volume whose pages Irving frequently was turning, determining from the index the material he wished, and sending for it piece by piece. It was his custom to work to the point of diminishing returns, and then seek relaxation. During that month of May he saw several bullfights, and from notations in his diary it is evident that he thought himself something of a critic of the methods of the matadors. Sometimes he went to the theater or the opera; often he spent an evening at a *tertulia* at the home of Williams, the English merchant, or that of Wetherell, another wealthy Englishman who had a tannery in the suppressed Jesuit Convent of San Diego. Frequently for exercise he walked to the top of the Giralda Tower, and he never tired of sauntering through the enchanted streets. Often, that summer, he felt the need of rest from his intensive labors. 'Feel enervated,' he wrote in his diary. 'Incapable of writing anything' — this more than once.

HIS requirements for relaxation and pleasure were quite simple. He never was surfeited by aimless rambles through the streets at night, letting his imagination play on the softly spoken conversations through barred windows, listening to the tinkling of guitars on balconies or in hidden nooks, and to the murmuring of fountains in odorous patios. But his favorite promenades were on the Alameda de Hercules, the Delicias on the banks of the Guadalquivir, and to the famous cigar factory, immortalized later by the 'Carmen' of Mérimée and the opera. Perhaps the Alameda saw him most.

In 1828 this was a fashionable promenade. Today one

still may walk in the Alameda as a century ago, but the atmosphere is quite different. The great stone pillars of Hercules still stand sentinel at the entrance. The street still is the widest in the city, with the wide parked space with trees in the center and with roadways on either side. The houses behind their iron fences with their little front gardens remain, but the aristocracy that once inhabited them have moved to other quarters, and some of the fine old houses are not above suspicion. No doubt some of the trees and shrubbery are gone, and the parked space is rather parched and drear. A fashionably dressed man strolling alone along the Alameda now would arouse the curiosity of the passer-by, but in Irving's day everyone took his stroll there as naturally as in the Prado in Madrid.

Irving loved it because it offered a change from the narrow streets of the city and gave him the wide expanse of star-studded sky he loved. Day after day he found his way hither, often alone, frequently in company with a friend, sometimes with a child as sole companion.

Now and then he went to the Delicias, a grove of flowering trees and plants about a mile down the river, much favored by lovers of the beautiful. Irving has left no description of this promenade, but another traveler of the same period has given us a picture of geranium-bordered walks, of avenues lined with acacias, of weeping willows, of orange and lemon groves just beyond and within view — delicious shade for a Sevillian summer with the perfume of flowers and plants. Here Irving occasionally was found walking alone, but the Alameda was much more convenient.

Nineteen years were to intervene before Prosper Mérimée would give immortality to the famous cigar factory of Seville with his tale of 'Carmen,' but Irving found it an interesting place to walk at night or late in the evening. This immense pile of stone, resembling a fortress, was then a favorite rendezvous for the young in the evenings. The scene with laughing youth was gay enough as friends and lovers prome- naded the broad walks around it under the trees. After a century it still is in use, though a part of the immense building is now a barracks for soldiers; the young have found more desirable places, and only the old and middle-aged find it an agreeable lounging-place.

But at all hours of the day or night, and especially when the moon was full, Irving found the great cathedral fascinat- ing. He haunted its library, and more frequently perhaps than any other in Seville walked to the summit of the Giralda; but he was awed and deeply moved, non-Catholic though he was, by the interior of the church. Time and again when the city was flooded with the moonlight, which seems softer and sweeter in Andalusia than elsewhere, he would walk around the church, finding the architecture more beautiful in the soft glow of the moon. Living close to the cathedral, he seldom passed a day without a visit, preferring to get his im- pressions alone, and not infrequently he made more than one visit a day. In a letter to Antoinette he vividly reflected his mood regarding the ancient church.

If ever you come to Seville be sure to visit its glorious cathedral. That, however, you will be sure to do; your good taste will not suffer you to keep away; but visit it more than once; visit it in the evening when the last rays of the sun, or rather the last glimmer of the daylight, is shining through its painted windows. Visit it at night, when its various chapels are partially lighted up, its immense aisles are dimly illuminated by their rows of silver lamps, and when Mass is preparing amidst gleams of gold and clouds of incense at its high altar. Visit it at those times, and if possible be alone, or with as few gay ladies and gentlemen as possible, for they are the worst kind of companions for a cathedral. I do not think altogether I have ever been equally delighted with any building of the kind. It is so majestic, ample, and complete; so sumptuous in all its appointments, and noble and august in its ceremonies.[1]

On San Fernando's Day, when the city was aflame with lights and the Giralda was brilliantly illuminated, Irving walked the streets in boyish delight, and in the cathedral he saw the body 'of the sainted King exposed in a coffin of gold and silver, with a glass side, the body enveloped in rich brocade.' The face seemed very dark to Irving, resembling that of an Egyptian mummy. And having looked upon the body of the long-dead king, he finished the day with a bullfight. Three hundred and fifty-one years before, Queen Isabella had knelt in the same spot before the monument of her ancestor.

Even the preparations for Corpus Christi delighted Irving, and he meandered about the fair with its toys and cakes. And then on the great day, after an early breakfast, he strolled through the streets protected from the sun by awnings, and rejoiced in the riot of color from the red damask that concealed the fronts of the houses and hung from the balconies. He eagerly found his way to the cathedral, where boys in old Spanish dress were dancing before the altar as Isabella had seen them three and a half centuries before, and he followed the procession with the crosses and images of the saints, immensely impressed by the great silver shrine with the Host. In the evening he went again to the cathedral, delighted by the grace of the boys dancing before the altar, with the high altar and grating richly gilded, and by the velvet of crimson wound around the great columns.

Then he went again to a bullfight, stopping on his way home for ices.

[1] Irving, *Life*, II, 118.

Thus Irving observed the celebration of Corpus Christi in Seville in 1828.

The cathedral, the Giralda — these were, to Irving, the choice things of Seville. He does not appear to have been so much impressed with the Alcazar, which in his mind was overshadowed by the Alhambra, but occasionally he walked in its venerable gardens, losing himself in the maze of the boxwood, and breathing deeply as he walked under the orange, the lemon, and the pomegranate trees.

THROUGH the sultry heat of June, July, and August he labored incessantly over his manuscript, feverishly writing on his 'Conquest of Granada,' making corrections in his 'Columbus,' occasionally writing some of the stories that later were to go into the 'Spanish Sketch-Book.' Frequently in the library of the cathedral, often in the Archives of the Indies, the greater part of his time, however, was passed in the house in the Santa Cruz section bending over his desk. At times the heat oppressed and weakened him, and he became very nervous and discouraged over his lapses in inspiration, sometimes recording in his diary that he felt 'desperate.' But these were moments of moods, and the day of depression was followed by one of exaltation over some discovery in a book or manuscript.

With Wilkie back in England, and his Russian friends in Madrid, he was thrown upon his resident English friends for companionship, and they responded freely to his needs.

Unhappily the exclusiveness of the Sevillanos deprived him of the social contacts he would have enjoyed. This was much more pronounced in Seville than in Madrid or Granada. Fond of the society of women, and fascinated by the Spanish women he had met, he was soon complaining to Dolgorouki of his failure to meet them in Seville. He wrote:

> I am convinced that the great fascination of Spanish women arises from their natural talent, their fire and soul, which beam through their dark and flashing eyes, and kindle up their whole countenance in the course of an interesting conversation. As I have but few opportunities of judging of them in this way, I can only criticize them with the eye of a sauntering observer. It is like judging of a fountain when it is not in play, or a fire when it lies dormant and neither flames nor sparkles. After all, it is the divinity *within* which makes the divinity *without*.[1]

I T WAS Everett who had introduced Irving to the Marquesa de Arco Hermoso and opened the way to the understanding friendship of two kindred souls. But before he met her Irving had been prepared to like her because of his social and literary intimacy with her father, Johan Nikolaus Faber, who had been a close associate at Cadiz. This German scholar had married a Spanish woman and had settled in Spain, where he was the manager of a wine company. Nature had designed him for literature and scholarship rather than for commerce. He was a man of

[1] Irving, *Life*, II, 120, 121.

real distinction and robust character, and Irving had the benefit of his conversation and his splendid library. It probably was his friendship with Faber that had drawn him to Santa Maria.

Cecile, the daughter, had married for the second time a little before Irving met her, and was living in Seville when Everett presented the American. Irving found her fascinating and congenial at the first meeting. She had beauty, spirit, animation, and charm, but it was her intellectual qualities and literary tastes and ambitions that appealed to the American writer. That first day she delighted him with anecdotes of the simple and superstitious peasantry of the village of Dos Hermanas, and he urged her to write what she had told him. To the father he sent a glowing account of the experience:

> She related them [the anecdotes] with wonderful spirits and discrimination, and in fact her conversation made such an impression on me that I noted down as much of the substance and point of it as I could recollect. I do not know when I have been more delighted with the conversation of anyone, it was so full of original matter, the result of thinking, and feeling, as well as observing.[1]

At Cecile's house, where interesting people gathered, he was to spend many happy hours, and soon the two were exchanging confidences regarding their literary aspirations; Irving was pressing her to write, and reading her manuscripts, criticizing and encouraging her, and probably influencing her literary career, which was to flower much later when, as Fernan Caballero, she would become a famous Spanish novelist of her time. The fact that both were romanticists, sharing a common idolatry of Byron, made them congenial. Through the long talks with her in the house at

[1] Letter to J. N. Böhl, from Seville, April 7, 1829.

8 Calle Jesus — or was it the Plaza San Vicente, as some insist? — Irving for the first time began to understand the psychology of the Spanish masses. Cecile's portrait by Madrazo, which hangs in the library of the University of Seville, has caught something of her charm and beauty. Not long ago I drove through the village of Dos Hermanas, with whose simple peasants, their superstitions, and folklore she had acquainted Irving. The streets were thronged with peasants, but times have changed, and those I saw bore no resemblance to the obsequious and superstitious forebears that Cecile had known.

But for the most part his friendships in Seville were confined to the small English colony there, and to but a few of these. Williams, the rich merchant, and Wetherell, the wealthy tanner, and their families contributed much to his enjoyment. This was especially true of the Wetherells, at whose hospitable home he attended numerous concerts. 'In the evening at Wetherells',' he writes in his diary. 'Mad Passarini there, the prima doña seria. Sings several airs for us. Her husband with her, an Italian prince.'

During the summer of 1928 Irving devoted several Sundays to picnics, and he had his favorite picnic grounds. More than once he drove to Italica, four leagues distant, to view the Roman ruins, the amphitheater, and the palace, and now and then he drifted down the river between tree-lined banks to the country place of Mr. Beck, another Englishman, to have lunch in the orange grove and to stroll under the orange trees in the moonlight. But his favorite picnic grounds were at San Juan de Alfarache and Alcala de la Guadaira.

THE village of Alcala de la Guadaira was famous even in the days of Irving for its bread, and Irving refers to it in his diary as Alcala de los Panaderos. After a century it is estimated that fully half the bread consumed in Seville comes from the bakeries of Alcala. In Irving's time it was carried by mules the full distance to the city, where deliveries were made from house to house on the backs of mules, and even now bread-laden mules deliver it from house to house, but they ride in a train to the city. The bread retains its popularity because richer in nourishment than most of that of the bakeries, owing to the kneading of the dough longer and more vigorously, thus excluding water, and to the use of more flour.

But it was not the bakeries that so often took Irving and his friends to the village and its environs.

The road to Alcala de la Guadaira today is one of the best, and for a distance shaded by trees on either side, but this road is comparatively new, and the one used by Irving is no longer in use.

The little town, which had, and has, a more prosperous air than the average village, is situated on the picturesque little river of Guadaira, which joins the Guadalquivir near Seville. Then, as now, on the outskirts of the town and on a hill are the ruins of a great Roman fortress which the Moors took over and used for war purposes for many years. Winding away from the village is the river, its green banks shaded by trees and lined with the ruins of old Moorish mills.

On Sunday mornings, Irving with his friends, with well-filled baskets, drove to Alcala in time for a fragrant breakfast on the greensward under the trees on the banks of the winding river. After breakfast it was always Irving's impulse to revisit the ruins of the old castle, whence he could survey the country for miles around. By this time everything Moorish fascinated him. And after lunch he would walk for miles along the riverbank, pausing now and then for a curious inspection of some of the ruined mills, to sit on the grass and listen to the songs of birds and the ripple of the water — the only sounds that one hears even now. 'Nothing can be more charming than the windings of the little river among banks hanging with gardens and orchards of all kinds of delicate southern fruits, and tufted with flowers and aromatic plants,' he wrote enthusiastically to Antoinette. 'The nightingales throng this lovely little valley as numerously as they do the gardens of Aranjuez. Every bend of the river presents a new landscape, for it is beset by old Moorish mills of the most picturesque forms; each mill having an embattled tower — a memento of the valiant tenure by which those gallant fellows, the Moors, held this earthly paradise, having to be ready at all times for war.' [1]

Here is a spot that has scarcely changed since Irving walked upon the banks of the river. The walk is beaten with the tramping of generations, the mills are just as picturesque and isolated, the serenity of the scene as sweet, and the shade almost as abundant. The flowers still bloom and the birds still sing, though I heard no nightingales.

Here, weary with the writing of the 'Conquest of Granada,' Irving came frequently to commune with Nature, to escape the heat of the summer's sun in the shade of the trees on the banks of the gently flowing stream. It was his favorite picnic ground.

[1] Irving, *Life*, II, 110.

A little nearer the city, and almost as popular with Irving for picnic purposes on Sundays, was San Juan de Alfarache, in the fertile valley of the Guadalquivir, which usually bore him and his party to the picnic grounds. Now and then he ascended the heights above the village to visit the monastery: frequently he and his party lunched from picnic baskets on the banks of the river, and on one occasion they dined at 'Valparaiso,' the country seat of Beck, the Englishman. This pleasant place was one of several in the neighborhood once used as retreats for the wealthy Moors. So charmed was Irving with Beck's country place that he often drifted down the river to spend a late afternoon or evening with his friend. Enthusiastically he proclaimed the beauty of the vicinity to Antoinette. 'You cannot imagine scenery more soft, graceful, luxuriant, and beautiful,' he wrote. 'These retreats are built along the side of a ridge of hills overlooking the fertile valley of the Guadalquivir, and the serpentine windings of that river, with Seville and its towers rising at a distance, and the Ronda Mountains bounding the landscape.' A 'perfect garden' he found it, 'filled with oranges, citrons, figs, grapes, pomegranates,' with 'the aloe and the Indian fig in blossom — the whole country covered with flowers, such as in other countries are raised in hothouses, but here growing wild.' [2]

After a century there has been much change. San Juan de Alfarache still is a village, but because of speedier means of locomotion more of a Sevillian suburb. The old monastery still stands upon the hill; the river still winds its way toward the sea, but its banks where Irving picnicked are no longer timbered as before. Even so, picnickers from Seville still use it as a picnic ground, though now a little *venta*, where I had a mug and a sandwich, relieves them of the burden of the basket.

[2] Irving, *Life*, II, 109.

Irving was to know this region well, for in this general neighborhood, the precise spot unknown today, he found the summer house to which he escaped through July and August from the heat of Seville.

B Y JULY the city was sweltering in the sun. In the region of Santa Cruz scarcely a breath of air was stirring. Irving found it impossible to sleep, and was yearning for the open spaces in the night where he might catch a breeze. It was just then that he found a friend whose necessities determined him to find a country place.

John Nalder Hall, the newly acquired friend, who roomed at Mrs. Stalker's, was a young man of education and charm who had sought the serenity of Spain for his health. A broken blood vessel had imperiled his life and left him in delicate health, and he hoped through a long period of rest and quiet lounging to hasten the completion of his convalescence. But in the scorching heat of Santa Cruz he failed to find the relief he sought, and Irving set about to find a country house that he could share with the invalid. For days he scoured the country roundabout in search of a cottage near enough to town to permit of easy excursions to the library of the cathedral and the Archives.

At length, Wetherell offered his cottage of Casa Cera, and on the first of July the two friends took possession. It was within walking distance of Beck's seat of Valparaiso, and the surrounding country offered numerous attractions. Casa Cera was a cottage with a little garden where they could rest in the shade of orange and citron trees. The little porch was shaded by grapevines and jessamines. A high brick wall surrounded the house and grounds, and with the setting of the sun the servant carefully locked the gates for the night against the robbers that were not unknown in the region. Sebastian, the servant, seemed a simple soul, but they were to find that he was not the soul of virtue, since on occasion in returning unexpectedly from a short journey they found him in a joyous state of inebriation. They noticed, too, that a mysterious stranger on horseback appeared occasionally before the gate for a moment, and then as mysteriously rode away. It was not until after the friends had given the cottage up that Sebastian was arrested for harboring robbers. Happily Irving was usually low in funds, else he might have ended his life with a slit throat.

Utterly oblivious to the danger, the two friends enjoyed their cottage. Irving was working doggedly through the two hot months, constantly walking to Seville to labor in the library and the Archives, and writing constantly at the cottage. It was there that he finished his story of the siege of Malaga and wrote the death of the Duke of Cadiz.

But he found time for the companionship of Hall when, in writing, he reached the point of diminishing returns. Frequently the two fared forth in search of adventure and of the interesting points of the neighborhood. Because of his frail health, Hall usually would mount the one horse they had, and Irving would plod along by his side. Many times in the late afternoon or early evening they explored the banks of the river Guadaira, and the old Moorish mill drew them often. Once, when they walked from the ruins of the mill on to the seat of Beck and sought a short cut home, they found themselves lost among the bushes. In the evenings their friends from Seville would drive out to sit with them and chat in the breezes of the little garden. 'Full moon, beautiful night,' he wrote after one such visit. At times Hall seemed very ill.

With one faintly hearing the flapping of the wings of the angel of death, it was not unnatural for them to sit in the quiet of the moonlit garden and speculate on eternity and a future life. Was there a future life? Hall was skeptical — wishing to believe, but doubtful. Was there such a thing as a visitation of the dead? They wondered. One evening they made a bargain on Hall's suggestion that the survivor of the two should try under the most favorable circumstances to recall the spirit of the departed friend. Irving was not to forget.

IT WAS while living at the Casa Cera that Irving made his sentimental and inquisitorial visit to Palos and to the monastery of La Rabida. He wished to visit Moguer on the way, for it and the region had been the seat of the Pinzons from the far-off days when they rallied to the support of the Columbus expedition. The family still was prominent and powerful, its members holding official positions and retaining the property which had made them so potent in the discovery of the New World. The head of the family was Juan Fernandez Pinzon, an old man of seventy-two with numerous sons, who lived after the patriarchal manner of his ancestors. Irving wished to talk with him, to inquire about family records, and to go with him to the spots associated with Columbus.

And so, leaving Hall in the care of the Wetherells, Irving on an August day drove in a *calesa* for Moguer with a letter from one of the younger sons of the patriarch to his father. It was to mean some days of hardship and hard driving. After a century, one may leave Seville at eleven or later, and driving over the most perfect roads, visit Moguer, Huelva, Palos, and the monastery easily in an afternoon. It was not so simple then. The *calesa* lumbered out of Seville and through Triana, a seafaring town favored by the gypsies, whence came the sailor of Columbus who first sighted the New World; and after a long afternoon of driving through a country of vineyards, olive orchards, fig trees, and impressive pines, he entered a lonely valley in which bats flitted about, and whence could be seen the fires flickering on the Sierra Morena.

That night he found a bed of three chairs in a solitary *posada* which had no side walls — just a roof supported by stone pillars. There he supped on a ham he had brought along. Even now this region seems more isolated and lonely than other parts of Spain, and that night Irving tossed on his improvised bed of chairs listening to the passing of flocks of sheep, to the sheep bells, to the barking of dogs. Even the morning disclosed a lonely countryside. Not even a bird was singing. At Villarosa he lingered for six hours to dine on eggs and grapes and to take a siesta, and at three he entered the grain and wine country. Passing the very ancient town of Nieblo he did not pause, merely making a notation of its 'Moorish walls and towers built around the crest of a rock.' He did not dream that after a century the excavations of archeologists would reveal a civilization there extending far beyond the Roman period and impart a mysterious charm to the town. He did not turn from the highway to see.

But Irving had other things to occupy his mind. The

roads were rough, and just before reaching Moguer the *calesa* tumbled over into a narrow defile. That night he found lodgings in a little *posada* where he slept in a room ten feet square.

It was at Moguer that Irving presented his letter to the patriarch of the Pinzons, seated with his family in a little court fragrant with flowers. There he had supper, and a friar of Santa Clara was summoned to open the monastery of La Rabida on the morrow.

Irving's journey to Palos in the morning was quite similar in its scenes to that one now makes luxuriously after a century. The same roads, only well paved today; the same Tinto River, running with its red water; and, in Palos, the same wide stretch of salt bar where the water reached when Columbus sailed. No docks or wharves then or now. A lonely abandoned seaport, and yet from no other port in all the tide of time has such a fleet been launched as that which sailed toward the sunset before the anxious eyes of men and women on the shore. Palos was largely covered with vineyards when Irving viewed it with the head of the ancient house. He went into the little village church of Saint George, and saw what may be seen today — the little iron pulpit whence the orders of the Catholic monarchs authorizing the expedition had been read, the little altar where Columbus heard Mass just before marching to the boats, the exquisite little Virgin before which Columbus prayed. Today this historic church is threatened with destruction by the hill behind it, which, with time, is pressing more and more upon it. The ceiling in the chapel of the Pinzons is partly down. The curate, with a keen appreciation of the historical richness of the church, now tells the stranger of his apprehensions for its fate. The curate in Irving's day was found going forth on his donkey with a gun for a day of shooting.

Thence it was only a little way to the monastery of La Rabida. It was evidently closed at the time of Irving's visit, since it was necessary to summon a friar from the church at Moguer for the key. It is now open, with five monks in attendance. Irving found it lonely, shut in as it was by pine trees. The century has witnessed the disappearance of most of these, but the pine tree still dominates the landscape. The olive orchards, once close about, were destroyed by the French. Most of the cells are closed now as when Irving was a visitor, and the cat he found has left no descendants, but a dog is there to cringe before a stranger. A kindly, gentle monk had permitted us to eat our lunch in the small dining-room of his brethren, busied himself with the bringing of knives and forks and plates, and then proudly turned on a radio on a little table, that we might lunch, in the monastery known to Columbus, to the music of 'Carmen' carried from Seville. La Rabida has recovered its place in the sun, but it was desolate when Irving trod its cloisters and peered into its deserted cells.

He had thoroughly enjoyed the hospitality of the venerable Pinzon, a burly old fellow who loved the chase and was wont to spend from four to eight days in the forest astride his horse. Returning from the monastery to Moguer, Irving noted the reverential respect with which the people in the streets saluted the veteran. The town plaza was thickly sprinkled with loungers, all wrapped in their Spanish cloaks, many of them with the swarthy face and garb of the gypsies. He was introduced to a dashing young Spanish cavalier — the world's concept then of a Spaniard. On prancing horse, with a white round hat, with broad satin ribbons and cockades, with light jacket and colored breeches, he realized all Irving's boyhood imaginings.

That night Irving sat in the open under a starry sky listening with the eagerness of a child to a discussion of bullfights, the prowess of the brigands and contrabandists. And on his return journey, one night in a wretched *posada* he learned something of the part bulls and matadors played in the lives of the masses. At first the discussion between two women was on the relative virtues and weaknesses of popular matadors, and the talk ran smoothly in a friendly groove. But when the relative merits of bulls came up, the clouds gathered and the storm broke. The conversationalists came from different sections, and each did battle for the bulls of her region until both were indulging in what Irving describes as 'violent words and gesticulations.'

Reaching Seville, he walked to Casa Cera, where he found the Wetherells keeping Hall company.

AGAIN he haunted the Archives of the Indies for a while, and then, toward the close of August, he and Hall embarked on the steamboat *Conario* for the Port of Saint Mary. The accommodations were none too good, and wrapped in their cloaks, pestered throughout the night by the buzz and bites of mosquitoes, they slept indifferently through the night. Reaching Cadiz in the morning, the two friends crossed in a ferry to Saint Mary's and found lodgings in the home of a saddler at 4 Calle de Palacios. That night, in festive mood, they went to a circus to see a tightrope walker.

But the saddler's place was in the heart of a noisy town,

and the stiff breezes made the white city black with dust. Irving passed 'a comfortless, wretched day,' and realized that work would be impossible in the apartment he had taken. The next day he made a virtue of necessity and drove to Jerez, the 'home of Sherry,' to visit the wine cellars of Domecq, with whom he breakfasted. He visited the wine vaults, and proudly recorded in his diary that he had tasted wine of the vintage of 1764.

Meanwhile, he was looking for a place in the country near Saint Mary's. In the interval he sent part of the manuscript of the 'Conquest of Granada' to Murray by the steamboat the *Duke of York*, and made arrangements for the publication of a new edition of 'Father Knickerbocker.'

At length he found a comfortable cottage about a mile from the town. It was the property of R. S. Hackley, once the American Consul at San Lucar and later for a time at Cadiz. He had made much money and retired to live in Cadiz, and his country house of 'Cerillo' was placed at the disposal of Irving and Hall. It was charmingly placed on a hill whence could be seen miles of land and sea, with the old Phoenician city of Cadiz looming eight miles away, and with the mountains of Ronda in the distance.

For a few days Irving was happy. In a short time he had written his story of the Pinzons and the introduction to the 'Conquest of Granada' and, crossing over to Cadiz, he had left the manuscript of the first half of the volume with A. Burton, the American Consul, for transmission to Murray. He liked Cadiz, but without the enthusiasm with which his imagination had acclaimed Seville. He loved the marine views from the ramparts, the white-sailed ships of the harbor from all quarters of the globe, the cleanliness of the streets, the whiteness of the houses, the hospitality of the people, the beauty of the women. But he missed the country, since,

because of its situation, there was no country within easy
reach. 'The women of Cadiz are beyond question the finest
in Spain,' wrote another traveler of that time.

But it was Burton, the American Consul, who contributed
most to Irving's enjoyment. For many years he was the
Consul there. He was a man of parts, whose intellectual
qualities appealed to Irving. He was slightly to be identified
with the publication of the 'Conquest.' But there is no record
of his career or personality. One may get an impression of
the man by turning the pages of the manuscript volumes
of the Consulate, now in the Consulate at Seville, but only of
his official character. The evident charm of his personality
cannot be recaptured after a hundred years. But Irving
liked him, and during his sojourn at Saint Mary's he frequently ferried over to Cadiz to dine and walk and talk with
Burton.

But scarcely had Irving and Hall become settled, and taken
a few walks to the seaside and an old tower, when the fever
fell on Cadiz and those who had property elsewhere hurried
from the stricken city. The owner of 'Cerillo' had children,
and he required it as a refuge. Irving hastened to Cadiz to
consult with Burton about another house. In sheer disgust
he thought at first of returning to Seville, but found that the
river boats had been discontinued in service. At length he
found a country house in an olive orchard known as 'Caracol,'
which he secured for fifteen shillings a month, partly furnished.

There he settled down to dogged work, poring over the
manuscripts of Vasco Nuñez, writing some sketches later to
be used in the 'Tales of the Alhambra,' copying the 'Conquest of Granada.' At this time he would sit in the shade of
the olive orchard and read aloud to Hall from the story of
the 'Conquest.' But he was suffering with a strange affliction

— excessive pains in the face and ear that made sleep difficult. Hall grew worse and was spitting blood. Irving was nervous and unable to work. He sought to throw off his depression by ferrying to Cadiz for a chat with Burton, but on returning just before sundown he was forbidden to land, and it was of no avail to send his passports to the Governor. Thus, making his bed on a sail he passed the night on deck.

September passed, and October. A letter came from Murray offering him the editorship of an English magazine with a salary of a thousand pounds, and the offer of liberal pay for articles besides. He was scarcely tempted. He was more interested in books.

Early in November he took the steamboat *Betis* for Seville, leaving Hall in the country house. He was not to see him again.

ON REACHING Seville, Irving called upon his friends and began a search for a house for Hall. Every day found him bending to his literary tasks; every night found him at the Italian opera where Passarini was singing. For a time he was disturbed by the loss of two chapters from the 'Conquest' and feared he would have to go to England to supply the loss. But by mere chance, as he recorded, he found a memorandum in lead pencil covering the missing chapters, and he was able to rewrite them in Seville.

Weary with his incessant writing, he found himself fre-

quently unable to work at all. Then he would chat with the
Marchioness of Arco Hermoso of the villagers of Dos Hermanas, rummage about old bookstalls, stroll around the
tobacco factory in the evening, ramble afield to view the
bulls intended for the fights, and see the fights in the arena.
More than once he walked with a friend to San Juan de
Alfarache, and one day in January he dined on the grass
there in the open air on a day as mild as spring.

It was during these winter days in Seville that he wrote
the story of 'The Enchanted Soldier' and the legend of the
tower of the Infanta. Though frequently he passed sleepless
nights and days of inertia, which he could not throw off, he
was happy over the success of his 'Columbus,' which was
much greater than he had expected. One day he went to
the magnificent palace of the Duke of Medina Sidonia to
call on Ramon Gelieu, formerly a Minister of the King, but
then the steward of the Duke. In one of the apartments of
the enormous palace he found Gelieu at home. He found
'a small, ugly man' with 'an abominable mouth' and 'hanging lip,' but with pleasant eyes, and the conversation persuaded Irving that he was a man of 'great talent.' At the
time he was preparing a dictionary of 'Don Quixote,' and it
was from him that Irving learned that his old friend, the
brilliant Diego Clemencin, who, as the head of the Royal
Academy of History, had been responsible for Irving's
membership in that learned body, was working on his
monumental commentaries on 'Don Quixote.'

MEANWHILE, word reached Irving from Cadiz that Hall had died. A few days later the horse that Hall had ridden while Irving walked at his side both at Casa Cera and at Caracol was delivered to him in Seville. He recalled the discussions in the twilight at Casa Cera concerning the possibility of calling back the spirit of the dead. Hall had turned suddenly to Irving and asked if he would be willing to receive a visit from him after death. Irving had consented.

'Why, Hall,' he had replied, 'you are such a good fellow, and we have lived so amicably together, that I don't know why I should fear to welcome your apparition, if you are able to come.'

'Then it is a compact,' Hall answered, 'and, Irving, if I can solve the mystery for you, I engage to do it.'

One evening, after the setting of the sun, Irving mounted Hall's horse, and not without emotion rode alone to the cottage of Casa Cera. All about him were scenes associated with the happy days the two had passed together in the walled-in garden, and he hoped, in these surroundings and mounted on his friend's horse, to create the right atmosphere for the experiment. He breathed an earnest prayer for the presence of the dead and waited. But nothing happened. 'The ghosts have never been kind to me,' he would say, in telling of the experiment afterward.

Then Prince Dolgorouki arrived in Seville by diligence from Madrid, and he revived Irving's spirits. Again he made the rounds of his favorite resorts with the Russian, parading him about the cigar factory, promenading him in the Alameda, taking him to the top of the Giralda, to the cathedral for the pictures and one night for the 'Miserere,' walking the narrow streets with him by moonlight listening to the tinkling of guitars from beyond the latticed balconies.

Soon they were busy with their preparations for their journey through the mountains to Granada.

Chapter 5: A KING IN

THE ALHAMBRA

IT WAS sunset on a beautiful May
evening that Irving and Prince Dolgorouki, on horses, and
accompanied by a loquacious notary of Granada they had
met at noon, rode into the romantic streets of Granada.
Their long and sometimes dangerous journey from Seville,
despite their gaiety and determination gracefully and happily
to adjust themselves to any circumstance, had given them an
ardent desire for a comfortable bed that night, and their
newly found cicerone was eloquent with assurances. How he
envied the two strangers their waiting wonders — such
streets and squares and palaces, and above all what women!
'But what of the *posada?*' asked Irving, breaking in on the
enthusiastic flow. Ah, they would be taken to the best,
where there were luxuries and beds of down such as King
Chico would have envied in the Alhambra of ancient days.
And so the gay but travel-stained travelers dismounted at
the portals of the Posada de la España at nightfall, delighted
with their adventures through Andalusia, and excited over
the prospect of the Alhambra. It was Dolgorouki's first
journey into these magic regions, and that night after dinner
the two went forth to see the magnificent monument of the
Moors in the light of a full moon.

Thrown together intimately for days, under circumstances sometimes trying, Irving had found the Prince all he had thought him, witty, humorous, tolerant, patient, and prone to make a lark out of such hardships as might come his way. Never were either to forget that equestrian venture over *vegas* and rugged mountains from Seville. Hardships they had found, but these had been expected, for they knew the way would be through a wild country in part, and over roads that often were little better than mule-tracks. It was in the days when brigands sallied forth with reasonable security from the mountain fastnesses to pounce upon the traveler and relieve him of his treasures; and the two men, prepared for such encounters, had forwarded their valuables to Granada and carried just sufficient money to meet their actual needs. But, warned by the experiences of others, they carried a sack with some silver with which to placate the robber should he appear. They had reached their destination without having met one of the dashing daredevils of the brigands' brood. With them had ridden a Biscayan youth as guide and servant and defender. This boastful young man with more than a touch of bravado was to brighten the journey and to bear with unconcealed delight the name of 'Sancho.' Like the lowliest of the Spaniards, he knew in broad outlines the story of Cervantes, but assumed it to be a true tale of a thousand years before.

At Alcala de los Panaderos, where on so many Sundays Irving had picnicked with Sevillian friends, they paused that the Prince might see the old Moorish mill that had so fascinated the weaver of fanciful tales; and later at Gandul, to view the ruins of the Moorish castle. There, while awaiting the preparation of their lunch at a tolerable *posada*, they went forth in search of the once-famous palace of the Marquis of Gandul, to find only heaps of stone. Thence, after a hearty meal, they rode out into the *campiña*, a vast untimbered wilderness with scarcely a sign of the habitation of man. The skies darkened; the rain poured down upon them in torrents. They could but wrap themselves in their picturesque Spanish cloaks and bend their heads to the lashing rain. And then the sun, hot and brilliant, would come from behind the clouds and the steam would rise from their drying garments. And then the rain again. That night they rode into the village of El Arahal in the hills.

THE village was much disturbed, for strangers seldom ventured there. A number of muleteers were at the *posada* scouring the country about for robbers. The passports in a foreign language puzzled the simple dignitaries of the place. And while the two friends stretched their legs, a number of villagers gathered in a group to study the strange writing. Sancho joined them, proffering assistance. But more satisfying than the explanations of Sancho was the distribution of cigars by Irving and Dolgorouki, and soon the entire village, its fears dispelled, was according them a warm Spanish welcome. A great armchair was pantingly carried into their room by the smiling wife of the landlord.

At dinner the commander of the patrol, a seasoned veteran who had seen service in South America, ate with them, and diverted them enormously with his boasting. And as they listened to the commander's gasconading, the landlord was scouring the village for the musicians and the belles, and when the travelers finished their repast and stepped into the patio it was filled with dancers, many with castanets, and there was one guitar which passed freely from hand to hand. Meanwhile, the landlord's pretty daughter, who had disappeared to make her toilet, emerged as the belle of the evening with red roses in her hair, and Irving has preserved the charming picture of her dash and grace in dancing the bolero with a handsome young dragoon. The two friends were delighted and entered whole-heartedly into the spirit of the occasion, ordering that wine be served in abundance. As Irving surveyed the colorful scene — the soldiers in their uniforms, the girls in their bright dresses and some with roses in their hair, the peasants wrapped in their brown cloaks — it seemed to him as a scene taken from 'Don Quixote.'

The next morning they mounted and rode on through the countryside, of great fertility, teeming with grain, and at noon they found a beautiful meadow by a clear stream and here they dismounted to lunch. They sat on the green grass and looked up at the blue Andalusian sky and breathed the rich fragrance of the flowers and herbs, and listened to the rapturous singing of the birds in the trees above them. Sancho, who proved an excellent provider, offered them abundant food, and a greater abundance of fine Valdepeñas wine. Pretending ignorance, Irving plied the doughty squire with questions about Don Quixote, while the Russian diplomat listened to the amusing answers with a smile. There, after a siesta in their cloaks, with the birds singing them a lullaby, they rested. Then they pressed on and reached the goodly town of Osuna on a hillside, dominated by a church and a castle.

The *posada* outside the town seemed bleak, for it was cool, and the natives, grouped about the warmth of the *brasero*, eyed the strangers with suspicion as they entered. Noting the distrust, the travelers smiled their broadest and entered with a friendly swagger, touching their sombreros in salute. It was enough. Clearly they were *simpatico*, and instantly they all were friends. It was apropos of this reception that Irving was to write: 'I have never known a Spaniard, whatever his rank or condition, who would suffer himself to be outdone in courtesy.' Cigars were passed around. It was a merry evening.

THE next morning they entered a range of mountains and rode along paths, picturesque but lonely, and remembered that this was the happy hunting ground of the robbers of the King's highway. Irving recalled that, many years before, the robber chief of the Moslems, Omar Ibn Hassan, was the terror of the region, and though that was a thousand years before, the gossips warned, with reason, that the tribe of brigands was not yet extinct. Their eyes were alert for strangers, and Sancho's courage drooped a bit, but nothing happened, and by evening, without mishap, they reached the historic town of Antequera, famed for the valor of its warriors. But approaching its gates they passed through hedges and gardens to the song of a nightingale. That night they slept at the Posada de San Fernando.

Remote from the usual course of travel, the friends were agreeably surprised at the abundance of well-cooked food and the perfect cleanliness of the rooms and beds. The next morning Irving sauntered forth alone to view the remains of an old Moorish castle built on the site of an ancient Roman fortress, and, sitting on a stone, let his imagination riot. For this was the country of the heroic struggles of the Spaniards and the Moors. From where he sat he could see the gate whence the cream of the chivalry of Andalusia had gallantly ridden forth in the struggle for the redemption of Granada, to be entrapped and massacred among the mountains of Malaga.

That noon they lunched near the village of Archidona in the shade of an olive grove by the side of a murmuring brook, and, thanks to the cunning of Sancho, they found a feast before them — partridge, salted codfish, ham; and for dessert that day they had oranges and figs and walnuts, with the choice wine of Malaga. A venerable man approached, eyeing the repast hopefully, and they gave him of their abundance and were rewarded with the courtly thanks that only the poor of Spain, even when illiterate, can phrase so well. 'It is cordial to an old man's soul,' he said as he drained his glass of the wine from Malaga. And the old man pointed out the ruins of the castle which Queen Isabella in the war for Granada had stormed in vain. And that afternoon they passed through the rugged defile of the mountains through which the glittering army led by Ferdinand, the King, marched to the conquest of the last refuge of the Moors.

That night found them in the very old town of Loxa, once the stronghold of Ali Atar, whose daughter married the unfortunate Boabdil who finally lost Granada to the Moors; and hereabout he had collected his troops for his last stand against the Christians. But Loxa had been loyal to the Moor and had sent Ferdinand in a hurry about his business.

The travelers passed the night in the Posada of the Crown, entranced, we more than half suspect, by the beautiful young Andalusian widow who was its mistress. Irving was to note the fire in her eye, the spring in her step, the coquetry of her manner, and the ornaments on her person. It was a scene to delight Irving's soul, for soon there clattered up to the *posada* a horseman of bold and daring manner and handsome appearance. Irving was sure he was the favored suitor of the widow. Was he a contrabandist? The two travelers thought him one. The whole atmosphere of the place proclaimed it the rendezvous of these bold riders of the plains and mountains.

That night Irving and his friend listened to the cavalier singing mountain romances to the accompaniment of his guitar, until other travelers, despoiled by robbers and left penniless, appeared. Dolgorouki, with his usual generosity, ordered them supper and a bed and gave them money to help them on their way. The two friends' interest in the evening grew when, a little later, an old man of powerful frame, and bearing a huge saber, swaggered into the midst of the group. Sancho whispered to Irving and Dolgorouki the magic name of Don Ventura Rodriguez, the hero of the community, who in the war with the French had killed or captured single-handed a company of six soldiers. The group looked upon the old man with evident relish and approval as he exclaimed with gusto, pointing to the saber, 'When I draw it the earth trembles.'

And then, with the old man in their midst, the picturesque and incongruous group sat far into the night listening to tales of the daring and the crimes of contrabandists and bandits, and to the never-failing legends of the Moors. That night, stirred by the stories he had heard, Irving could scarcely sleep, and just as he was drowsing a dreadful din, suggesting an attack from the legendary Moors, aroused him again. He hurriedly dressed to investigate and found the attack was nothing more sinister than a charivari in celebration of the marriage of an old man to a young and buxom girl. Irving congratulated the pair and wished them joy, and slept the remainder of the night.

It had been a colorful, memorable journey with an ideal companion, and all this — the *vegas*, the mountain passes, the picturesque costumes of the lowly, the stirring stories they had heard — was part of the background of their introduction to Granada as they stood that night before the Alhambra, flooded with the light of the moon.

THE next morning Irving and Dolgorouki hurried to the palace of the Moorish kings. Centuries of neglect had fallen upon the historic building. Not so very long before, these ancient rooms, associated with so much of romance and tragedy, had been taken over by tramps, thieves, and smugglers who nightly sallied forth to crime. But these had been sent upon their travels, and though the inhabitants were of lowly station they were no longer of the criminal classes. A small garrison of a hundred superannuated soldiers now guarded the premises. Under its commander, Don Francisco Serna, they were kept in the best state of repair possible with the limited appropriation. Though the Governor of the province had rooms there for residence and official duties, he preferred to stay in the center of the town. He had no imagination, and, being a practical man, found the town more convenient for business. After lingering throughout the day at the palace, the two friends made a call of ceremony on the Governor, and expressed astonishment that he did not avail himself of what, to them, seemed the precious privilege of dwelling within the storied walls of the Alhambra. The Governor smiled. It was well enough for the old kings who needed the protection, but for business, he explained, it no longer was feasible.

'But,' he continued with an amused smile, 'if you think a residence there so desirable, my apartments in the Alhambra are at your service.'

Of course, it was only a courteous gesture. Was it not the custom for the owner of any article to offer it gracefully to an admirer? But alas, it was a mandate of good breeding to express thanks with a declination. But to their amazement the Governor was persistent:

'You will find a rambling set of empty rooms, but Tia Antonia, who has charge of the palace, may be able to put them in some kind of order and to take care of you while you are there. If you can make any arrangement with her for your accommodation, and are content with scanty fare in a royal abode, the palace of King Chico is at your service.'

Amazed and thrilled by the prospect, the two friends hurried up the hill and through the Great Gate of Justice to see Tia Antonia. Indeed, she said, she could arrange it. Though of the crudest sort, she did have some furniture she could put in the rooms. The eager listeners assured her they gladly would sleep on the floor. And the fare, added Tia Antonia, would be very simple. Ah, thought the friends, they could live on the songs of the nightingales. As for a maid, little Dolores, a niece, could wait upon them.

Walking on air, the two friends returned to their *posada* for the last night there, and early the next morning they moved into the palace. They took possession of the Governor's apartment facing La Plaza de los Algibes. Though modern, it adjoined a number of small Moorish chambers occupied by Tia Antonia. This was to serve for a time.

Since never was Irving to know such joy as that of his residence in the palace of the Moorish kings, we must enter into the spirit of the place by meeting the other inhabitants with whom he was to be associated. Foremost, of course, was Doña Antonia, the châtelaine. It was her function to keep the place in order, and in return she was allowed the tips of visitors and the produce from the garden. Occasionally it was expected that she would send some fruits and flowers to the Governor. Irving was to find her always gracious, friendly, considerate of his wants and comfort — a merry soul who often had her friends in on an evening, when Irving sat in their circle and listened to the gossip of the town and the legends of the past. With her lived little Dolores, a niece, and Manuel Molina, a nephew with ambitions.

But it was Dolores who was to make the liveliest and most indelible impression on Irving. A plump young girl, healthy and happy, her black eyes twinkled constantly with good humor and amusement when they did not imply amazement at the peculiarities of the guest. She was to be the sole heir of her aunt, which meant that in time she would come into possession of a hundred and fifty dollars a year, and that gave her a special distinction. The two friends had been shown through the palace on their first visit by this charming, friendly soul, and, since both were kindly and gracious, all barriers had been broken down. Thenceforth so long as Irving remained she was to be for him the angel of the Alhambra. It was she who kept his rooms in order, and made his bed and served him at his meals. Despite her youth, she soon was mothering him, protesting with frightened eyes against his disposition to explore deserted chambers, dark stairways, and the dungeons where ghosts and evil spirits lurked and threatened. Day by day, her little fingers plucked the choicest flowers she could find and they were conveyed proudly to Irving's chamber. It was she who first got his morning greeting when she bore his breakfast, sometimes to the magnificent Hall of the Ambassadors, where the table was spread in front of one of the windows offering a breathtaking vista of town, *venta*, and mountains, and sometimes to the Court of the Lions, where the falling waters furnished music for his repast. When, after a brief sojourn, Dolgorouki left to continue his Andalusian travels, he enjoined Dolores to take good care of Irving, and the bright-eyed little damsel was to figure in the correspondence of the two friends. Irving wrote the Prince:

> Little Dolores is very grateful for your remembrance of her and desires me to say a thousand kind things on her part. She is an excellent little being, with a great deal of natural cleverness united with great naïveté. She takes good care of me in consequence of your parting recommendation.

Quite as useful in another way was Mateo Ximenes, described by Irving as 'my valet de chambre.' The two friends first met this strange creature as they were entering the Alhambra on the morning after their arrival at Granada. A tall, slender youth, wearing a rusty brown cloak whose mission seemed to be the concealment of the rags beneath, had detached himself from some equally ragged soldiers,

Holman Print Shop, Boston

THE ALHAMBRA

dozing in the sun, to offer his services as a guide. Unimpressed at first, and assuming the youth an ignoramus intent on tips, Irving had asked him if he knew anything about the palace.

'I am a son of the Alhambra,' he replied proudly.

It appeared to be the truth, for after much questioning Irving was convinced that his family literally had lived in the fortress since the days of the Conquest. No other of the inhabitants had greater claim to the boast. To his delight, Irving soon found that not only did Mateo know the palace, but that he was soaked with its stories and legends. In the first days he was Irving's shadow, making himself so useful in an intelligent way that in the end he crept into Irving's service as 'valet, cicerone, guide, guard, and historiographic squire.' Irving made a sally into the town, and soon the rusty brown coat was discarded with the rags and the eager youth was startling his fellow residents of the King's palace with a nifty Andalusian hat and jacket. Conscious that because of Irving's scanty needs his job hung by a thread, Mateo exerted his ingenuity in finding services to render. Thinking himself alone, Irving would start on a new tour of the palace, and there, emerging from the shadows, was Mateo to accompany him as cicerone. Should the master crave a ramble in the surrounding hills, there at his heels was Mateo, apologetically explaining that he would go along as a guard, though Irving suspected that in case of danger the long legs of his valiant protector would take to flight. And alas, when Irving was thriving in a flirtation with a pretty Polish lady sketching — or pretending to — in the Alhambra, there again was Mateo — and that was not so good.

Soon, however, he was found most useful. Though simpleminded, he had a happy carefree disposition, and as the two wandered about the hills, Mateo, who had the 'loquacity and gossip of a village barber,' and who knew the stories of most of the inhabitants of Granada, would chatter to his companion's infinite entertainment, and often profit. Through this simple soul's imagining every human being about was a rich mine for the novelist. And every cave and corner of the palace was good for a thrilling story not written in the books. He became a torch-bearer for the legends. For his grandfather, also a 'child of the Alhambra,' had lived to be a centenarian, conducting his little tailor shop where princesses once had disported. His friends, among the oldest men of the community, were wont to gather in the shop in the evening and gossip far into the night of the legends of the palace and of the bizarre characters who had dwelt therein. And thus Mateo as a small child was saturated in the tales coming down by word of mouth from the last days of the seventeenth century, and long before.

Irving's interest in strange people led him to visit the family of the omnipresent Mateo, who lived in a hovel built of reeds and plaster just above the iron gate. The father, then seventy, was a ribbon-weaver and his tastes were simple. Irving found there little but 'a crazy bed, a table, and two or three chairs,' and 'a wooden chest containing the archives of the family.' Mateo himself was married, and numerous children clambered about at the grandfather's feet. On holidays the wife, bearing one child in her arms while others clung to her skirts, regularly took her stroll on the *paseo* of Granada, and the eldest daughter was already adorning her hair with roses and dancing to the music of the castanets.

Like a conscientious baron of feudal times, Irving called on all his tenants, and thus he found living in a closet under the outer staircase a little old woman calling herself Maria Antonia Sabonea, and by others dubbed 'La Reyna Coquina.' Irving could not have escaped her, for from dawn to dark she sat in the cool stone corridor sewing and singing. Indeed he cultivated the ugly old woman, who, despite her poverty and rags, was ever merry, for a chat or two disclosed that she too was a rich mine of legends and folklore. He found she had a gift for story-weaving and that she had as many stories at her tongue's tip 'as the inexhaustible Scheherezade of the Thousand and One Nights.' She had buried five husbands and she was merry.

Among her neighbors was another 'child of the Alhambra' boasting the proud name of Alonzo de Aguilar and insisting on a direct line of descent from the great Gonzalvo of Cordoba. 'Poor as a rat and proud as he is ragged,' observed Irving. But this old man with an ample paunch and a 'bottle nose' strutted about in rusty clothes, wearing a cocked hat of oilskin and a red cockade, with a haughtiness that even his alleged ancestor, the great captain, could not have exceeded in the days of his triumphs.

Irving knew them all, and found in all something that lifted them above the commonplace. He too was now a 'child of the Alhambra.'

For two weeks Irving and Dolgorouki lived in state, such as it was, in the Governor's apartments, marveling at the beauties of the palace, lounging in its courts, enjoying the marvelous vistas from the balconies, devoutly attended by Dolores and satisfactorily, though simply, fed by Tia Antonia. And then the parting came, for the Russian, on limited leave from the capital, had to press forward on his Andalusian travels. Irving's nephew had joined them a little while before, and he too left. Irving found the parting painful, and from the Tower of Gomares, with the aid of a spyglass, he followed the departure of his nephew until he was lost to view behind the foot of the mountain of Elvira.[1]

To intensify his discomfort, the rains set in, the sunshine no longer brightened the old courts, and the Alhambra was cold and damp. Not a little lonely, Irving was confined a few days to his quarters, where he sat wrapped in his cloak. He consoled Dolgorouki with the observation that had he remained he would have found it 'a cheerless life to stroll about the cold marble halls even of a palace.' But Irving had work to do. He was eager to hear the legends of the Alhambra from its humble residents and he was putting the finishing touches to the 'Conquest of Granada.' While the rain splattered in the courts he sat at his desk oblivious to the weather, busy with his manuscript.[2]

Then the sun shone again, and again Irving rambled about the venerable pile to satisfy his curiosity. One day in a remote gallery he came to a door leading into regions he had not yet explored and found it locked. Only the reverberation in empty chambers responded to his knock. Here was a mystery, perhaps the haunted chamber! Should he seek a secret entrance in the night, or appeal to the good-natured Tia Antonia for a key? Little Dolores he found utterly ignorant of the interior, and even Mateo confessed the limitations of his knowledge, 'child of the Alhambra' though he was. Tia Antonia graciously opened the apartments and Irving found himself in empty chambers, with rich, old,

[1] Irving, *Life*, II, 155.   [2] Letter to Dolgorouki, Irving, *Life*, II, 156.

though European, architecture. The ceilings were lofty and of cedar, paneled and deeply carved with fruits and flowers, with here and there a grotesque mask or face. The walls, once covered no doubt with damask, were now bare, and desecrated with the scribbled names of tourists of other times. The windows opened on a charming garden. He found that years before when Philip V was planning a sojourn there with the beautiful Elizabeth of Farnese, Italian artists had fitted these apartments for the Queen and the ladies of the court. Here in the loftiest room were Elizabeth's sleeping quarters, and here was her boudoir.

Irving was enchanted. The Governor's apartment now seemed dull and drab. Instantly his decision was made. If possible he would move into Elizabeth's apartments, for here he would be shut in as in the days of the Moorish kings. But when he proposed the change, Tia Antonia was astounded. To the good woman and her family these apartments, remote and lonely, seemed dismal enough. The eyes of little Dolores opened in mingled fright and wonder. It was so lonely there! Bats and owls flapped their wings ominously. In a vault of the baths near-by, a fox and wildcat were confined by day and roamed about at night. Tramps haunted this section and gypsies lived in the caverns of the neighboring walls. There were no locks on doors or windows, and the criminally minded, learning that a foreigner, who must be rich, was dwelling there alone, would break in at night to rob him and do him hurt. Should he find himself in danger his cries could not be heard by the other denizens of the palace.

But the romantic glamour of the apartments and the beauty of their outlook determined Irving. Soon Mateo and a carpenter were busy securing the doors and windows. When Mateo offered to sleep as a guard and protector in an anteroom the offer was declined. When the apartments had been made burglar-proof, the entire family of Tia Antonia solemnly marched with him in procession as he took possession.

Their manifest fears had not been without effect on Irving's imagination. He was to confess the uneasiness and mild terrors of the night. The sense of solitude, the moaning of the wind in the citron trees beyond the windows, the gloom of the darkness without, impelled him to close the windows. The entrance through a broken pane of a bat with flapping wings in the darkness was a bit disturbing, and finally in a desperate effort to divest himself of his uneasiness he determined to make a tour of the apartments and its galleries.

With a lighted lamp which threw himself into relief and all the surroundings into deeper gloom, he started on his travels. And then he heard weird sounds, as of moans and clanking chains that seemed to come from the Hall of the Abencerrages, where men had lost their heads in the great stone or marble bowl. And then he heard shrieks and inarticulate mutterings. It was too much! Irving hurried back to his bedchamber and bolted the door. Finally he slept. When the worried Dolores brought his breakfast in the morning the little lady was able to clear the mystery of the groans and ravings. In a vaulted room beneath the Hall of the Ambassadors a brother of her aunt, a maniac, was confined. Irving had not yet met this member of his family.

Thereafter all fear vanished, and the charms of his apartments grew upon him. 'I never had such a delicious abode,' he soon was writing Dolgorouki. 'One of my windows looks into the little garden of Lindaraxa; the citron trees are full of blossoms and perfume the air, and the fountain throws up a beautiful jet of water.' From another window he could see the Court of the Lions, and still another spread before him the rare beauties of the Generalife. He loved the place so much he could 'hardly force [himself] from it to take promenades.' [1] He came to love the garden of Lindaraxa. Long before, the Moors had found it enchanting and had rhapsodized about it:

> The beauty and the excellence that are in me proceed from Mohammed. His goodness surpasses that of beings that have passed, and that are to come. Among five stars, three turn pale beside his superior brightness; my master gives lightness to the murkiest atmosphere; the stars sicken with love of him; and to them, he communicates the perfume of plants, and the sweet odor of virtues. Their business is to enlighten the firmament, else would they dart from their places and seek his presence. By his commands, stones are firmly rooted; it is his power that communicates to them their delicate workmanship; and by his will do they remain firm. The marble softens at his voice; and the light of his eyes scatters darkness. Where is there a garden like unto this? Its verdure and its fragrance excel all others; and its freshness is diffused far around.

The days now passed rapidly and rapturously. Happy in his surroundings, Irving did not neglect his writing, but he would sit for hours looking out into the scented and murmurous garden, listening to the songs of nightingales. From a near-by gallery looking down upon the old town he enjoyed studying the life of the people through a spyglass. At the foot of the hill was the Alameda, long fashionable, and while the more elegant *paseo* of the Xenil had recently supplanted it as the promenade of the more elegant, it remained the favorite of the middle and poorer classes. Through his glass, Irving liked to study the promenaders — soldiers and friars, peasants and gypsies, the dark-eyed belles and the beaux of the lower order, the girls in gay Andalusian cos-

[1] Irving, *Life*, II, 164.

tumes and with the inevitable fan. Thus life was spread before him for his delectation. Now and then some figure, clearly of the higher classes, half muffled in his cloak, could be seen unostentatiously threading his way among the merry-makers of the common people. No doubt a secret love affair, thought Irving. Mateo could tell him the life history of the people dwelling in the houses, and about them Irving wove fantastic stories for his own amusement.

Seldom now did he descend into Granada. In early June he had completed his 'Conquest of Granada,' and now he was busy with his 'Tales of the Alhambra.' He wished to complete these under the spell of the old palace associated with them, that they might 'bear the stamp of real intimacy with the charming scenes described.' [1]

Once, however, he was persuaded by the eager Mateo to join the gay throng during one of the religious festivals in the town. It was the fête of Corpus Christi. The night before the religious procession, when the town was crowded with mountaineers from the villages and the peasants from the *ventas*, he permitted his faithful squire to lead him through the merry crowds to the historic square of the Vivarrambla, where a gallery had been erected for the morrow's entertainment. The square was brilliantly lighted, bands played, the beauty and fashion of the town promenaded side by side with the belles of the poorer classes, whose beautiful flashing eyes, flirting fans, and colorful Andalusian dresses imparted charm to the scene. Here and there a swaggering contra-bandist could be seen, and here and there a popular bull-fighter strutted through the throng, the cynosure of feminine eyes. Irving was enchanted. On the outskirts of the crowd were peasants seated at their repast upon the ground. There many of them would sleep that night.

[1] Irving, *Life*, II, 163.

It was scarcely sunrise on the morrow when Irving, with Mateo, appeared again in the square. He saw the village deputations march into the town bearing banners and images of the Blessed Virgin and led by the priests. He witnessed the grand procession — the religious orders, the civil and military authorities, the churches and the convents with their fluttering banners, their images and relics. He saw the archbishop walking under a damask canopy surrounded by subordinates. He heard the music of the bands, the tramping of the multitude marching toward the fine cathedral. Thus in Granada in 1829 Irving joined in the celebration of Corpus Christi, and Mateo was delighted with his master's pleasure.[1]

One night Irving on his balcony listened to the tolling of many church bells in the town. The consort of King Ferdinand was dead.

EVEN in the Alhambra Irving's associations were not to be confined solely to the family of Tia Antonia and to his squire. One morning he awakened with a start to hear shooting in the palace, and he hastened forth to ascertain the nature of the attack. In the Hall of the Ambassadors he found a group of domestics surrounding an old man who had been satisfying his passion for sportsmanship by shooting at swallows from the balcony. It turned out to be the Count of Luque, a wealthy and veteran member of

[1] *Tales of the Alhambra*, pp. 147–51.

the nobility who, with his numerous family and retainers, had migrated for a time from his great palace in Granada to enjoy the coolness and the fresher air of the Alhambra hill. The zeal of his servants in loading his gun had made it possible for the old man to keep up an almost continuous fire, but Irving observed that he shot not a single bird.

Thus Irving's undisputed kingship in the ancient palace was disputed, but the two monarchs divided the kingdom between them in the best of humor. The Count and his family would take over the Court of the Lions and the adjoining halls, leaving Irving in undisputed possession of the apartments of the Bourbon Queen and the garden of Lindaraxa. They all dined together in the arcade of the court to the music of the falling water. In the evenings the Countess, a second wife, and much younger, would visit the head of the house in the palace, bringing with her a beautiful sixteen-year-old daughter, Carmen. Constantly the Count's employees, his chaplain, and his lawyer were coming and going, for great were the old man's possessions.

To Irving the most interesting of the family was the young daughter, whose form had not yet matured but the symmetry of whose graceful body promised an early flowering. Soon she became one of Irving's sources of entertainment, for she played the guitar and other instruments with exquisite grace, and with unstudied spontaneity she danced the dances of the region. While the Count and Countess with the chaplain or secretary sat in the arcade at their cards, Carmen, with the idolatrous Dolores as maid, would sit by one of the fountains singing to the accompaniment of her guitar.

But the old Count grew in interest when Irving found that his family had played an heroic and romantic part in the great days of the Alhambra. He was a lineal descendant of the great Captain Gonsalvo of Cordoba, whose feats before

Granada's walls were not unknown to him who had just finished within the Alhambra the story of the Conquest. More fascinating still to Irving was the discovery from an old Arabian manuscript that his venerable new-made friend had in his veins the blood of the Moorish kings. In the old days the Prince of Almeria had married the daughter of King Berejo, and the third daughter of the union had married a son of the House of Luque, of which the ancient Count now was the head. Soon Irving was visiting the palace of the Count, who conducted him over the whole of it, for the old man was proud of the palace he himself had planned after a fashion not known to architects. The great sword of the Grand Captain was displayed in the archives, causing Irving to marvel at the strength of the wrists and arms of the olden days. He even penetrated under the old man's ciceronage into the dusty garrets, where under the débris he found a number of huge blunderbusses with matchlocks that he concluded must have 'made a great noise' at the time of the conquest of Granada.[1] Irving became fond of the friendly old Count and his family, and always he was to remember Carmen as 'a lovely little being sporting in happy and innocent girlhood in the marble halls, dancing to the sound of the Moorish castanets.'

MORE valuable to him, however, was another friend of Granada whom he met at the Alhambra. It was the Duke of Gor, who lived in the palace in Granada, which after more than a century is still in pos-

[1] *Tales of the Alhambra*, pp. 185–90; Irving, *Life*, II, 174.

session of the family. He was a grandee and one of the most
intelligent and public-spirited of the nobility of Spain. He
more than any other single person was said to have been
influential in persuading Ferdinand VII to turn over the
enormous wealth of priceless paintings of the royal family
for the establishment of the Prado Gallery. When Irving
first met him in the halls and galleries of the Alhambra he
was between thirty and forty years old. His appearance
was most attractive, for he was a handsome man. And his
manner was frank and friendly. Because he was a true
aristocrat he had the simplicity of democracy. A brief conversation in the Alhambra disclosed to Irving a kindred soul.
The Duke was interested in Irving's work and pleased with
his personality. Soon Irving was dining *en famille* with the
Duke at his palace in Granada. The host asked two or three
men who he knew would be congenial to the dinner, and
Irving was enchanted. The Duchess he found 'perfect
amiability,' and as usual with him he was delighted with the
interesting family of children.

Soon he was on such terms that he could run in without
ceremony. 'I have since called at the house in the morning,'
he wrote Dolgorouki, 'and found the Duchess surrounded by
her beautiful children, and occupied in teaching some of
them to write.' With helpful courtesy, the Duke showed him
through his 'curious' library containing many old chronicles
and curious manuscripts. The library was placed at his
disposal, and he was given permission to take such manuscripts and chronicles as he wished to his apartments in the
Alhambra. This room in the Duke's house became his
second home while in the historic town.

Not least among the services rendered Irving was the
securing permission for him to have access to old manuscripts and books in a number of the convents, and especially

in the Jesuit library of the University. Time and again in those early summer days of 1829 he found his way down the hill to the University, where he was allowed to shut himself in with the keys to the bookcases; and more than once he spent the entire day thus without lunch, rummaging among the treasures. He found the Duke 'an acquaintance exactly to my taste.' Now and then he found himself at his friend's table, and once he had the courage to invite the family to the Alhambra for the day. The Duke, the Duchess, and all the children appeared in time for breakfast, which was served in the Court of the Lions among the flowers and fountains. 'They came to breakfast and stayed until night, and a pleasant day we had of it,' he wrote his brother.[1]

It was inevitable that he should choose a child and a girl for his special affection, and in the nine-year-old daughter of the Duke he found another for his gallery of favorites. Years later, when he returned to Spain as Minister of the United States, among his first callers was the Duke of Gor, then living in Madrid.

SOMETIME before, at Malaga, Irving had met a sturdy soul resembling a rough diamond named William Kirkpatrick, a Scot by birth and an American by adoption, then serving the United States as Consul. Through him he had met the Count of Teba, a veteran to whom the wars had been unkind, for he was crippled and

[1] Irving, *Life*, II, 166.

he had lost one eye. This lusty old warrior had become enamored of Kirkpatrick's pretty daughter, and had married her. His home was in a castle near Granada.

And now that he was in Granada the acquaintance was renewed, and Irving was invited to the castle for a visit. He rode forth to his engagement little thinking that he was to meet one of the most fascinating characters of history. The old Count he found refreshing in his breeziness, but he was especially interested in a little lady of three summers. With his usual appeal to children he speedily made friends, and soon he was holding her in his arms and on his knee and telling her thrilling stories. The time passed pleasantly and he returned to the Alhambra.

Some years later, when Irving was Minister from the United States to Madrid, the little miss of three was one of the toasts of the town, but even then he did not appreciate the privilege he had enjoyed in the country place of the Count of Teba. This was not to come to him for some years when, as an old man in retirement at Sunnybank, he read the reports of a royal wedding in Paris. Then, with some satisfaction, and meditations on the whirligig of time and chance, he wrote Mrs. Storrow of the new Empress of the French:

> I believe I have told you that I knew the grandfather of the Empress — old Mr. Kirkpatrick, who had been American Consul at Malaga. I passed an evening at his house in 1827 near Adra, on the coast of the Mediterranean. A week or two after, I was at the house of his son-in-law, the Count Teba of Granada, a gallant, intelligent gentleman, much cut up by the wars, having lost an eye and been maimed in a leg and hand. His wife, the daughter of Mr. Kirkpatrick, was absent, but he had a family of little girls, mere children, about him. The youngest of these must have been the present Empress. Several years afterward . . . I was invited

to a grand ball at the house of the Countess Montijo, one of the leaders of the *ton*. On making my bow to her, I was surprised at being received by her with the warmth and eagerness of an old friend. She claimed me as the friend of her late husband, the Count Teba (subsequently Marquis Montijo), who, she said, had often spoken of me with the greatest regard .... She subsequently introduced me to the little girls I had known at Granada — now fashionable belles at Madrid.

After this, I was frequently at her house, which was one of the gayest of the capital. The Countess and her daughters all spoke English. The eldest daughter was married, while I was in Madrid, to the Duke of Alba and Berwick. The other now sits on the throne of France.[1]

An old man's memory betrayed him as to dates, for it was in 1829 that he was the guest of Teba near Granada. But undoubtedly it was the future Empress who sat on Irving's knee and listened to his stories in the old Count's castle.

So PASSED that memorable early summer in Granada. Writing his 'Tales of the Alhambra,' pacing the empty galleries and the courts at night, peering through his spyglass on the contemporary drama of the town, spending occasional evenings with the family of Tia Antonia, and enjoying the story-telling art of the ugly old lady beneath the stairs, chatting with the adoring Dolores, watching with approval the development and fruition of her romance with her cousin, the young medical student, visiting

[1] Irving, *Life*, III, 238, 239.

the Duke of Gor, and wandering through the hills with Mateo as his guide, he never had felt such sheer happiness in his life. Though the gypsies even then were living in the caves where after a century they now display their art to those who pay, there is nothing on paper to imply that he ever sought them out. In the great Square of Corpus Christi he saw them dance in the street, and he watched them curiously through his spyglass from his gallery, but that was all. There was art and romance enough in the great dwelling-place of the Moorish kings. The death of the Queen had given pause to the activities of the town. Such amusements as were usual were now closed. The activities of the great houses were suppressed. Irving was ineffably happy, forget-ful of the passing of the days, content to live on indefinitely in the 'sweetness and tranquillity' of his apartment.

And then the blow fell — from Washington.

Chapter 6: A KING BEGINS HIS EXILE

N EVER had Irving been so happy
and contented and so loath to change his mode of life
as when letters arrived from Washington and New York
announcing his appointment as Secretary of Legation in
London. No ambition could have been more remote from
his mind. But a friend was to be Minister in London, and
Martin Van Buren, with abundant cleverness and charm,
wished his companionship and assistance. To Irving it all
seemed wrong. Everett was going home, for a new Administration had come in, and Everett would have liked to stay;
and now Irving was going to London, far from sunny skies
and the music of castanets and fountains. His first feeling
was one of perplexity, for he was 'extremely reluctant to
give up [his] quiet and independent mode of life.' [1] He tried
to reason himself into a happier frame of mind about it.
He looked with horror on the exchange of the hurry and
bustle of the world for 'the delicious quiet and repose of the
Alhambra.' But, after all, could he afford to linger indefinitely in the siren's arms? Only 'self-indulgence' pleaded
for it. Had he not found 'the climate, the air, the serenity and
sweetness of the place almost as seductive as that of the Castle

[1] Letter to Wetherell, *Life*, II, 167.

of Indolence' and found his ambition melting to a 'mere voluptuousness of sensation'? [1]   But his feelings continued to struggle with his judgment, and he continued to lament that 'Never in my life have I had so delicious an abode, and never can I expect to meet with such another.'   The heat of midsummer was now on southern Spain, but Irving had found 'a delightful retreat in the halls of the baths, which are almost subterranean and as cool as grottoes.' There was real grief among his subjects in the Alhambra when they learned that he must go.

His arrangements were soon made, for he carried little baggage, and he left no household problems behind. A young Englishman was leaving at the same time, and they arranged to travel together. It was much too hot to ride horseback. The travelers engaged a tumbledown *tartana*, a two-wheeled vehicle into which they piled two mattresses on which to loll as they jolted over the hot highways. A tall, lank Portuguese, who had been a contrabandist and might have been a robber, was engaged as guide and guard.

As the hour for departure approached, some excuse or other was found for a postponement. But the parting had to come. So warmly attached had Irving become to the people of his meager kingdom that he could not bear the thought of farewell. Tia Antonia was deeply moved, and when Irving saw that little Dolores was on the verge of tears he could only shake hands in silence and walk hurriedly down the Alhambra hill as though intending to return. But Mateo and Manuel, the nephew of Tia Antonia and the future husband of Dolores, together with two or three old broken soldiers with whom Irving had loved to gossip, did not propose that the beautiful Spanish custom of accompanying a departing guest a way upon the road should be set aside.

[1] Letter to Peter Irving, *Life*, II, 169.

Thus the melancholy cortège moved. At the foot of the hill north of Granada, Irving alighted and walked slowly to the top with Manuel, who had received his medical diploma and had confided his engagement to Irving's favorite and his ambition to become the physician of the fortress. At the top of the hill sad farewells were uttered, and the little group slowly descended it. From the top, Irving waved a last farewell. The King of the Alhambra was on his way to exile.

As the travelers approached Gaudix, where the Duke of Gor had extensive estates, they were met by the Duke's administrator in a carriage and driven to his comfortable house in the town, where they were urged to remain as long as possible. That evening several canons from the cathedral called, ices were served, an elaborate supper was spread. At daybreak they again were on their way, but when they reached the village of Gor, nestled in a green valley at the foot of a grim mountain, they paused to escape the midday heat, and in the castle of the Gors, even then almost a ruin, they were entertained, wined, and dined.[1]

Thereafter the travelers entered upon the rough and dangerous stage of their journey. No one traveling through the region today with its perfect hard-bottomed roads, the best in Europe, would be able to conceive the conditions of little more than a century ago. Then the roads were execrable, full of ruts and rocks, and in rainy weather all but impassable because of the mud. The accommodations were inconceivably crude. The *posadas* were impossible. The food was wretched and scant, unless carried by the traveler, and beds were a luxury seldom found. And by common consent the route the travelers took was perilous because of robbers who infested the hills. Murders were commonplace,

[1] Letter to Peter Irving, *Life*, II, 177.

and Irving was impressed by the innumerable crosses mark-
ing the spots where travelers had been murdered by the
bandits. Here and there he found the skulls of robbers hanging in iron cages. In one village, while Irving was there,
four robbers who had been captured were brought in; and
in another village he viewed the dead body of a robber who
had just been shot by the alcalde. Through certain sections
it was agreed that a mere private guard, though armed,
would not suffice against the brigands, and that only four or
five armed soldiers could furnish adequate protection.
Irving, however, in the spirit of a gambler determined to
rely on his Portuguese, though in no sense convinced of his
dependability, and, as fortune had it, he made his way
through the wildest country without molestation or annoyance. At the inns he and his companion spread their mattresses on the floor and slept soundly.

As they approached Murcia, they found the roads increasingly intolerable until within a short distance of the
town, which they entered through a wide avenue bordered
with magnificent trees for a distance of four miles. The
streets of the town were as clean as those of Seville, but they
could not linger. As soon as the travelers could catch their
breath, they started for Alicante through scenery as beautiful
as could be found anywhere in Spain, admiring the groves
of palm trees; and then on to Valencia, noted even then for
its rice fields, its rice dishes, and its charming women,
described by another traveler of the time as 'the most charming triflers in the world.' It was a community of extremes,
the mass of the population very poor, the proprietors of the
rich lands very rich. There the Duke of Medinaceli drew a
revenue of seventy-five thousand dollars annually from his
estates, and the families of Villa Hermosa and Benavente
almost as much. But these high dignitaries lived elsewhere,

and the workers were left to the none too tender mercy of the overseers.

At Valencia, Irving and his companion parted with their lank Portuguese and his trusty musket and took the diligence for Barcelona. The roads and inns were now much better, but soon they rattled into the most turbulent city in Spain. There they lingered a little while.

B ARCELONA had long been the center of revolutionary risings. Even then the Rambla was the fashionable promenade, but Irving's most interesting experience there was his dinner at the palace with the famous Conde de España, the rigorous Captain-General.

Spain in those days had few men so lusty, gusty, picturesque, or powerful. Ardently devoted to the King, the Conde was forced by circumstances to call on every possible resource in the defense. There had been revolutionary troubles across the French border and the populace of Barcelona was in constant danger of infection. The French soldiers had taken up their quarters in the town a little while before. A little cloud heralding the Carlist war was on the far horizon. Ferdinand himself was not an inspiration to his supporters. He had come to rely largely on the ruthless methods of the Conde. Deliberately he set about to terrorize the people into peace. Men had been banished without trial. Rumor bruited it abroad that there had been too many secret executions. An inquisitorial policy and oppression were adopted. No more than four people could dine together at a coffee-house. Spies circulated freely in public places, and the gossips were convinced that not a few of these waited at table in private houses.

Thoroughly hated by those who feared him, and in constant danger, the Conde de España seldom appeared in public, and thus he had become a symbol or a legend. His box at the opera seldom saw him, though nightly it was brilliantly lighted and sentinels stood at the entrance as though in expectation of a royal visit.

Two years before Irving saw him, he had incurred the displeasure of the Archbishop of Toledo. That year occurred the Catalan insurrection of the Carlists. Fifty thousand armed men threatened the province with anarchy, and Barcelona was in imminent danger of capture by the enemies of Ferdinand. The Conde de España knew that a large number of the bishops were all too familiar with the conspiracy against the King, since he was in possession of the documentary proof. At this juncture he had persuaded Ferdinand to visit his city of Barcelona for a conference. He then called a convocation of the bishops, the ostensible reason being the King's desire to consult with them on the state of the province. The King appeared, the bishops entered and took their seats, and the Conde de España took the chair. There was a moment's silence as he rummaged among his papers. Then, selecting one and turning to one of the bishops, he said in a cold tone:

'My Lord Bishop, you know this —— '

And then taking up another document and turning to another:

'And you, my Lord, know this —— '

Thus, then, paper by paper and bishop after bishop, he exposed without histrionics the complicity of each and all in the conspiracy to drive Ferdinand from his throne. Then, brushing the papers aside, he gave his ultimatum:

> You perceive I hold in my hands proofs of treason; you who have fomented this rebellion can put it down; and I have instructions from His Majesty, if the rebellion be not put down within forty-eight hours — I am sorry for the alternative, gentlemen — but my instructions are peremptory, to hang every one of you; and it will be a consolation for you to know that the interests of the Church shall not suffer, for the King has already named successors to the vacant sees.

The old master of dramatics had staged the scene perfectly and timed it right. There was much grumbling, but no one but knew that de España would carry out his threat. Within forty-eight hours the insurrection ended.

Such were the stories that had thrown a halo of mystery and awe about this strange personality. He was now about fifty. Though slightly less than the medium height, he was powerfully built and he had the energy of a dynamo. His head and face were large, the latter dominated by most expressive eyes which revealed the character of the man, his violent passions, his cold courage, his penetration, the strength of his mentality, and the cunning of an Oriental potentate. Irving was to find that he had a rather cruel sense of humor.

Though of French extraction, he affected at least a bitter distaste for the French and spoke English fluently. He occupied the royal palace. On reaching Barcelona, Irving met a few English friends who were on terms of cordiality with the Captain-General, and thus an invitation to dinner was easily arranged. The company consisted of three Englishmen and Irving. His imagination fired by the lurid tales circulating about the man, Irving was to feel that he was 'entering the abode of a tyrant.'

Ushered into the presence of the host, he found before him a man of middle age and size, well set up and evidently robust, and attired in military dress. His face impressed the visitor as handsome, and his manner was the last word in Spanish courtesy. At the table the 'tyrant' became jocose and familiar, exchanging rather coarse jokes with his intimate English friends and laughing uproariously after the manner of Henry VIII. Irving thought he could detect 'a lurking devil in his eye,' and in his laugh something 'hardhearted and derisive.' His sense of humor was not subtle. In the midst of the laughing and joking an interruption threw a vivid light upon his character.

From the balcony at the Alhambra, Irving had heard the church bells tolling the requiem of the late Queen, and now, almost too soon, Maria Christina, the beautiful Princess of Naples, was expected in Barcelona any time en route to Madrid to marry Ferdinand. Every conceivable courtesy was to be extended the Princess, and officialdom was on tiptoes. The dinner was over and the company was seated at the table with coffee and cigars when one of the petty functionaries of the city was announced. The Conde de España smiled and winked at his guests, foreshadowing a joke at the expense of the well-meaning wight. Into the room with an air of suppressed excitement bustled the functionary, with the information that he had just learned by letter of the movements of the Princess and had lost no time in reporting to the chief. Though long in full possession of the information, which he had in truth been relating at the table, the Conde assumed an air of the utmost gravity and the keenest interest. Solemnly he had the petty official repeat his information, and then again, and again, all the while intensifying his expression of gratified interest. Then, with the ceremony with which he would have conducted the King, he bowed the proud informant out of the court and to the great staircase.

The Conde returned to his guests convulsed with laughter over his mockery of the well-meaning functionary. He stood to mimic the voice and manner with which the information had been conveyed, punctuating his recital with roars of metallic laughter, converting the incident into a rollicking farce which reminded Irving of the 'gamboling of a tiger.'

Such was Irving's last festive scene during his first sojourn, and the next day he resumed his journey over the Pyrenees to France.

Thirteen years were to intervene before he would again tread the Spanish soil. The Conde de España would be in his grave — murdered by his enemies. Though unable to await the initial coming of Maria Christina in 1829, he would be among the diplomats and functionaries to greet her on her return from exile under the tent in the field beyond Aranjuez. Again he would visit the palace in Barcelona, but this time to pay his respects to the girl Queen Isabella, the daughter of the Neapolitan Princess. And as he passed up the grand stairway to the royal presence, the scenes of his last dinner on his first Spanish sojourn would flash like a picture before his mind.

THUS began Irving's exile. Two years in England among old friends and driving in leisurely fashion with Martin Van Buren, a congenial companion, through country lanes, and then back to the United States to be fêted and acclaimed as the first professional writer of that country to receive European recognition. His 'Life of Columbus' had been published and favorably received before he had left Spain. The 'Conquest of Granada' went to press the year he left and while he was in London; in the year of his return to his homeland the famous 'Tales of the Alhambra' was published and received with enthusiasm. With no thought of wandering more, and with numerous literary ventures in his plans, he built his attractive home of 'Sunnybank' beside the Hudson River. Soon, however, he was making a western tour, and out of this at length came the book 'Astoria,' dealing with the establishment of the fur trade on the Columbia River.

Meanwhile, he had been meditating a biography of George Washington, and he hoped to base his claim to lasting fame on this. And just then, in 1842, he was offered the post of Minister to Spain. John Tyler, the President, equaled by few of the American executives in a love for literature, had long been a warm admirer, and Daniel Webster, the Secretary of State, was a friend. As a youth, Irving had written for the Federalists, and then the Jacksonians sent him to the Legation in London, and now the Whigs were asking him to accept the mission in Madrid. For a moment he hesitated. 'Sunnybank' was now so pleasant, and that 'Life of Washington' was yet to be written. But then the lovely memories of the beauty, the glory, and the charm of Spain came to him in a flood and drew him toward the scenes he loved so well. There would be leisure at the Legation, and there, as well as at 'Sunnybank,' he could write his book. He accepted and sailed. The book would not be written in Madrid as he had hoped; but that is another story.

M ATEO'S sons grew up; and long after Irving left his friends of the Alhambra a tourist in Granada would be given a card, which may be seen today in the Astor Library in New York City:

Granada.

José Jimenez
(Son of Mateo Jimenez
Guide of Washington Irving)
Respectfully offers his services to
accompany strangers.

For by this time the traveler, American or European, would be apt to be interested in the Alhambra because of the tales recorded by the man who lived in the apartments of Queen Elizabeth of Farnese, in the palace of the Moorish kings.

Chapter 7: BACK TO SUNNY SKIES

ARRIVING in France, Irving proceeded to Paris, where he awaited his official household consisting of Alexander Hamilton and J. Carson Brevoort. The former was the grandson of the great American statesman. He had been selected as Secretary of the Legation, and Brevoort, a member of the family with which Irving was most intimate in New York, was taken along as an attaché. The Minister was eager to reach Madrid and settle down. For months he had passed hurriedly from scene to scene with maddening distractions, and he was no longer young. 'I am too old a frequenter of the theater of life to be much struck with novelty, pageant, or stage effect,' he wrote.

But the young members of his household were in no hurry to tear themselves away from the diversions of Parisian life, and it was not until July 25, 1842, that Irving reached Madrid. Vail, his predecessor, met him and conducted him to the elaborate apartments in the palace of the Duke of San Lorenzo he was to occupy for a short time. This palace, since razed to make way for the Plaza, was very old and very large and stood in the older section of the town. For a while Irving was to occupy one wing of the palace, and the other wing was occupied by Cavalcante de Albuquerque, the Brazilian Minister. This contributed not a little to Irving's satisfaction in the beginning, since Madame de Albuquerque, who was a New York woman of the family of the Oakeys, was both amiable and intelligent. Not far away was the royal library, where in other days he had bent laboriously over books and manuscripts, and the royal palace was but hard-by. To add to his initial satisfaction, he had scarcely installed himself when a visitor was announced and his heart leapt at the appearance of the Duke of Gor, his friend of Granada days. The old friends fell into each other's arms, and then for a long while Irving listened eagerly to gossip about his other acquaintances in Granada. The Duke had taken up his residence in Madrid, where he was a prominent member of the Moderado Party, which was in opposition to Espartero, the ruling Regent. Mild and reasonable, gracious and generous, he numbered his friends in every party, and his liberality in the trying times inspired his election to the presidency of the distinguished Ateneo Club (Athenaeum) that very year. More than ever he was interested in public affairs, political and otherwise, and the charming Duchess, remembered by Irving as surrounded by her children, was at the head of numerous charitable organizations.

Irving lost no time in presenting his credentials, and thus at the beginning he was called upon to make a decision of policy. Spain had passed through perilous and tumultuous days since Irving had bidden it a sad farewell. The Neapolitan Princess Maria Christina, whose advent for the marriage with Ferdinand he had barely missed at Barcelona, had known vicissitudes. At the time of the King's death she was the mother of two daughters and no sons, and the dying monarch had set aside the Salic law and promulgated the 'pragmatic sanction' to make the older of the daughters his successor. Don Carlos had raised the banner of revolt, and for seven years the war of the succession had divided the nation into warring camps. The liberals had rallied around Maria Christina as the Regent Queen, and she had proved herself unworthy of the noble opportunity before her. Soon her most ardent supporters were alienated by her stubborn opposition to all salutary reforms and her contemptuous hostility to constitutional limitations on power. Many ascribed this to the domination of Louis Philippe of France, her uncle, who despite his ascension to power as a liberal was a stubborn foe of reform. More fatal to her popularity was her infatuation soon after the King's death for one of her bodyguards, whom she advanced in station. One day a mob demanding a constitution broke in upon her at the palace of San Ildefonso with the demand that she sign. When she refused, her lover was taken to the court of the palace, and to save him from the firing-squad reluctantly she signed. Thereafter she appeared less defiantly with her lover in public, but gossips bruited it abroad that goodly portions of her enormous income were lavished upon him. Thus with waning popularity she drifted along for three years.

Then in 1839 the Carlist war collapsed before the guns of the patriot General Espartero. Don Carlos fled the kingdom. And Maria Christina took advantage of the general rejoicing to agree to an order vesting the appointment of all municipal officers in the Crown. Again the fire of liberalism flamed, and the Queen Regent hurried to Barcelona, where Espartero was stationed with his victorious army in the hope of receiving his sanction for the decree. The warrior refused, and warned her of the inevitable popular reaction to her act. Disregarding the warning, she signed, and before the furious reaction she abdicated the regency and crossed to France, where, on Irving's arrival in Spain, she still was stay-

ing in the court of Louis Philippe. Espartero conducted the
two young princesses to Madrid, and to general applause
installed them in the royal palace. There he gave them a
guardian in Agustin Arguelles, a brilliant and patriotic
Spaniard who had suffered exile in the days of Ferdinand,
and as governess he selected Countess Mina, widow of a distinguished general, much loved for her amiability and
spotless character. Their education was entrusted to
Quintana, one of the most learned men of the kingdom, and
Espartero became the Regent of Spain.

But the ambitions of Maria Christina, sustained by her
enormous wealth and encouraged by the French King, were
alert and active. The fruition of her intrigues came with the
insurrection at Pamplona. Seizing upon the citadel, General
O'Donnell proclaimed Christina the Queen Regent. To
strengthen the insurrectionary cause it was planned to capture the two Infantas and conduct them to the insurrectionary camp.

The night of the attempt the soldiers on guard at the
palace were under the domination of the insurrectionary
chiefs. It was a night of tempests, of wind and rain. The
leaders of the plot with a few companions entered the palace
by the main portals and rushed up the grand stairway, with
confident expectation that no one would bar their way to the
little Queen's apartments. There at the doors stood eighteen
hardy veteran halberdiers who made resistance, and some of
the invaders fell before their fire. When the assault party
hurried away for reinforcements, the halberdiers took refuge
in the apartment and fired through the doors. Many fell
mortally wounded.

Meanwhile behind the doors the scene can be imagined.
The royal children screamed and wept and prayed, fearful
of their lives. The little Queen threw herself into the arms of

Countess Mina and cried out: '*Aya mia*, who are they? Are they rebels? What do they want of me?'

Such was poor Isabella's introduction to queenship. Her sister was in convulsions. Meanwhile there could be heard pounding at doors, the firing of guns, the shouts and groans of combatants. Mattresses were spread in an out-of-the-way corner, safe from random shots, and the children, in exhaustion, slept.

Happily the gallantry of the halberdiers sustained the defense until the news of the attack had reached the people of Madrid. From all quarters of the town the regular troops and the National Guards rushed to the palace and surrounded it. The two officers leading the attack deserted their followers and escaped, though one, betrayed by his general's uniform, was caught and shot. All this happened but nine months before Irving assumed his duties in Madrid.

THOUGH Irving was sure that 'the brutal attempt has been to throw complete odium on the course of Maria Christina, to confound the enemies of the Constitution,' the bitterness of the enemies of Espartero was not diminished. Just a little while before, the French Ambassador had reached Madrid and demanded admission to the Queen to present his credentials. The effect intended was the discrediting of the regency of Espartero. The Spanish Government pointed out politely that the constitutional method prescribed that the credentials should be presented to the Regent. The Ambassador haughtily refused and then interrogated Paris. Louis Philippe, with Maria Christina at his side, supported his Ambassador. Again the demand for an audience with the Queen was made, again refused. The Ambassador grew wroth. Unless his demand were granted he would ask for his passports and leave the country. More, he would remove the escutcheon of France from above the gates of the Embassy. The Government calmly sent him his passports. He went away in a holy huff, but left the escutcheon on the gates and one of his secretaries in charge of the Embassy.

It was immediately after this comic incident that Irving reached Madrid. Would he, too, demand permission to present his credentials to the Queen? Though they were addressed to her, Irving had discussed the situation with Daniel Webster before leaving Washington and had been told to use his judgment on the ground. He was determined to bow to the constituted authority. Soon after his arrival he called on Count Almodovar, the Minister of State, presented his credentials, and asked for instructions. He was informed that they should be presented to the Regent. With all eyes on him to note whether he would follow the precedent of the French Ambassador, Irving drove to the palace of Buena Vista, once the habitat of Godoy in the days of his domination of Maria Luisa and Spain, and after a century the War Office of 1936. Alexander Hamilton accompanied him as he entered the portals of the historic palace in the midst of its stately trees. At the entrance to the grounds sentinels saluted. Within the palace as he passed from one spacious salon to another, more soldiers stood at salute. At length he entered the impressive anteroom where he was to await his summons. In two corners of the room he observed busts of Espartero, and on the wall a painting of the Regent in one of his great battles. Here scattered about the room were a few officers and aides-de-camp. Here too was Cavalcante de Albuquerque, the Brazilian minister, on the same mission as himself. Unsympathetic toward the dominant party, he had just been spared by the action of the American Minister the humiliation of the French Ambassador, with whose position he sympathized. At length the door was opened and Irving found himself in a small salon. There, at the far end of the room, stood Espartero with Count Almodovar at his side.

Irving advanced, bowed, and read his brief address:

> I have the honor to deliver into the hands of Your Highness, as Regent of this Kingdom, a letter from the President of the United States of America accrediting me as Envoy Extraordinary and Minister Plenipotentiary to this Court.
>
> In presenting this letter I do but echo the sentiments of the President in accompanying it with assurances of the high respect and regard of my Government for the Sovereign of this country, for its political institutions, and for its people; of its sincere desire to draw more and more closely the ties of amity which so happily exist between the two nations, and of its ardent wish that Spain under her present constitutional form of government, administered with wisdom, firmness, and patriotism, may open for herself a new career of prosperity and glory.
>
> Your Highness will permit me on my own part to express the extreme satisfaction I feel in being appointed to a mission, the sole object of which, I trust, will be to promote mutual good understanding and good-will between my own country and a country for which I have ever entertained the highest consideration.

With the French exhibition in mind and conscious of the potentialities of a blunder, he had cautiously worded his address to convey the thought that he accepted as an outsider the constituted authority of the moment.

Espartero, who made a profoundly favorable impression on Irving by his manner and appearance, replied:

I appreciate in the bottom of my heart the assurance of approbation which the President of the United States of America manifests in favor of my reign and my country.

The bold, open countenance of Espartero, his frankness, his soldierly directness, his manly demeanor, and the fine courtesy of the Regent captured Irving's admiration in that brief time, and he was ever to remain an admirer. At the conclusion of the ceremony Irving was informed that the little Queen would now receive him at the royal palace.

Reaching the palace, Irving had to wait awhile in the apartment of the Minister of State. Then, for the first time, he ascended the grand staircase, scarcely equaled in beauty and magnificence by any other in Europe. Thence he was led through one spacious apartment to another. The casements were closed to exclude the July heat. Most of the rooms were silent and vacant. Thus he passed in silence through twilight more suggestive of a convent than of a royal abode until he reached the Porcelain Room, with its high vaulted ceiling floridly designed, and its silken tapestry. It, too, had the softness and the sadness of twilight.

Then into the room noiselessly glided the little figure of the twelve-year-old Queen, with the benevolent and good Madame Mina and Agustin Arguelles by her side. All were in black, mourning for the Duke of Orleans. With superb poise the child Queen advanced a few steps into the room and paused. A little behind her Madame Mina stood. The Minister of State then presented the envoy in his official capacity.

Irving from that moment became a partisan of Isabella II. His heart was touched by the little mite, who seemed so much alone in the midst of so many ugly passions and ambitions. He saw before him a little girl scarcely twelve, but fully developed for her years. Her complexion was fair, though pale; her eyes seemed blue or a light gray. Hating the ceremony as she must, her manner, though uncannily grave for one so young, was courteous and friendly. How Irving could have made her laugh with his amusing stories had she been just a little girl remote from thrones, as Eugénie of the French had seemed when some years before he had dangled her on his knee! His heart went out to the child Queen, 'separated from all her kindred except her little sister, a mere effigy of royalty in the hands of statesmen.'

As Irving passed from the presence of the little Queen into the adjoining room, he was surprised to find the famous Arguelles in hot pursuit, and even more astonished when greeted effusively and welcomed warmly to Madrid. The great liberal, a brilliant orator, unsurpassed in the parliamentary history of Spain, was known to him by reputation, though he had no recollection of having ever met him. But it seemed that when the dour Ferdinand forced Arguelles into exile he had gone to England, where his liberalism was both known and appreciated. Lord Holland, true to the liberal traditions of his blood, made him his librarian at Holland House, about whose table the foremost liberals of England had broken bread from the days of Fox, and the generous peer gave the exile a pension as payment against his needs. Occasionally in the scintillating circles of writers, artists, and politicians Irving had there frequented, his path had crossed that of the interesting Spaniard, but the latter's distinction and significance had been lost upon him. Delighted now to have the casual acquaintance refreshed, Irving that day looked forward to the cultivation of an intellectual friendship. But the great reformer was deeply engrossed in his duties at the palace, for which he received no pay, and the two men seldom met. Returning soon afterward from Aranjuez, where he had joined in the official welcome of Maria Christina, back from her exile, Irving learned that Arguelles had been stricken, and a few days later, in the midst of the festivities over the homecoming of his enemy, seventy thousand people reverently followed the great man to his grave. But Irving was to feel that it had been a privilege to know him.

Thus the day had passed pleasantly. Irving had been won by Isabella, and he was delighted to have made pleasant contact with Arguelles, but Espartero had made a profound impression upon him. The soldier-like bearing, the strong face denoting intelligence and determination, the flashing black eyes, were uppermost in Irving's memory as he drove back to the palace of San Lorenzo.[1]

MEANWHILE, Irving was not without annoyances incidental to housekeeping. When his trunks and baggage reached the Spanish frontier they were held by the customs officers, much to his annoyance. He politely called the Foreign Minister's attention to his embarrassment. Three weeks later he had not received the trunk and eight boxes, and his patience oozed away. A week before he had written Almodovar and there had been no answer. He wrote an indignant note saying that he was 'daily suffer-

[1] MS. Archives, report to Webster, August 2, 1842; letter to Mrs. Paris, *Life*, II, 407.

ing great inconvenience and incurring expense from the detention of articles indispensable to the daily use and the entire arrangement of my domestic establishment.' He could not refrain from observing that his mere official character had been sufficient to protect him against customs annoyances in France and England, though entitled to no privileges in those countries. At length he received his household effects.[1]

In the list of contents sent to Almodovar we get a glimpse into the domestic plans of the bachelor diplomat. In one box were two brass lamps with glass globes and other attachments. Another contained table linen and bedclothes. In another were two dozen crystal glasses, eight dozen wineglasses of various classes, eighteen decanters, and twenty-four fingerbowls. A fifth box contained a pair of gilded candelabra, another a set of white porcelain, and another a set of white gilded porcelain. The eighth box enclosed a set of porcelain for dessert. It was evident that Irving had no thought of entertaining more than twenty-four at dinner at one time.

At length the boxes were unpacked and Irving was prepared to dine his colleagues in the great palace of San Lorenzo. He waited impatiently now for the arrival of his books and papers, which had been shipped from New York to Cadiz. His impatience increased as the days passed. 'As soon as I receive them,' he wrote, 'I shall set to work at my "Life of Washington," and foresee that I shall have abundant leisure here for literary occupation.' In this he was to suffer one of the bitter disappointments of his life.[2]

[1] MS. Archives, Irving to Almodovar, August 24, 1842.
[2] Letter to Mrs. Paris, *Life*, II, 412.

IRVING had been plunged into the hottest part of a Madrid summer. Happily the great houses with their thick walls had been constructed as a protection against the heat more than against the chill of winter. Daily he rose at five, taking a mean advantage of the sun. Throwing open the windows and the doors of his chamber to admit a free circulation of the morning breeze, he sat down at his desk to read or write until eight o'clock, when royalty offered him a diversion. Afar off the sound of drums and military music announced the approach of the troops marching to the palace to relieve the guards. Invariably — for he loved pageantry — he took his stand at the window as the horse-guards pranced by, accompanied by a band on horseback playing lively military airs. The clatter of the horses' feet reverberated in the narrow street between the palaces of the nobility, and Irving watched them with childish delight until they turned out of view down a narrow passage leading to the royal abode. Then from a distance the swelling music of another band — the foot-guards were approaching. At a quick step to the enlivening music of a march or waltz the soldiers in their colorful uniforms swept by.

It was now time for breakfast. On the table before him he found, spread out for his delectation, all the Madrid newspapers, which, because of the stringent governmental regulations, he soon found scarcely ever contained anything of interest. Then music again, the soldiers returning, the foot-guards first this time, to some gay air, and Irving would leave the table to enjoy the scene, for he never tired of the spectacle. After glancing over his mail, Irving, Hamilton, and Brevoort would go to their different rooms for the routine business of the day. Frequently they would exchange visits — a bit of business — a little gossip.

The windows of Irving's apartment looked out upon the busy, noisy, narrow street that traversed the city from the Prado to the royal palace, and it swarmed with people. From one of his windows he looked down upon the choicest remnant of other centuries, the Plaza Mayor, so rich in the romance, the tragedy, the intrigues of both the lofty and the lowly. Standing in this fascinating little square after almost a century, one sees practically the same scene that delighted Irving. But the fountain in the center is now gone. In Irving's time this was surrounded throughout the day and far into the night with men and women water-carriers, and with the gossips of the neighborhood, for Spanish fountains are notoriously sacred to the exchange of news. Often Irving was entertained by the strife and turmoil of the water-carriers struggling to fill their jars, though a police officer indifferently sought to make them take their turn.

During the hot part of the day Irving would seek his bedroom, which was also his study, because it was lofty and large. The shutters were closed to keep out the warmth of the sun, and in a mild twilight, making it just possible to read, he found August not unbearable in the thick-walled palace. Thus passed the afternoon.

At five o'clock Irving, with Hamilton and Brevoort, would dine, and then the three would seek their couches for the inevitable siesta, or lounge at ease until the breeze from the Guadarramas had cooled the streets. Sometimes Irving would brave the long walk through the town to promenade in the Prado, and often he would walk to the esplanade of the royal palace for his exercise. When the heat persisted after the setting of the sun despite the breezes from the mountains, he would draw an easy-chair onto his balcony where he could catch whatever air might be in circulation, and find vast entertainment in observing the people in the streets.

On such evenings he was usually rewarded with a fleeting glimpse of the little Queen. A footman rushing through the streets blowing a bugle announced the approach of the child Isabella. She was returning from her drive in the Retiro. Three or four horsemen on prancing steeds rode on ahead, and then, in the royal carriage with six horses, came the Queen and her sister, with Madame Mina. The carriage, an open barouche, passed just below Irving's balcony, and he had an excellent view of 'these poor innocent little beings in whose isolated situation' he took a keen interest. Officers on horseback rode beside the carriage; and then came a troop of horse; and then another carriage and six bearing the functionaries of the court in attendance on the monarch.

And Irving would linger on the balcony, for the night was growing cooler, until midnight, when he would go to bed.

Such was the routine of his days during the hot season of 1842 when he dwelt in the palace of San Lorenzo.

But the Madrid of 1842 was not, to him, without its alloy of sadness. It was already a Madrid of memories. The old friends with whom he had held sweet converse in former days were gone. He was to pass the old house of the D'Oubrils on the Alcala with wistful longings, for the diplomat and his children and the charming niece no longer were there to give him welcome. D'Oubril was then in Frankfort as the Russian Minister; the children were grown up; the niece no

doubt was married and with children of her own — or so he
thought. Prince Dolgorouki, who had left Madrid long before to become Minister in Persia, was never to be seen again
by Irving, though occasionally they exchanged letters. In
pensive mood Irving stood before the former home of the
D'Oubrils, where once he had romped on the floor with the
children, and gossiped with the Minister as he elegantly
sniffed his snuff, and delighted in the conversation of
Mademoiselle Antoinette, and observed carpenters and
masons at their work doing the house over for the habitation
of a millionaire who had made a fortune in speculation.

And the delightful commingling in society that he had
known had ceased. The war of the succession, the venomous
hatreds of the conflicting politicians, and the fear of spies
had forced Madrid society to close its doors to all but intimates. Of the Spaniards of Madrid Irving had known and
admired the most during his first sojourn, only the scholarly
Navarrete was on the stage, and he, grown old and feeble,
spent scarcely any time in the capital and Irving did not see
him. Among those he had met and admired fifteen years
before he found much of disillusionment. 'Time,' he wrote
Dolgorouki, 'dispels charms and illusions.' How well he
remembered the charming society belle of exquisite beauty
who had captivated his fancy in a social tableau as Murillo's
Virgin of the Assumption. Then she was young and but
recently married, and he assumed that she was 'pure, lovely,
and innocent and angelic in womanhood.' He had made
inquiries about her on his return to Madrid. One night at
the theater she was pointed out to him. In the box of a
fashionable nobleman he found her, still handsome, with a
riper beauty, seated with her daughters and the nobleman,
who was younger than she. He was shocked to learn that the
young nobleman, though rich in material goods, was poor in

intellect and in morals, and was the lover of Murillo's Virgin of the Assumption, and that the liaison was quite open. 'The charm was broken, the picture fell from the wall,' he wrote Dolgorouki.

Soon he was to make new friends and to adjust himself to change, but never again in Madrid was he to find the magic circle within which he had moved in the gladsome days when he was an industrious author.

PERHAPS it was because of his marked partiality for children that Irving was so interested in Isabella and her sister. He had been in Madrid little more than two months when he saw her again at the opera. She sat in the box with her sister, with Espartero seated on her right. He noted that she was fond of theatricals — was she not later on to add a theater to the Palace of the Pardo? — and 'appeared to take great interest in the performance.' He noted also that she was growing rapidly and would soon be quite womanly in appearance, though only twelve years old. Real beauty he failed to find, but in her sister he discovered enough of prettiness to satisfy the most exacting notions of how a princess should appear.

It was soon after this that Isabella observed her saint's day with the members of the House and Senate and the diplomatic corps in attendance. The members of the Cortes filed into the palace at two o'clock and the diplomats followed at three. To Irving it was a spectacle; to little Isabella it was to be the most exquisite torture, for she was to pass down the line of gray-haired diplomatists and say a word to each. Sympathizing with her terrors, he was almost as much flustered as the child Queen.

The scene was more cheerful than on the occasion of his first visit. Instead of the oppressive silence and the twilight, he found animation and the cheeriness of full daylight. The dark dress of mourning for the Duke of Orleans had been laid aside and Isabella was garbed in white. He observed now that she was matured in form beyond her years; that she had light hair and eyes, scarcely to be expected, he thought, in a Spaniard; that her skin was noticeably rough and had a 'mealy look,' owing to the neglect of Maria Christina. The dark hair and eyes of her sister gave Isabella an advantage, though he understood that she was paler and not quite so pretty as she had been. He was sure, however, that the baths Isabella was taking for her skin would soon rid her of the 'mealy look' and that the little Princess would 'grow up very handsome.'

Irving sympathized deeply with the little Queen as with evident embarrassment and reluctance she started toward the line of diplomats. Happily, the first in line was the British Minister, Aston, with whom she was fairly well acquainted, and she regained something of her composure; and then came Count Lima, another old friend, and she was smiling. She had recaptured her self-confidence before she reached Irving. It was he who for a moment was at a loss as to what to say. He had been so engrossed in studying the child that when she stood before him he realized that he had thought of nothing special to say. He covered his lack of foresight by expressing regret that his inadequate knowledge of Spanish made it impossible for him to talk with her as he would wish. There was always something maternal in

Isabella, and this came to the surface instantly. Giving her fan a flirt, she smiled.

'But you speak it very well,' she said.

Irving shook his head in dissent.

'Do you like Spain?' she asked with perfect composure.

The little miss realized that she was mistress of the situation, and she may have felt sorry for the embarrassed diplomat. And then, the benevolent friendly look of Irving invariably won the confidence of children.

'Very well,' he said.

Again she smiled, gave her fan another flirt, bowed, and passed on.

The little Princess followed, less mature than her sister, more the child.

Irving expressed the hope that she had enjoyed the opera.

'Yes, I like the theater,' she said timidly, and glided on in the wake of her sister.

Having gone down the line, the little mites on whom so much of the hopes of a great nation then depended returned to their places and stood motionless. A functionary of the court gave them their cue. They bowed. The line of diplomats bowed from the waist, and then backed out of the room.

It is significant of a certain appealing quality in Isabella which she never was to lose that Irving never was to see her without finding his sympathy grown stronger.

And then came the insurrection in Barcelona.

Chapter 8: WIGS AND FANS

SOON Irving was sending sprightly and penetrating dispatches on the Spanish scene to Washington, and Daniel Webster, the Secretary of State, was laying everything aside on their arrival to read the entertaining gossip of the master-weaver of graceful tales. For Irving's dispatches were not the stilted dry-as-dust reports of the average diplomat. If a government fell, it meant a portrait of the fallen Minister, a clever analysis of the reason for his fall, and penetrating studies of the successor, along with the gossip of the town. Fortunately, though there were several changes in the Department of State in Washington, all the successors of Webster were men capable of appreciating Irving's unique letters. Hugh Legaré, one of the most accomplished scholars of the South, and Calhoun were as appreciative as Webster of Irving's observations on the court of the young Isabella.

In August he found many rumors of foreign machinations and internal conspiracies, but thought the Government would have a 'breathing spell.' The finances, however, were all awry. The very high protective duties had encouraged smuggling on a colossal scale and the Treasury was not collecting. All suggestions of reduced customs duties met with the clamorous opposition of the protected interests that dolefully declared reductions would 'throw thirty thousand men on charity.' The war of the succession had not been liquidated, for throughout the land roamed armed marauders who fell on villages and the traveler on the highway. In Catalonia, where the robbers were most arrogant, a robust, ruthless officer called General Zurbano was moving against the brigands without regard for law. A robber found had short shrift, no trial, no incarceration, and only a firing-squad. Much grumbling was heard in political circles against these 'atrocious' and 'sanguinary' measures, but Catalonia was soon rid of robbers, and kidnaped victims held for ransom were released. But party bitterness had reached fever heat. Espartero and his hand-picked Ministry had their enemies, and a powerful coalition had been formed to effect their overthrow. An act for press control to moderate the licentiousness of the times arrayed most of the gazettes in furious opposition.

And the little Queen became the storm center of a venomous controversy.

NOTHING concerned the politicians more than the determination of the time when Isabella, aged twelve, should be declared of age and entrusted with the responsibilities of ruling a kingdom. It was a battle between the liberals, insisting on the Constitution, and the absolutists, dreaming of the joyous days of the sixteenth century when kings were kings and the people were the rabble. Isabella was of the age of susceptibility to environment. About her were Arguelles, a liberal and progressive, and Madame Mina, who had no one's axe to grind. The absolutists wished to sweep these aside and to surround the child with reactionary minds. The liberals wished to hedge her about with liberal minds until her own views were mature and her habits and opinions formed. With the conservatives clamoring for her immediate assumption of full authority, the liberals were whispering that she should not be burdened with the cares of state until her eighteenth year, in accordance with the defunct Constitution of 1812.

The absolutists' fire was now directed on Espartero. His head was turned by almost regal power, they said. He wished indefinitely to prolong his reign. How impossible for this vain man complacently to contemplate the loss of his dazzling station and his retirement to drab private life!

Irving listened to the gossip and formed his own conclusions. He sought information from the Regent's intimates. They assured him that Espartero was 'sincere in his professions and honest in his intentions; little skilled in intrigue; more the soldier than the statesman.' They added that he was 'prone to sink into apathy on ordinary occasions,' but energetic when a real emergency appeared. Irving concluded that 'at such moments of rallying energy the prompt soldier now and then needs the warning voice of the wary statesman, to keep him from trampling involuntarily over the boundaries of the Constitution.'

MORE agitating to many states-
men, both within Spain and without, was the subject of
Isabella's marriage. Though she was only twelve, the web
of intrigue was being woven in the dark in the palace of
Louis Philippe, and on Downing Street in London there
was much concern. The greater part of the Spanish people
resented the interference of other nations. They felt the topic
unsuited for the young monarch's age. They had learned a
lot through the centuries of the futility of alliances based on
matrimony. While Isabella was playing with her dolls,
superannuated roués of diplomacy were linking her with
this prince or that as though she were their daughter.

When Irving reached Madrid, however, there was an
active Spanish candidate in the person of the Duke of Cadiz,
the son of the Infante Francisco. Though not so bothersome
and dangerous to the Crown as Don Carlos, Don Francisco
kept the waters of intrigue boiling. This was due in large
measure to his ambitious and cunning spouse. He had married the Princess Luisa Carlota, the sister of Maria Christina
— a woman as daring, aspiring, contriving as the widow of
Ferdinand. The very summer of Irving's arrival, the hectic
flutterings of Luisa Carlota in the drawing-rooms of Madrid
had impelled the Regent to suggest that the health of Don
Francisco demanded treatment at some remote watering-
place. Making a virtue of necessity, the troublesome family
were soon jolting over the roads to a resort in the north of
Spain. The people there were pleased by the presence of

members of the royal family, and the young Duke of twenty gained warm adherents to his cause. Moving familiarly among the people, Don Francisco by his easy manners and plebeian air made a profoundly favorable impression on the lower classes. Meanwhile Luisa Carlota concentrated on the people of more pretension and better intellects.

The lady soon was conducting a campaign as though her impotent son were aspiring to a seat in the Cortes, rather than to the hand of a young miss scarcely in her teens. At Saragossa the enthusiastic reception of the people determined her on a more audacious course. Soon hired *claqueurs* were assembling under the windows of the palace where the family was staying, wildly acclaiming the young Duke, proclaiming him the hope of Spain, singing in serenades in which the name of the Duke and the little Queen were coupled. Snatches of the songs were being printed, for pay, in journals throughout the country. When Irving reported the incident to Webster, the highest authority had not only intimated that the air of Saragossa was bad for Francisco's health, but that the coming winter in Madrid would be too rigorous for his delicate constitution.[1]

Meanwhile Irving had left the huge old palace of San Lorenzo, where the noises of the streets disturbed him, and had taken the principal apartment in the imposing palace of the Marques de Mos, the owner

[1] MS. Archives, to Webster, November 5, 1842.

PALACE OF THE MARQUES DE MOS, IRVING'S OFFICIAL
RESIDENCE AS UNITED STATES MINISTER

retaining bachelor quarters in one wing. No one apparently
has known of the association of the author of the 'Tales of
the Alhambra' with this palace, for no plaque proclaims the
connection to the passer-by. A large four-story stone house
with thick walls and many windows with iron balconies,
it extends for a block on the Calle Victor Hugo, once the
Calle San Jorge, and its windows look out also on the Rosales
de Castro, formerly the Calle de las Infantes, and on the
Calle Gomez de Baquero. The other side of the palace then
looked out, as now, on an old garden. The entrance then,
as now, was midway of the palace on the Calle Victor
Hugo.

Still the property of the family of the Marques de Mos,
the palace was leased some years ago as the headquarters of
the Dirección General de Seguridad — the Scotland Yard
of Spain. Wandering through its long corridors today, one
finds little to suggest the palace Irving knew and described.
The exterior and the entrance are unchanged. But the necessities of the police have torn out some partitions and made
others, and the cold, hard severity of the bleak stone walls
is now depressing. I am convinced that Irving's bedroom
was at the corner of the Calle Rosales de Castro and the
Calle Victor Hugo, and that the little study where he groaned
because of the doctor's orders against writing was the adjoining room. The salons where he received and entertained all
face on the Calle Gomez de Baquero. The surrounding
streets are narrow and given now to commerce. The garden
with its fountain and its goldfish is gone. The serenity, charm,
and elegance of the old establishment are as dead as the
goldfish that Irving knew. By night the streets are lighted
by electricity and the charm of the torches has been lost.
But in the evening it is easy to re-create in fancy the scene
on the nights of Irving's dinners when servants stood with

torches at the wide entrance to light the guests into the building and up the broad stone stairs.

'I have such a range of salons,' he wrote his niece, 'that it gives me quite an appetite to walk from my study to the dining-room.' From the windows of his study, looking south, he could enjoy 'a little dilapidated garden, in the center of which is an old, half-ruined marble fountain with goldfish . . . and a superannuated Triton in the middle blowing a conch-shell, out of which, in his younger days, there no doubt rose a jet of water.' At one end of the building was his study and bedroom. His sleeping apartment in former times had been the family chapel. It was octagonal in shape, with a glass cupola or dome through which he could see the luminous Spanish stars. When the sunlight in the morning poured through the windows into the charming little room done in pink, yellow, and pale green, the effect was magical. 'You have no idea what a splendid waking up I have sometimes in the morning,' he wrote. From the windows of his adjoining study he could look into the half-ruined garden and meditate on the vagaries of life and catch a view near-by of the historic palace, once Godoy's and now the residence of Espartero, and of the not distant groves of the Retiro. Thus he was to find the Prado within reach for his promenades. For the first time he had found a house where he felt at home. Near-by on the Alcala were the homes of a number of his colleagues.

THEN came the insurrection in Barcelona on which hung, for the moment, the fate of Espartero. Irving, who admired the Regent, was keenly interested in the outcome. Following the developments in Catalonia with eager eyes, he was sending elaborate reports to Webster. He had noted the increasing irritation in Barcelona. There was bitter resentment because of the vigorous repressive measures from Madrid; and the ruthless, if effective, methods through which General Zurbano was putting down sedition, robbery, and contraband had infuriated the desperate criminal element. Irving noted also that the prospective cotton treaty with England which would admit British manufactured goods to compete with the woolen products of Catalonia had alienated the sympathy of the manufacturers. At length the pot boiled over. There was a 'general and spontaneous rising of the populace'; the troops, after a sanguinary engagement, were driven out of the town, and the few who had taken refuge in the citadel were forced to capitulate and surrender their arms. It was a defiant challenge to the central authority in Madrid.[1]

On the day Espartero rode forth personally to assume command, Irving joined the immense throng drawn to the neighborhood of the palace of Buena Vista to witness the stirring scene. It was a day of brilliant November sunshine. On the esplanade of the Prado the National Guard, fully armed and equipped, marched and countermarched to the

[1] MS. Archives, dispatch to Webster.

music of military bands. It was when Espartero emerged from his palace and rode down the Prado between the lines of soldiers that Irving, who was not superstitious, could not but tremble for the fate of the Regent. Scarcely had Espartero ridden through the gates of the palace grounds astride a superb, spirited white charger with long flowing mane, when a solitary raven, bird of ill omen, mysteriously flew into the picture. And as Espartero, in his full uniform, with towering feathers in his cap, started along the heads of the columns, saluting the cheering soldiers with his gauntleted hand, the raven followed not far above his head, flapping its wings. Irving was among those who noticed that it flew directly above the plumes of the Regent's military cap, and then disappeared as uncannily as it had come.

Irving, who thrilled easily to spectacles, enjoyed the scene. Never had Espartero seemed so magnificent, so militant, so competent, so impressive. He saw the Commander pause to speak familiarly with some of the cavalry. He saw him wheel his horse and return to the center of the esplanade and then draw his sword. He saw it flashing in the sunshine. He felt the dead silence that fell upon the restless crowd, anxious to hear Espartero's words. 'I do not know that ever I was more struck by anything than by this sudden quiet of an immense multitude,' he was to write. Here, he thought, was colorful history in the making, as the General rode back and forth a distance of thirty yards, waving his sword in the sun, and addressing the soldiers, who then adored him, in robust tones that reached the uttermost ring of the crowd. Irving heard his declaration of intent — to defend the Constitution, to protect the liberties of the people against the machinations of despotism, to maintain public order and put down the anarchy of the mob. Could he entrust the peace of the capital and the life of the young Queen to the loyalty of the Guards? The soldiers roared their promise. The spectators joined in the fervent demonstration. Espartero sheathed his sword, smiled, and with all the pomp and circumstance of war rode through the great gate of Alcala.

Irving walked back through the crowd to the palace of the Marques de Mos.

Eager as a star reporter, Irving now listened to the gossip in cafés and streets, exchanged views with his colleagues of the diplomatic corps, inquired for news from the War Office. Soon he was writing Webster that the trouble was localized. Saragossa and Valencia held aloof from the contagion. Generals Zurbano and Van Halen, though driven from the town, were encamped near Barcelona and were being reinforced. There were no desertions. Warships were anchored off the city. From the heights of the fortress of Monjuich a bombardment had commenced and the French and British were holding parley with Van Halen.[1] Four days later Irving's pen nervously was scratching paper on another dispatch to Webster. Resistance in Barcelona was tightening. The original 'popular Junta Directiva,' composed of men of little character or standing, and some foreigners, had been displaced by another composed of some of the richest and most substantial citizens of the town. Van Halen had given an ultimatum that without a surrender within two days he would open a bombardment.

It was two weeks before Irving could report the suppression of the insurrection. There had been a severe bombardment. Espartero had sought to persuade surrender without this measure, but his toleration had been scoffed at as weakness by his enemies. The political foes of the Regent seeking his ruin were flooding the Madrid gazettes with unmeasured denunciations. Irving predicted that every effort would be

[1] MS. Archives, dispatch to Webster, November 22, 1842.

made to cast odium upon Espartero. He was amazed at the intemperance of the press.

Through the crisis in Barcelona there was perfect serenity in Madrid. The National Guard kept faith with Espartero, if indeed there was any sentiment for insurrection. To reassure a niece, Irving wrote that even in the event of a popular commotion he would be in no danger. He was not the sort, he said, 'who goes abroad in riotous times in quest of adventure,' and the national arms above the portal of his house would be respected 'even by the rabble.'

He added a warning against taking the press campaign against Espartero too seriously. 'As far as I have had an opportunity of judging, he is an open, frank, well-meaning man, more of the soldier than the statesman, but sincerely disposed to uphold the present Constitution; to protect the throne of the little Queen.'

THE nobility and aristocracy of Madrid for many generations had held aloof from the society of foreigners, and, a century before, diplomats were complaining of their exclusion from the social circles of the natives. During Irving's diplomatic career there was but modest entertaining, even among the members of the corps. The richest member of the group was Aston, the British Minister, who often was giving dinners in which the American, who had been honored by Oxford, was almost invariably included. Irving found the Englishman frank, open, cordial, and the soul of hospitality. 'But to cope with him,' he wrote, 'is out of the question; besides his ample salary he has a large private fortune.'

He wrote in the midst of 'a little domestic hubbub,' since he was giving a diplomatic dinner of his own that night to repay in part his indebtedness to Aston and the staff of the British Legation. The brass lamps with the glass globes were lighted, the gilded candelabra threw their mellow light upon the table with its white gilded porcelain and its wineglasses 'of various classes,' and the decanters were filled for the Scotch and soda. Soon Aston would be gone and Bulwer-Lytton would hold forth in the Legation of the British. And such is the ephemeral life of the average man that after less than a century the name of Aston, who then set the social pace for the diplomats that none could equal, means nothing to those who represent the great empire in the Madrid of today.

A FEW days before the dinner, Irving had seen the 'little Queen' presenting prizes on a formal occasion at the Liceo, which he describes in a letter to his sister as 'a numerous and fashionable society instituted for the cultivation of art and literature.' Extraordinarily brilliant in its day, it long since passed from existence. In 1836, in the midst of the discouraging and destructive war of the succession, when Spaniards were slashing zealously at each other's throats, Don José Fernandez de la Vega had conceived a plan to divert attention from the bloody scenes of dynastic ambitions to more ennobling phases of Spanish life. This was six years before Irving returned to Spain as Minister. Gathering about him his companions from literary and artistic life, Don José formed the Liceo for the cultivation of literature and art. The happy thought made an instantaneous appeal to a war-worn people, and soon the most illustrious painters, sculptors, writers, architects, actors, actresses, and musicians were enrolled. They met at first in Don José's house at 13 Gorguera, but so many clamored for admission that the meetings were moved to a larger house in the Calle de Leon; and then, as the interest grew, to another house on the Calle de las Huertas, and then to a still larger quarter in the Calle de Atocha. Finally they settled in what Irving describes as 'an old ducal palace,' which was the palace of Villa Hermosa, at a corner on the Prado. This fine old palace still stands, an impressive brick block with many windows brooding on the Prado, but the ground floor on the main streets is now occupied by business offices. In the rear, on a very narrow thoroughfare, is the entrance to the part of the palace still occupied occasionally by the noble family. A high brick wall conceals the garden, and the casual tourist passes by without suspecting that the imposing building with its severely simple façade was once one of the great palaces of the capital when Isabella was a child, or that any portion is reserved to this day for its original purpose.

The cream of the nobility and intellect of the capital soon were enrolled in the Liceo, and in Irving's time there were six hundred members of both sexes. The society was divided into six sections, devoted to literature, painting, sculpture, music, dramatics, and architecture, and each section was expected to contribute seriously to maintaining the brilliancy of the weekly meetings. The palace became interested, and members of the court appeared always at the sessions and participated in the programs. On certain occasions prizes were awarded on a gala night when the monarch appeared personally to bestow the awards. Fortunate the stranger who on such a night could gain admittance, for there assembled were the notable figures of the court and the no less interesting notables of the Court of Intellect. Distinguished statesmen, high officers of the army, brilliant men from the ranks of the nobility, the most beautiful women of society, all were there to make the scene one of the utmost animation. And the diplomatic corps was included in the invitations.

Irving had been in Madrid six months when he attended the first of these gala sessions. It was the anniversary meeting of the Liceo, and prizes were to be awarded and presented by the little Queen, attended by her sister, the pale Princess. When he entered the 'immense and lofty salon in what was formerly a ducal palace' (it still is), he found before him at the end of the room a stage with scenic decorations. The great room was crowded with the brilliance and fashion of the town. Immediately before the stage seats had been reserved for the diplomatic corps, and on either side were raised daises richly carpeted, with two chairs of state for the Queen and her sister. Irving liked these spectacles.

At length the Queen was announced.

Everyone rose, and not a few of the women stood on their chairs or benches to get a better view of the little lady. This pleased Irving too, and he observed that 'many a beautiful Spanish face with dark, flashing eyes was to be seen peering anxiously over the heads of the crowd.'

Down the center aisle passed Isabella and her sister, the faithful Madame Mina with her, along with a few of the functionaries of the court and a number of loyal halberdiers.

As they passed along, the Queen and the Princess saluted acquaintances right and left, and Irving thought 'in very gracious style.'

They ascended the dais and sat down in the chairs of state. A halberdier with his musket took his stand on either side of each chair. The halberdiers stood immovable as statues.

Then the Duke of Osuna, one of the richest of the grandees of Spain, and unmarried at thirty, conceded the palm as the greatest dandy in the capital, presided in his capacity as President of the Liceo and master of ceremonies. He announced the prizes one by one and placed the award in the hands of the little Queen. The recipients were then conducted down the aisle to the foot of the improvised throne and the girl monarch presented the prizes. The happy man or woman — two girls won prizes — then knelt and kissed the plump hand of Isabella.

Irving was curious as to how Isabella and her sister would conduct themselves, and concluded that they both acted 'with great grace and decorum, not laughing more than was becoming in a queen and princess.' But he could see that the royal sisters were enjoying the situation immensely and were much amused in a childish way.

But as the evening advanced Isabella was seen to yawn behind her fan, for the hour was late, even for a child monarch. The courtiers and the Duke of Osuna also noticed, and the program was therefore hurried through. The actors spoke so rapidly that Irving could scarcely understand them.

At length the curtain fell. Isabella rose, bowed to the assembly, and then passed down the center aisle again, nodding as before to her acquaintances as she passed out. Irving went outside and saw the Queen and her sister enter their carriages in the light of many torches, and then sweep out of sight to the clatter of 'a glittering troop of horse.'

Meanwhile that fall Irving was not unmindful of his more prosaic duties. The commercial relations of the United States and Spain were far from satisfactory. Irving had discussed the possibilities of a treaty with Count Almodovar, and had learned that quite soon the latter was planning to ask the Cortes for changes in the regulations of commerce. Thereupon Irving prepared an elaborate letter to the Minister of State. He reminded the Minister that for a long while the United States had been urging the mutual benefit of a better understanding but without encouragement from Madrid. Discriminating duties had led to competition in the restraining of the natural flow of trade. The interchange of goods between the United States and Cuba and Puerto Rico had been seriously hampered by restrictions that had operated unfortunately for both nations. And the trade between Spain and the States was 'in a sad state of decline, sinking under the prohibitory and protective system.' The recent Spanish tariff act almost completely excluded American products from the marts of Spain. The result was that Spanish ports once familiar with American merchantmen were 'almost entirely deserted by the flag of the Republic.' At Bilbao, where twenty-six years before there had been seventy-nine vessels of the United States registering 8299 tons, two vessels of but 321 tons were now registered, and neither of these had carried Spanish cargoes on the homeward voyage. In Barcelona no vessel from the States had been seen in years. The once flourishing trade with Alicante had dwindled to utter insignificance. For six years American vessels entering the port of Alicante had averaged but four a year. And 'Cadiz, once so enriched by American commerce, is now little more than a port of transit.' Cadiz was being starved.

True, at Malaga American commerce 'still lingers.' During the previous four years exports to the States from the port of Malaga averaged $1,200,000 a year. But, warned Irving, 'I find the products of the United States permitted to enter in exchange for these five millions did not amount to more than four hundred thousand dollars. No trade can prosper where there is so little reciprocity.'

But Irving was gratified to learn from Almodovar that measures were in preparation to permit free trade in tobacco. Had not the high duties defeated their purpose by making smuggling profitable? Irving pleaded at length for the tobacco industry of his country. The United States was a 'young country of vast consumption and constantly increasing demand.' 'Yet it is an ominous fact,' he wrote impressively, 'that in this country, so favored by Nature, possessing as has been well observed "a genial climate, an active population, a soil of boundless fertility, a seacoast of great extent, numerous harbors, the noblest colonies ever enjoyed by any nation and boundless treasures of the precious metals," not two merchants of the United States unconnected with some official employment from their Government are resident, and the ships of the Republic are gradually disappearing from the ports.' [1] It was a persuasive document and the Minister of State was sympathetic, but Ministers in those days were birds of rapid flight; scarcely were they seated comfortably on a bough when the winds of faction blew them far away. Irving was to be disappointed in his hopes.

That first autumn he was writing notes to secure the release

[1] MS. Archives, November 8, 1842.

of an American from a Havana jail, and in protest against the withdrawal of the right of American vessels to make repairs in the shops at Mahon. The affair of the Americans was long drawn out, but the protest had an immediate effect when it reached the authorities in Madrid.

In December Irving was confronted for a moment with an unpleasant duty imposed by the unauthorized action of the Chevalier de Argaiz, the Spanish Minister in Washington, in ordering the Intendant in Cuba to discontinue payments of interest due the United States under the Treaty of 1834. The Minister had filed a claim against the United States wholly unconnected with the treaty obligation and, failing to receive an early reply, had taken it upon himself to order the discontinuance of the interest payments. Webster's note of inquiry had brought a curt reply, and Irving had been instructed to ask the Minister in Madrid if the Chevalier had acted under instructions from that quarter.

Irving invariably was to find the Count Almodovar courteous and friendly. On calling, in compliance with instructions, he had found the Minister astounded at the act of the Chevalier. Meanwhile, however, the latter had changed his mind and the interest had been paid. But the Count was not insensible to the reflection upon his country implied in the query, and had spoken sharply of Webster's delay in replying to the claims note of the Chevalier. It was a tempest in a teapot.[1]

[1] MS. Archives, dispatch to Webster, December 5, 1842; note to Almodovar, December 6, 1842.

ON CHRISTMAS DAY Irving, who more than once had known the meaning of Christmas cheer in England, was invited for his Christmas dinner to the British Legation, with the hospitable Aston as host. He enjoyed 'the good old Christmas luxuries of plum-pudding, mince pies,' and passed a happy day in familiar conversation with a congenial company remote from his friends in the States.

But soon thereafter Irving in consequence of a cold was confined to his house, and his indisposition soon took the form of an inflammatory disease of the skin similar to that which had laid him low twenty years before. The physicians diagnosed his ailment as a nervous disorder due to overwork. He had written many lengthy dispatches to Washington and many long notes to the Minister of State, and he had employed his leisure in writing many long letters to his friends. No one ever found greater joy in composing fascinating letters to his correspondents, and he had written incessantly when fagged. Nature exacted the penalty. Though the malady was not dangerous, it was obstinate and annoying, and the orders of the physician were more painful than the disease. Not only was he confined to his house and denied the ever-colorful pleasures of the streets, but he was forbidden to write, since the slightest mental excitement caused an aggravation of his trouble. Even books were denied him. For some weeks he was a recluse.

It was during this period that his fondness for the Duchess

Victoria, wife of the Regent, increased. He had found her
a woman of beauty and infinite charm, owing in large measure to her graciousness of manner and the sprightly quality
of her mind and conversation. Soon he was to be impressed
with her courage, loyalty, and fortitude in the face of danger
and reverses of fortune. That one of her cultivated mind
should have found in Irving a companionable friend was to
have been expected. Unfailingly he had attended her receptions at the palace of Buena Vista. He had thought her the
ideal mate for a public man. Throughout her life she was to
follow the political fortunes of her dashing husband with
keen intelligence and to be the repository of his most secret
thoughts and plans. No one can peruse the charming letters
to her from Espartero covering some dramatic years, and
incorporated by the Count de Romanones in the appendix
of his biography of the great liberal, without an appreciation
of the really distinguished woman who inspired them.

Throughout the four months of Irving's seclusion he was
to receive many tokens of her interest and esteem. Frequent
inquiries were made concerning his condition. Flowers and
books were sent to brighten and enliven his bondage. And
Irving was not to prove ungrateful in the solemn hour of her
misfortunes that was hurrying on. She was then but twenty-
eight, but of the heroic mould of the Roman matrons in the
days when Rome was truly great.

For the enemies of Espartero were numerous and powerful.
The old aristocracy abhorred him for his liberalism, and it
was mobilized for the assault whenever the hour should strike.
From the court of Louis Philippe, the intriguing Maria
Christina was exhausting her resources to undermine him.
Never would she forgive him his failure to give the sanction
of his sword to her violations of the Constitution. Forces
the most incongruous, drawn together solely by their com-

mon hate of the Regent, were now making common cause. The press campaign against him had long passed the stage of the merely licentious. The bombardment of Barcelona was being used with deadly effect against him. The day he had ridden into Madrid after successfully repressing the insurrection he had been received with what Irving thought a strange coldness. True, the municipal authorities and the National Guard had waited upon him with ceremony and acclaimed him with apparent warmth and enthusiasm, but Irving could feel in the air the waning of his once enormous popularity. 'It could hardly be otherwise,' he wrote, 'considering the falsehoods and exaggerations concerning those events, which have been industriously propagated through the opposition papers and the false colorings given to the conduct of the Regent in the affair, who is held up as a perfect Nero.' [1]

Irving thought his treatment hideously unfair. Studying the Regent's character, he could find nothing to justify the description of 'cruel' or 'tyrannical', and even the bombardment he felt had been warranted by conditions. 'A bombardment is a noisy process,' he wrote Webster, 'terrible to the eye and ear, but I doubt if the insurrection would have been put down, and the threatened anarchy of the country prevented, as promptly and effectually and at as little cost and bloodshed by any other mode.' [2]

In January he was sure that the suppression of the insurrection had diminished Espartero's popularity while increasing his military power. The proposal to reduce the army was no longer heard. The disaffected had been disarmed. Wherever the loyalty of the National Guard with reason had been suspected it had been disbanded. Would this sense of military power go to Espartero's head? Irving wondered. His ene-

[1] MS. Archives, dispatch to Webster, January 7, 1843.   [2] *Ibid.*

mies were seeking to pique him to extreme measures. Even
his friends were urging him 'to make the Government respected.'

In the Cortes a combination of parties had been formed
against Espartero, and rather than submit his measures to
an organized majority he had dissolved the body and ordered
elections. The contest would be bitter. The Moderados,
comprising the old nobility and men of great wealth, were
preparing to take the field. For more than two years they
had refused to participate in the government, and had
contemptuously denounced the régime as a usurpation.
Some of the nobility, however, were urging a return to public
life and the seeking of an understanding with Espartero, lest
by permitting their power to rust in inactivity they ultimately
sacrifice their interests.[1]

One month later the alert eyes of Irving found factions
thriving more than ever. Money in abundance from mysterious sources was available for the encouragement of seditious
movements and for the subsidization of the press. Agitators
in Barcelona constantly were prodding the people to another
insurrection, and only the iron hand of the military kept the
populace in bounds. 'The city remains like a half-extin-
guished volcano,' Irving reported, 'ready at any moment for
another eruption.' To meet the attacks upon him Espartero
had issued an election manifesto of doubtful wisdom. Until
the elections were over Irving reported that no progress could
be made regarding negotiations and discussions with the
Ministry of State.

[1] MS. Archives, dispatch to Webster, January, 1843.

Chapter 9: PERILS AND PAGEANTRY

THE campaign against Espartero increased constantly in bitterness. Forces the most incongruous and irreconcilable momentarily joined under the common banner of 'Down with the Regent!' The elections had not turned out happily, and while Irving did not feel that the complexion of the Cortes meant the downfall of Espartero, he reported to Webster immediately that it did mean the overthrow of the Ministry, which had been hand-picked by the Regent. One of the new deputies was the Infante Don Francisco, who entered the capital with much fanfare of trumpets and beating of drums. He hated Espartero, who had courteously exiled him from Madrid. Irving did not think he had much 'energy of character,' but that Luisa Carlota, his wife and a sister of Maria Christina, was a 'scheming, ambitious, intrepid little Queen.' With the couple when they entered in triumph into the capital was 'an unprincipled dangerous man, Count Parsent, who is always with them, supposed to be a paramour of the Princess.' He was thought to have 'great influence with the lower classes.' Irving had no doubt that their arrival would accentuate the controversy over the marriage of the child Isabella. Luisa Carlota was determined that her son should share the throne with his cousin. And that spring Jerome Napoleon, son of the former King of Westphalia, had made a mysterious appearance in Madrid and was assumed to be another candidate for the hand of Isabella. Judging from the gossip in high circles, Irving was persuaded that the twenty-year-old youth's aspirations were not frowned upon by the Government, since he was favorably received by Espartero and was given a private audience with the young Queen.[1] Luisa Carlota nursed her wrath.

Meanwhile, throughout the months of May and June conditions grew more threatening. The air was charged with electricity. The seed of insurrection was being sown industriously throughout the provinces, and the crowds in the Madrid streets and chocolate shops were seething with excitement, as rumors of plots and conspiracies circulated by word of mouth. In Barcelona the old passions began to boil.

It was just before the crisis came that Irving attended the soirées of the Regent at the palace of Buena Vista. Illness had deprived him of that pleasure for four months, and he was shocked to find how few were in attendance. Where once the salons were crowded with a gay company he was distressed to find how thin was the attendance now. Upon the faces of the loyal few he noted 'a general gloom.' Espartero was too constantly engaged in council to appear, and Irving's heart went out to the Duchess, who had been so kind to him. She was pale and seemed dejected, and while she explained that she had a headache, Irving was convinced that it was a heartache instead. A woman of keen intelligence, who followed with more than wifely interest the fortunes of her husband, he was sure that she felt their 'hazardous position and the pitfalls that surround them.' Never had she seemed to him more lovely or amiable, and he wrote that her pallor

---

[1] MS. Archives, dispatch to Webster, April 1, 1843.

and dejection 'heightened her beauty in my eyes.' He thought she would rejoice in a descent from the dizzy height where her husband was exposed to all the shafts of malice.[1]

Soon insurrection was rearing its ugly head in various parts of the kingdom and Espartero was making his preparations to take the field in person. Many predicted that Madrid would never see him more. On the day Espartero left the city, Irving attended a levee at Buena Vista and listened to the Regent's 'frank, manly address' to the diplomatic corps. He wished to maintain the most cordial relations with other nations, and particularly with those that were represented at the court, and recognized the Constitution, the throne, and the regency. He declared his sole ambition was to maintain the Constitution and in sixteen months to turn the reins of government over to the Queen with the nation peaceful, prosperous, and happy. In the meantime, however, he would maintain order, suppress the insurrection, and defend the throne with the valor of a soldier.

That was at noon, and four hours later Irving witnessed again the review of the national militia in the Prado. Again the prancing horse, the plumed cap, the military music, the flashing sword, the cheering soldiery, and again through the gate of Alcala, Espartero rode forth to battle. Irving was not a little sad, for the harvest of insurrection was more abundant than before and he had some doubt of the Regent's triumph.

Two weeks later there had been no battle. Armies were marching and countermarching throughout the country; city after city was declaring itself in a state of insurrection. An insurgent army under General Espiroz was hovering near Madrid. The capital was humming with suppressed excitement, and hourly the people were alarmed by persistent

[1] Irving, *Life*, III, 24; letter to Mrs. Daniel Paris.

rumors. It was said that General Narvaez was hurrying from another quarter to join Espiroz and that Generals Zurbano, the iron man of Barcelona, and Soane were hastening toward Madrid to defend the capital. The city was declared in a state of siege. The gates were closed and guarded — the people of Madrid were prisoners.

Seated at his desk writing one afternoon, Irving was interrupted by clamorous voices in the streets. He hastened to the window. The scene before him was disturbing. Men, women, and children were scurrying wildly in the streets, running in all directions, as far as the eye could see. He summoned the faithful Lorenzo, his servant, for an explanation. Did not Señor know that there was a revolution? The alarm had been sounded, and this meant pressing peril. Word had reached the city that General Espiroz had arrived at the Puerta de Hierro, or the iron gate which one may see today on the way to the country club. From his window, Irving observed the development of the fascinating drama. The National Guards, arranging their equipment as they ran, were seen emerging from every quarter and running to their posts. Distracted mothers, with terror on their faces, were wildly searching for their children to gather them in from the perilous streets. Soon Irving was assured that eighteen thousand men were under arms within the city's walls. The Puerta del Sol and the Plaza Mayor and all other squares were packed with soldiers; the gates were guarded. Cannon were placed within the squares commanding the streets that entered them. The shops were closed. Soon the streets were deserted and an ominous silence fell upon the town. Warned of the dangers without, Irving thought it discreet to remain cooped up in the palace of the Marques de Mos. But when darkness fell and the town was brilliantly illuminated, the boy instinct within him would not be quelled.

Thus, with a boyish bravado, Irving ordered his carriage and drove to the Prado. Fashion was not on promenade that night as usual, and the great preening-ground of vanity was filled with soldiers. But two other carriages were to be seen as he drove from gate to gate. And then he alighted and walked among the troops. They seemed in high good humor. Delighted with the adventure, Irving was loath to return home. As the night advanced, he drove through the Alcala, the Geronimo, all the principal streets, enjoying the brilliant illumination of the houses from street to roof. Few Madrileños ventured into the streets, but at almost every door he found groups of neighbors gathered excitedly discussing the situation. Troops patrolled all the thoroughfares, and when Irving reached the Puerta del Sol and other important squares he found the soldiers bivouacked on the pavement. As Irving's carriage, in solitary grandeur, rumbled noisily through the silence of the night it attracted general attention, but he was not molested.

Having sufficiently exposed himself and satisfied his curiosity, Irving drove to the palace of San Lorenzo to drink tea with Madame de Albuquerque, and then, satisfied that he had never seen Madrid 'under more striking and picturesque circumstances,' he returned to his own home.

A T SIX the next morning Irving was awakened by a general alarm. The insurgents had approached another gate of the city, and it was bruited abroad that General Narvaez had reached Guadalajara with his army. Again the city was under arms, and the shops again were closed. Irving was enjoying the sensation of being in a besieged city, but he had his grievance. 'The greatest evil I have as yet experienced,' he wrote, 'is the cutting off of the supply of butter and cows' milk for my breakfast, both coming from the royal dairy beyond the Puerta de Hierro, or Iron Gate.' The very absence of news was thrilling. The opposition papers had been suppressed and the government gazettes were exercising a censorship on themselves. But lurid gossip filled the void. Everyone, including Irving, listened eagerly, if incredulously, to weird stories of savage plots, of plans to kidnap the Queen and to fire the powder magazine.

And where was Espartero? Some said he was in La Mancha, the land of Don Quixote, and hurrying to the relief of the capital; others insisted that he was going to Cordoba, and still others, to Granada to put down an Andalusian insurrection. Irving heard one moment that his troops were bubbling over with enthusiasm and confidence, and the next that they were deserting him in great numbers.

Two weeks later there had been little change. 'We have been in a state of siege,' Irving wrote a niece, 'the enemy at the gates; the whole body of the National Guards under arms; the main streets barricaded; every house illuminated at night; the streets swarming with military men; the shops shut; the publication of newspapers suspended and the public ear abused with all kinds of lying rumors.' There was growing impatience among the insurgent soldiers without the walls. Now and then Irving could hear sporadic, meaningless musketry fire at the guarded gates. Expecting treachery within the city walls, with the National Guards going over to the insurrection and throwing the gates wide open to the enemy, the besieging army had not brought up its artillery. And the National Guard still stood four square.

From one of his upper windows Irving could see one of the gates of the city and the flash of the guns by night. Day by day he fared forth gaily into the barricaded streets to meet the siege face to face. He learned that soldiers had been stationed in all the houses on the main streets to pick off the insurgents with rifle shots should they gain access to the town. The ground was to be contested inch by inch, from street to street, and, at the worst, the final stand was to be made at the royal palace. There the Duchess of Victoria had repaired from her more exposed palace of Buena Vista to be with Isabella and the Princess.

As the insurrectionists gained accessions and more troops gathered about the gates with every indication that ultimately they would penetrate the city, with all that would mean of savage fighting, Irving became apprehensive for the little Queen. Perhaps the presence of the Duchess of Victoria in the palace may have added to his concern. Should the insurgents break through and the final battle of the streets and barricades be waged for the possession of the royal palace, the danger to the royal sisters would be deadly. The innate chivalry of Irving made his path clear.

Again Irving was in his carriage, driving from one of his colleagues to another with the proposal that should a struggle come for the possession of the palace, the diplomatic corps should urge upon the Government the adoption of every possible precautionary measure for the safety of the Queen, and, if invited, repair to the palace and surround the little Isabella throughout the perilous hours.

That Irving took the initiative there can be no doubt, and that he wrote the note to the Minister of State signed by the entire corps is quite as clear. But after the event, when the chivalrous proffer had won popular acclaim, it was reported in one paper that Irving had written the note 'under the direction of the French Chargé d'Affaires,' and by another that it had been prepared 'in concert with the British Minister.' We have the word of Irving that he wrote the note without consultation, and with the view to phrasing it so as to meet with the approval of both the English and the French. Irving had learned of the preparations to convert the palace into a citadel. He had heard that Mendizabal had boasted that in the last extremity he would 'sally forth with the Queen and her sister in each hand, put himself in the midst of the troops, and fight his way out of the city.' Though assuming this gasconading promise as a bit of idle swaggering, Irving did not know 'how far the defense would be pushed,' nor to what extent it would endanger the lives of the royal sisters.

The diplomats conferred and disagreed. Irving and the majority favored a protest against any extreme, 'either of attack or defense.' Aston, the British Minister, wished to strike out the word 'defense.' At length a compromise was reached on Irving's offer to repair to the palace in a body.

'My only view,' wrote Irving later, 'was, as far as our interference could have effect, to prevent the poor little Queen and her sister from being personally exposed to the dangers of any ruffian contest between warring and desperate factions.' But the offer was declined, and hastening events eliminated the necessity.[1]

[1] MS. Archives, dispatch to Legaré, July 22, 1843; *Life*, III, 35.

ONE night the people of Madrid were in a frenzy of apprehension. The report flashed through the streets and homes that there would be a general attack by the insurgent armies during the night. Irving had been meandering about the streets enjoying the novelty of the scenes of a city in a state of siege. Tired from his rambles, he went to bed and then noticed on the table beside the bed a note. It was from Mrs. Weismuller, the wife of the representative in Spain of the House of Rothschild and a connection of that family. Irving knew her well — a young and beautiful woman, but recently married. She and her husband occupied a large house on the street through which the insurgents first would enter the city in the event of a successful assault. Fearful lest the insurgents in the intoxication of success should run amuck and possibly attack her house, she had written to ask Irving for refuge in the Legation.

It was midnight, but Irving immediately rose and dressed, sallied forth into the streets with the companionship of the faithful Lorenzo, and found his way to the home of the Weismullers. At every corner soldiers and sentinels challenged and peered into his face. He found his friends in a high state of excitement. Information, thought to be authentic, had reached them that the attack would be launched at four o'clock in the morning. Irving offered them the hospitality of his home, and after some discussion it was agreed that at the first sounds of an attack the young couple should repair to Irving's house. By two o'clock he was again in bed.

At four in the morning, he was awakened by the rolling of drums in the street, the firing of shots in the distance. Assuming that the attack had begun, he prepared to rise and dress to receive his expected guests.

But the beating of the drums ceased. No more shots were fired. Soon all was quiet. It was not until afterward that Irving learned that instead of launching the assault the insurgent forces had marched away in the night. Intelligence had reached them that Generals Zurbano and Soane were marching upon the city from one direction and another force under Generals Iriarte and Enna were approaching from another. To prevent the meeting of the two insurgent armies General Narvaez had marched to meet Zurbano and Soane, and General Espiroz had hurried away to intercept Iriarte and Enna. The critical moment had come. Should the insurgent armies prevail, the capitulation of the city would be inevitable. The fate of Espartero's regency hung in the balance.[1]

The armies met. A few shots were fired. Then followed a strange fraternization of the soldiers, with the forces of Espartero going over to the insurgents. That evening, Zurbano, who had managed to escape capture, entered Madrid accompanied by three aides-de-camp — a melancholy figure of a fallen leader. The city was stunned by the turn of events. All the Ministers instantly tendered their resignations — all but Mendizabal. The municipal authorities assumed control and deputations were sent out to treat for terms.

The terms imposed by Narvaez were not easy to meet. He called for the disarming of the National Guard, and this promised a violent resistance and a free flow of blood. Irving thought Narvaez might hearken to the admonitions

[1] Irving, *Life*, III, 31 *n*.

of the more moderate members of his party.[1]   But Narvaez
was in no compromising spirit, and the city had surrendered.
Between forty and fifty thousand soldiers marched triumphantly into the town, and these took possession of every
strategic point and patrolled the streets.   The arms of the
National Guard were taken away.   The victors styled the
new régime 'The Government of the Nation,' and the
Ministry announced by Narvaez ten months before assumed
its functions.   The acting Minister of State, Joaquin de
Frias, formally notified the members of the diplomatic
corps of the advent of the new régime.

Some of the diplomats determined to await instructions
before recognizing the new régime, but with Irving, three
thousand miles from home, this was not feasible.   Acting on
the traditional policy of his country to recognize a *de facto*
government without inquiring into its history or origin,
Irving's first impulse was to enter into relations with the
new régime without ceremony.   But first he consulted with
Valdivieso, the Mexican Minister, in whose judgment and
integrity Irving had the utmost confidence and whose
situation was not dissimilar to his.   The two agreed that the
new Government, powerful in its armed forces, acknowledged
through the greater part of the kingdom, and recognized by
the Queen, could properly be accepted as the Government
de facto.   Thus the representatives of the two American
republics jointly replied to the note of Señor Frias.[2]

Meanwhile, Espartero was in the midst of his siege and
bombardment of Seville when a courier arrived with the
announcement of the capitulation of Madrid.   Immediately
raising the siege, the fallen leader would have turned his
army toward Cadiz, but his men deserted, his forces dwin-

[1] MS. Archives, dispatch to Legaré, July 22, 1843.
[2] MS. Archives, dispatch to Legaré, July 25, 1843.

dled to nothing, and, fearing he would be intercepted by a
force under General Concha, he turned off to the Port of
Saint Mary, where Irving had lived with Hall. There a
Spanish vessel conveyed him and his suite to a British ship
of war. As he stepped on board a salute of twenty guns
was fired — a farewell to one phase of that remarkable
man's career.[1]

IRVING had been puzzled by
Espartero's conduct in the crisis, his seeming lack of decision,
his apathetic failure to prepare for the struggle when there
was time, his apparent lack of a well-digested plan. But his
admiration for the fallen leader had not entirely cooled, and
his admiration for the Duchess of Victoria grew warmer.
'I have always esteemed and admired her,' he wrote, 'but
never so much as since her great reverse of fortune.'

When the insurgents took possession of the city she retired
from the royal palace and took temporary refuge with an
aunt living in the center of the town. Irving, unmindful of
possible criticism and faithful to his friendship, drove openly
to her house, where he found her attended by some loyal
friends. He was impressed by her calmness and self-possession, but most of all by her stoic, philosophical acceptance
of the alteration in her state. Indeed, she seemed far happier
than when he had seen her surrounded by courtly ceremony
at the palace of Buena Vista. Irving chatted with her a

[1] MS. Archives, August 3, 1843.

long while. She said her conscience was clear; that the elevation of her husband to the regency had not divested her of her sense of proportion, and that she had sought to make her conduct then conform to that of the wife of a simple general. Her husband's fall brought her no sense of humiliation. Only when she reviewed the charges against him of ambition, avarice, artifice, and love of power did her indignation flame. 'He,' she said, 'whose habits were so simple, whose desires so limited, who cared not for state and less for money, whose great pleasure was to be in his garden planting trees and cultivating flowers!' She told Irving that afternoon that it was a source of pride to her that they left the regency poorer than when they had entered upon it.

Irving observed with satisfaction the absence of acrimonious reflections on Narvaez and the open enemies of her husband who had triumphed. Only the fair-weather friends who had deserted invited her scorn. 'This,' she said, 'is the severest blow of all, for it destroys our confidence in human kind.' Thus when Narvaez and Serrano, the Minister of War, each wrote her offering her an escort out of the country and all possible courtesies and facilities, she discriminated in her response.

'General Narvaez,' she said to Irving, 'has always been the avowed enemy of my husband, but an open and a frank one; he practiced nothing but what he professed. I accept his offers with gratitude and thanks. As to Serrano, he professed to be my husband's friend; he rose by his friendship and favors, and he proved faithless to him; I will accept nothing at his hands.'

So Irving took his leave of the woman he so greatly admired.

A few days later the Duchess of Victoria, under an escort furnished her by Narvaez as a protection through Spain, journeyed to the coast and took a boat to England, where she joined the fallen leader in exile. 'I have no doubt she will be well received in England,' Irving wrote.[1]

Irving was now to meet new faces in the public life of Spain.

THE old nobility and aristocracy which had held aloof even from the court during the regency of Espartero now flocked back into the limelight with much fluttering of fine feathers. They swept into the capital with much elation and *éclat*, and in no mood to compromise their demands or to spare their enemies. Arguelles, the man of wide culture and strong liberal principles, had short shrift and was speedily driven from his rôle as guardian over the young Queen; and Madame Mina, to whom, at the time, the two princesses were devoted because of the kindness of her heart, was exiled from the palace. No one of those who had risen from the ranks and had found a place near the throne was permitted to remain, and the high nobility and the haughty aristocracy which had shunned the palace as it would the plague now rushed pell-mell up the grand stairway to group themselves about the wondering child Queen. The Duke of Bailen, who was not without renown, now took the place the unfortunate Arguelles had forfeited.

Meanwhile no time was to be lost in harvesting the fruit of the military victory. The thirteen-year-old Queen must

[1] Irving, *Life*, III, 44.

be declared of age with all facility and take in her childish fingers the scepter of the state. The constitutional provisions must be set aside. Too long her impressionable mind had been moulded by the liberals. Others of a more conservative brand would now guide her childish steps.

And then one memorable day when the diplomatic corps was summoned to the palace Irving drove up to the foot of the magnificent stairway, and it was as though he were in another world. He observed 'hosts of old aristocratic courtiers, in their court dresses, thronging the marble steps like the angels on Jacob's ladder — except that they were all ascending and none descending,' and he 'followed them up to this higher heaven of royalty.' At the portals opening into the royal apartments Irving paused.

On the marble casings were still the marks of musket balls; the folding door was as a sieve, riddled by bullets on the night when the courtiers of the moment were bent on the capture of the Queen. He glanced at these mementoes of a dead day, and then entered an immense and lofty *ante-sala* to pass through lines of halberdiers and servants of the court in colorful livery. The anterooms were packed with smiling courtiers, the sparkle of victory in their eyes. The contrasting costumes of the courtiers, the military officers, and the clergy enlivened the scene further.

Irving passed on into the Hall of the Ambassadors. When he was there before it was empty, silent, rather mournful; now it swarmed with the nobility and the aristocracy. He liked this spacious and imposing room, with its ceiling painted with pictures illustrative of the vast colonial possessions of the Crown, with its walls hung with crimson velvet, its crystal chandeliers, its furniture that Irving pronounced 'sumptuous.' In the center, on one side of the room, loomed the throne on a raised dais with a canopy of velvet

— all very much as it is today after ninety-three years have passed.

Irving, with the eye of a dramatist and a philosopher, surveyed the crowded room. It swarmed with courtiers, with scions of the houses of the oldest nobility. None of these had called upon the Queen in the days of Espartero. Now it was different. Happy days had come again. The uniforms and decorations of officers caught the eye. There was Narvaez, the victor. Yonder stood Espiroz, who had co-operated in the siege. And there too was General O'Donnell, 'the hero of the insurrection of 1840,' whose success in the North had inspired that night attack upon the palace. All were amiable enough today. 'In short,' thought Irving, 'it was a complete resurrection and reunion of courtiers and military partisans, suddenly brought together by a political *coup de théâtre.*'

Then, in the midst of the humming and buzzing of the beelike swarm, a voice rings out:

'*La Reina! La Reina!*'

A hush falls upon the room. An avenue is cleared in the center of the crowd. And thirteen-year-old Isabella advances, led by the Duke of Bailen, once General Castanos. Behind her, and bearing her train, is the Marchioness of Valverde. Irving knows her as of the highest nobility, and observes with satisfaction that she is 'splendid-looking.'

And, following the Queen, her sister, her train borne by the Duchess of Medinaceli of the grandees of the realm. And following these a number of beautiful women sparkling with jewels chosen from among the greatest aristocrats in Spain.

The Queen is helped to the throne by the Duke of Bailen. He takes his stand beside her. The Duchess of Valverde carefully and gracefully drapes the train over the back of the chair of the monarch, so that Irving thought it resembled 'the tail of a peacock.'

A little to the left of the throne and on the floor is another chair of state for the little Princess, and when she is seated the Duchess of Medinaceli takes her position behind the chair, and the ladies-in-waiting, shimmering with diamonds and jewels, range in a line to the left.

A little more remote, but seated in a chair of state, sits Don Francisco, the uncle of the Queen, but Irving is more curious about the Duke of Cadiz, the son who stands behind him. Had not the hired *claqueurs* at Saragossa serenaded beneath his window demanding his marriage to the little Queen? Irving had heard strange things about him, but as he looks upon him now, in his hussar's uniform, he seems quite personable, though a stripling.

Irving's eyes return to the two royal sisters, and he notes that they are dressed alike, the skirts a beautiful brocade elaborately fringed with gold and with an abundance of exquisite lace. The trains were of deep green velvet. They both wear diamond pendants and necklaces, with diamond ornaments in their side locks. The only difference between them is in the light crown of diamonds that rests on the head of Isabella.

Irving thinks the Queen 'looked well ... quite plump and grown much.' He noted with satisfaction that 'she acquitted herself with wonderful self-possession ... her manner dignified and graceful.' But he thinks the Princess 'her superior both in looks and carriage,' with 'beautiful eyes, an intelligent countenance, a sweet smile,' and giving promise of becoming 'absolutely fascinating.' He has not yet seen Maria Christina, but he understands that 'her looks and her winning manners' were 'inherited from her mother.'

The two girls appear to enjoy the scene — the first one

in which Isabella has been surrounded by the high nobility.

The drama unrolls. The Ministers of Spain station themselves before the throne. One steps forward to read an address explaining that 'circumstances' make it imperative that Isabella should be declared of age at the next meeting of the Cortes, when she should take the oath of office. Meanwhile she stands with her written reply in her hand, seemingly oblivious to what is being read to her, her eyes glancing about. Now and then she catches the eye of her sister and both seem to struggle to keep from giggling. The Ministers conclude. Isabella turns to her prepared reply and reads it.

'*Viva la Reina!*'

The throne room shakes with the shout of the courtiers. The Duke of Bailen, an old man, bends on one knee and kisses Isabella's hand. Don Francisco and his son follow in the same ceremony of allegiance. All others follow — all but the diplomatic corps. The little Princess has her hand kissed too. Irving notes that some kiss the hand of Don Francisco, but these were his partisans. It is a long ceremony.

Irving keeps his eye upon the young Queen and he observes her discriminations in her manner of receiving homage — a smile, sometimes a word to those she knows best. Irving thinks it 'curious to see generals kneeling and kissing the hand of the sovereign who but three weeks since were in rebellion against her government.'

This ceremony over, Isabella and her sister pass to the balcony in front of the great Hall of the Ambassadors, and there they sit under a rich silken awning with the high dignitaries of the court about them. In a balcony on one side are the ladies of the court, and opposite, the diplomatic corps. The windows of the royal suite are all thrown open and thronged with courtiers in court dress and uniforms.

To Irving the scene is 'remarkably brilliant.' In the square before the palace there is a great throng.

And now military music is heard in the distance. Through an archway on the other side of the square rides General Narvaez with his staff, followed by a troop of horse — and then the whole army that but recently had besieged the capital. Passing beneath the royal balcony they shout '*Viva!*'

That evening Irving writes his impressions:

> It was really a splendid sight — one of those golden cloudless evenings of this brilliant climate when the sun was pouring his richest effulgence into the vast square, around which the troops paraded. Here were troops from various parts of Spain, many of them wayworn and travel-stained, and all burnt by the ardent sun under which they had marched. The most curious part of this military spectacle was the Catalan legion — men who looked like banditti rather than soldiers — arrayed in half-Arab dress, with *mantas* like horse cloths thrown over one shoulder, red woollen caps, and hempen socks instead of shoes.[1]

THE ceremony over, Irving drove to the palace of Buena Vista to greet the rising sun. Espartero was gone, and gone the lovely Victoria. And Narvaez is now surrounded by the courtiers. Irving is not sure what the next act will be, or whether the audience will permit the play to go on. Like all coalitions of incongruous elements,

[1] Irving, *Life*, III, 41, 42.

this one carried, he fears, the germs of its disintegration. He notes that there were three ambitious generals in the capital, 'each watching with jealousy the honors accorded to the others.' The disbanded legions of the old regency, unemployed, uneasy, dissatisfied, are roaming about the country invited by want to the ranks of banditry. As he takes his long walks through the city, it seems to Irving that the people are unhappy and resentful of the soldiers from other regions strutting about with an air of masters, while their National Guard is disarmed, humiliated, pushed aside.

And the victors are chattering more than ever about the marriage of the child Isabella. Cold, cynical, heartless statesmen in other capitals are sticking their fingers in the pie. Policy proclaims that Isabella shall step from the cradle into the snow. Love is to be taboo. They are discussing the marriage of this thirteen-year-old child without a thought of her heart's promptings. And then, too, there is the shadow of foreign interference falling on Spain. The rivalry and jealousy of England and France threaten complications. The former, thought Irving, had been out-maneuvered by the latter, and then England's partiality for Espartero has become a handicap in the struggle for ascendancy in the Peninsula.[1]

Irving is finding it fascinating to watch the plays on the checkerboard of Spanish politics. He seeks information, listens eagerly to all the gossip, and reports to Washington. Already the coalition has been threatened with a schism. Narvaez, a soldier, with a soldier's impatience with the restraints of legality, has precipitated a crisis over his demand for an immediate declaration of the Queen's having become of age. Within the Ministry there is a clamorous protest on constitutional grounds. Only the Cortes can make the

[1] MS. Archives, dispatch to the Secretary of State, August 3, 1843.

declaration, Narvaez is told. At length the compromise is reached which is celebrated in the scene at the palace just described.

But the marriage of the Queen! Now that she has reached the ripe age of thirteen, it is agreed by the régime that no time can be lost about the marriage. And here again the coalition is at loggerheads.

One August day Isabella and her sister are hurried to the palace at La Granja and the tongues begin to clack. Irving hears the gossips say that within a few days Narvaez, disregarding the Constitution and the Cortes, will have her proclaimed of age there by the army, and that he has sent five thousand soldiers to the beautiful palace of the gardens, the fountains, and the statues. Irving is assured that thereupon the Queen will dismiss the Ministry and name another of Narvaez's choosing, and will become affianced to a prince of the choice of Maria Christina.

Other gossips are quite as sure that the two royal children have not been sent to La Granja for the air and the exercise, but that unmolested by the curious they may meet an emissary from their exiled mother. Maria Christina, whose ambitions have not cooled, is bent on having the young Queen married to one of the sons of Louis Philippe. This would give France an easy ascendancy, it is feared, over the affairs of Spain. It is out of these suspicions of France that still other gossips have drawn another explanation of the removal to La Granja. The Queen is to be spirited away to the Basque provinces, beyond the influence of the people of Madrid 'and within the influence of French policy!' All these rumors Irving sends on to Washington with the warning that they should be ascribed to the imaginations of the gossips of 'this idle and gossiping capital.'

But he trembles for the little Isabella. He finds her 'the

ISABELLA II
1845

only rallying point of national feeling,' but he fears that 'the moment her minority ends, and, as Queen, she favors either party, that moment she will become an object of hostility and her very throne may be shaken in the violent convulsions which are likely to occur.' [1]

BUT for the moment the paeans of triumph are still sounding, and soon after the ceremony at the palace with the army crying '*Viva!*' the diplomatic corps is invited to the palace to a religious ceremony in which the young Queen is to have the stellar rôle. This ceremony is to be staged in the royal chapel. The Cardinal Patriarch of the Indies is to pontificate. The Te Deum will be chanted in honor of the recent political and military events.

On the appointed day Irving, taking Albuquerque, the Brazilian Minister, with him, drives to the palace and again ascends the grand stairway between lines of halberdiers and courtiers in embroidery. It amuses him to find the latter 'hastening to pay their devotions to the throne rather than to the altar.' The octagon-shaped chapel in the rear of the palace is crowded when they enter. Most of the official characters, civil, military, and religious, are on their benches. Numerous ladies of the court, not on duty, are dressed in black, with mantillas attached to the backs of their heads. In the lofty recesses of the arches in small galleries dignitaries of the Church are seated. A short way from the high altar

[1] MS. Archives, dispatch to the Secretary of State, August 19, 1843.

on the right stands a magnificent state chair on a platform covered with a rich carpet, with a canopy of damask on which is worked the arms of Spain. On this little platform to the left of the chair is the royal prie-dieu, or praying desk, covered with a damask mantle, and there is a damask cushion for the Queen to kneel upon.

On a front bench facing the throne, seats are reserved for the diplomatic corps. Irving happens to be the ranking member on this occasion, and thus directly faces the throne.

There are some minutes of waiting. Women now crowd the recesses. There is much confusion. The seats reserved for the members of the court are pre-empted by the more audacious, and these are not easily ejected. Irving is delighted with the delay — it gives him ample opportunity to study the scene. He is charmed by 'the pretty and picturesque young female heads peering down from the galleries and windows,' and the 'dark flashing eyes of some of the ladies in veils and mantillas,' and the restless movement of their fans catch his fancy. He does not fail to note that the court dresses of a number of veteran courtiers are considerably the worse for wear.

His meditations on the fugitive nature of earthly power are now interrupted. In the great court of the palace, a blare of military music.

There is a rustling about in the gallery. The folding doors of the chapel are thrown open — the Queen announced. Through the great door now emerge the functionaries of the court, followed by the Queen, led by the venerable Duke of Bailen as before. Behind her files the handsome Marchioness of Valverde bearing her train. Behind her comes the Princess, her train carried by the Marchioness of Alcanizes, thought by Irving to be 'one of the most beautiful women in

Spain.' It is a veritable parade of Spanish royalty, for next
in line comes the charming but intriguing Luisa Carlota,
walking with her daughter; and then her husband, the
Infante Don Francisco; and then their son, the Duke of
Cadiz, campaigning for the hand of Isabella with the aid of
pamphleteers and press agents.

Isabella ascends her platform and sits in the chair of
state; her ladies range themselves on a bench assigned them
to the right. Beyond them in all the splendor of their
decorations sit the grandees of Spain. To the right of the
throne, Don Francisco and his son. To the royal tribune,
where usually the royal family sit, the little Princess, with
Luisa Carlota and her daughter, now repairs.

Irving can study the young Queen without appearing to
stare. Afterward he is to try to describe her dress for the
entertainment of his sister. Her gown he notes is of white
satin or brocade covered by a very rich lace. Her head is
encircled with a diamond diadem from which is draped a
splendid white lace veil. The train is of scarlet velvet
embroidered with gold.

The two-hour Mass is conducted with impressive dignity
by the venerable Patriarch of the Indies, assisted by dignitaries of the Church, and Irving is delighted with the
music. And again he is amazed by the poise of a child not
yet thirteen. Seated alone on a lofty throne, in the midst
of the dignitaries of State and Church, with all eyes upon
her, her grace and dignity are far beyond her years. To
Irving she has the physical proportions of a well-developed
child of fifteen. He thinks her appearance has improved,
indeed is 'quite handsome.' He feels a painter should have
preserved on canvas the memorable scene of the child kneeling at the prie-dieu with her prayer book, her long train
extending behind her across the throne.

And so the army and the aristocracy have duly celebrated the victory over Espartero and the policies he personified.

But Irving is unhappy. He is still ailing, and the excitement and heat of the July and August sun have weakened him a bit. He writes to Washington for permission to journey into France for a vacation.

Chapter 10: THE TENT NEAR

ARANJUEZ

AFTER the excitement of the insurrection and the pageantry of the celebration, Irving is in a state of deep depression because of the persistence of his ailment. His physicians have instructed him to discontinue writing and to read but little, and now that there is no excitement in the streets he feels his exclusion from his chief sources of enjoyment. He writes his friend:

> This indisposition has been a sad check upon all my plans. I had hoped by zealous employment of all the leisure afforded me at Madrid to accomplish one or two literary tasks which I have in hand. A year, however, has now been completely lost to me, and a precious year at my time of life. The 'Life of Washington,' and indeed all my literary tasks, have remained suspended; and my pen has remained idle.[1]

An inflammation of his ankles due to a nervous ailment adds to his misery, and his physicians advise him to try travel and a change of air. Acceding to the suggestion, he writes Washington of his decision to make a journey into France. He feels no misgivings about the affairs of the Legation since he has the utmost faith in the loyalty and competency of Alexander Hamilton, who will remain as Chargé d'Affaires.[2]

[1] Irving, *Life*, III, 48.
[2] MS. Archives, dispatch to the Secretary of State, September 6, 1843.

Thus, early in September, accompanied by the faithful Lorenzo, he fares forth from Madrid, and soon the beauty of the greenery of the mountains and valleys of the Basque country is reviving his spirits. His nights in this charming region are lighted by a full moon, and the air is fresh, and fragrant with the foliage.

But he hurries on to Paris and puts himself under the care of a physician, and for three months he lingers in the city on the Seine.

Meanwhile much is happening in Spain. An insurrection in Barcelona and Saragossa, with the insurgents for a time in possession of the cities. Revolt in Vigo. An attempt is made on the life of Narvaez, en route to the theater to join the Queen and Ministers in the royal box, and fails by a miracle, and the calm courage of the General wins popular acclaim. The Cortes declares Isabella, thirteen, of age, and Irving misses the picturesque ceremony when she takes the oath. A crisis is hurrying on in Spanish politics. And Irving toward the last of November starts for Madrid.

Lumbering in a mail carriage all along over the rough French roads, he listens to a lurid tale of the robbing of the mail coach between Bayonne and Madrid and the rough treatment of the passengers. Disregarding the advice to await an escort, he presses on, and as the coach enters the region of the robbers in the night the two musketeers for the guarding of the carriage sleep. Not wishing to stay awake and alarm himself with shadows, Irving arranges himself comfortably and likewise sleeps soundly through the perilous quarter. Soon he is in Madrid.

He ARRIVES in time to join in the festivities of the popular rejoicing over the accession of Isabella to the throne. As he drives through the town he finds the houses gaily decorated with tapestries hanging from the balconies, the public fountains flowing with milk and wine. For three days the fiesta flourishes, and Irving, with a boyish joy in a spectacle, spends much time in the streets curiously observing the jubilation of the people — watching the processions, colorful and picturesque, enjoying the graceful dancing in the squares of gay young blades and beautiful young women with flashing eyes, observing the games of the children. He finds it comforting to get back among his friends of the diplomatic corps, though he is saddened by the departure of Aston, whose Legation has been the gayest of them all, and whose personality had been so pleasing. Henry Lytton Bulwer is coming in his stead, but he has not arrived. It is at this time too that Irving forms an agreeable relationship with the handsome and clever wife of Calderon de la Barca, who is lingering in Madrid in expectation of an early appointment as Spanish Minister to Washington. As Frances Erskine Inglis she and her sister had conducted schools on Staten Island and in Baltimore until her marriage with the Spanish Minister at the age of thirty-four. Though Spanish by marriage and Scotch by birth, she has spent much time in the United States. But a little while before she has published a charming and entertaining book on her residence in Mexico. Because of her keen intellectual interests she enjoys the friendship of men of letters and is in constant correspondence with Prescott, the historian, who described her as 'a little lady with a bird-like voice.' It is in these early days of Irving's return that he reads the proof-sheets of Prescott's 'Conquest of Mexico' through the kindness of Madame Calderon. Irving finds her 'intelligent, sprightly, and full of agreeable talent,' and frequently he is found at the lady's tea-table enjoying her sparkling conversation. He almost hopes the Calderons will not be sent away.

He has returned to find the Moderados, the party of the old nobility and the higher aristocracy, triumphantly mounted and riding hard, and riding down their enemies ruthlessly, determined to maintain their ascendancy by the sword. General Narvaez is with them, and they count on his vigilance to hold the restless multitude in check. Irving notes that 'the capital gleams with bayonets as in time of war.'

But scarcely has he resumed his residence in the house of the Marquis of Mos when the party struggle ushers in a procession of hurrying events that sends him to his desk to write long dispatches to Washington. Only a few days before, Olozaga has formed a government, and with the best intentions in the world he begins to move with lightning rapidity. But he has the fatal weakness of fairness, and he soon trips on his sense of right. When he issues a decree suspending the reorganization of the militia, and another suspending the law regarding municipalities, the Moderados are jubilant enough, but when, by decree, he declares all grades and honors granted by Espartero up to the moment of his embarkation confirmed, he is assailed with frenzy. In the midst of the tumult and the shouting the town is shocked by the announcement of the official *Gazette* that Olozaga has been dismissed from office by royal decree. And then in the

Heraldo, the organ of the Moderados, the people read that by personal violence the Minister had forced young Isabella to sign a decree without a date empowering him at his discretion to dissolve the Cortes. It is then that the storm breaks in all its fury. The stage setting of Madrid is shifted; the gay processions vanish from the decorated streets, the dancing girls and boys find the dance is over, and in their place Irving observes 'dark knots of politicians muffled in their cloaks holding mysterious conversations at every corner,' while sober, somber crowds congregate in all the streets and squares in the vicinity of the Cortes.

When Olozaga goes, his colleagues of the Cabinet tender their resignations, and for a moment Luis Gonzalez Bravo holds all the portfolios himself. Irving is to find him fair, courteous, and friendly, a man of no mean ability, but the old nobility and aristocracy had hoped for something better when they forced the crisis. What! Such a man as Bravo in close proximity with the child Queen? He had risen from the ranks without aid of title or decoration, and soon Irving is hearing that his origin is 'low,' that some of his relatives actually were on the stage, and that his wife had really been an actress! What company for a queen! And had he not been the editor of a 'scurrilous' paper that had grossly insulted Maria Christina by probing not tenderly into her love life? Monstrous! And when the liberals in ribald mirth hold their sides in splitting laughter, the indignation of the aristocracy knows no bounds.

And then a blunder, born of zeal, embroils him further with the liberals. Soon it is known that, on his insistence, Isabella has reduced to writing the charge that Olozaga by personal violence on the Queen had forced her to sign the much-discussed decree. Though stated expressly in the statement that it should be deposited in the Archives of the

State, Bravo on impulse reads it to the Chamber of Deputies, and thus the fat is in the fire. Thus is Isabella made a principal in an attack upon a fallen Minister. The friends and some of the former foes of the disgraced statesman rally ardently to his defense. The accused man enters a general denial, and charges that the child Isabella has been swayed by a group of both sexes who so thickly hedge her about in the palace. The exchanges in the Chamber become bitter. And then the controversy spreads rapidly to the streets. Soon a throng before the town hall is shouting '*Viva Espartero!*' and 'Death to Narvaez!' and 'Death to all traitors!' When others shout lustily for the little Queen, hoarse voices from the shadows cry, 'Long live the sovereign people!' Both the contending factions hurriedly dispatch emissaries to the provinces to spread their propaganda, and the streets of the capital are again stained with blood. But Narvaez is equal to the emergency and holds the restless multitude crouching under the shadow of the mailed fist. Irving, walking through the streets, finds troops stationed at frequent intervals, and he sees 'the bayonet glitter in every street.'

While waiting for the reaction of the provinces, Irving recalls to Washington his prediction that the accession of the Queen so young would embroil her in party politics and dim her popularity. 'Let events go as they may,' he writes the Secretary of State, 'a fatal blow has been struck to the popularity of the youthful Queen, and with it to the stability of her throne.' Already, he reports, it is being charged in the streets that she has signed an 'arch falsehood' and 'stooped to deceit,' while the more moderate whisper that she has become a mere manikin in the hands of courtiers.

For days the controversy rages, with the friends of the fallen Minister in stout defense and with the unhappy man demanding an investigation. But in the midst of the wordy war within the Chamber the Cortes is indefinitely suspended, and soon thereafter Olozaga takes flight to Portugal.

Meanwhile the Bravo Ministry is filling up and reorganizing the army and seeing that it is well clad and fed and paid; it is cultivating the clergy, which has its grievances, and resorting to wholesale removals in offices great and small throughout the kingdom.

And then comes an ominous election. In the city and province of Madrid the exiled Minister, put up for the Cortes by his supporters, leads the poll. Even in the shadow of the palace his majority is impressive.

Meditating on the situation, Irving concludes that the weakness of the Moderados is in the mediocrity of their leaders. The best men in the party, shirking responsibility, are seeking posts in foreign lands. Martinez de la Rosa cannot be enticed from England.

MEANWHILE Maria Christina is planning a return from exile.

Irving hears that she is coming merely on a visit to her daughters, and that she will take no part in political affairs except to insist on the preservation of the Constitution. Some smile at the thought of the clever woman's remaining aloof from politics. Irving thinks the youthful Queen stands 'in need of such a friend and councilor as a mother of judgment, virtue, and experience might prove,' but he wonders whether her arrival will not awaken the old hostilities, and he thinks it of doubtful wisdom, just as the Bravo Ministry is forcing upon the nation the decree affecting the rights of municipalities which had sent the young widow of Ferdinand upon her travels.

But for the moment a calm falls upon the land, and Irving's interest is momentarily diverted by the arrival of two interesting new colleagues. Instantly he takes a liking for Count de Bresson, the French Ambassador. No other diplomat in Madrid bears such delicate responsibilities. The Government of Louis Philippe is 'deeply committed to the present state of affairs,' and de Bresson is expected in Paris to guide the new régime in the way that it should go. Will he be able to influence those in power 'under the watchful eye of a public jealous of foreign interference and cautioned against French ascendancy'? Irving wonders. And so does Count de Bresson, though he had been quite successful in Berlin. Irving thinks him 'completely confounded and dismayed by the political chaos before him, and at a loss how to proceed.'

But he finds the Count 'a man of probity and intelligence and sincerely disposed to do what is right.' Soon de Bresson is frequently in prolonged conferences with the Ministers, and Irving, more than ever convinced of his probity and judgment, is sure that his influence will be exerted 'toward restraining the impetuosity of the Cabinet and inculcating that measured and firm and sagacious policy by which Louis Philippe has been so successful in tranquillizing France.' But Irving and the Ambassador frequently exchange visits, and Irving is persuaded that the Count considers the political affairs of the country 'in a desperate state and beyond the reach of remedy.'

Not least among the charms of the ménage of the Count is the attractive and sprightly Countess, with whom Irving will soon be mingling with a mob in the spirit of a lark.

The new British Minister is the celebrated Sir Henry Bulwer, then in his forty-third year and a bachelor, with an interesting background. Madame Calderon recorded his arrival 'with a train of men and women and birds and monkeys.' For a time he had been a cavalry officer before entering the diplomatic service in which he had served as Attaché in Berlin, Vienna, at The Hague, and Brussels. He had gone to Greece on a romantic Byronic mission, carrying with him eighty thousand pounds sterling for the patriots in their war for independence, and one of the fruits of his brief sojourn was a charming little volume called 'An Autumn in Greece.' He had been Chargé d'Affaires in Constantinople and in Paris just before he was sent to Madrid in the rôle of Minister.

He has many things in common with Irving, for, in addition to his book on Greece, he has written an ambitious work in two volumes on 'France — Literary, Social, and Political,' in which he has disclosed a keen penetration and no mean literary judgment. The two Ministers have many mutual friends in the literary and political circles of London, and both are bachelors. Irving delights in his companionship. At first he is astonished at Bulwer's seeming indolence and indifference, but soon he is to find that no one knew better how to be keenly observant without inviting observation, and that an air of languor could serve as a mask for tremendous energy. Only the Foreign Office in London knew that he was infinitely more serious than his apparently idle lounging in the salons of the Continent would indicate. Even so, Irving was amazed by his social errors, due to the precipitancy of his social activities before acquainting himself with the tone of the town. Irving is to find him an amusing playmate. In social circles his infinite tact and droll manner, emphasized by the solemnity of his long face, make him immensely popular, and he is one of the most skilled conversationalists of his time. Irving likes to listen to his fascinating anecdotes, told with an almost affected languor, and the *bons mots* he scattered lavishly, together with the subtle irony of his whispered observations, were a source of constant delight to the American.

At first Irving is deceived by Bulwer's air of aloof indifference to the Spanish drama, and reports to Washington that his task is much easier than that of his French colleague. For did he not tell Irving that the 'tissue of perplexities' in the Spanish situation was one in which Britain had no responsibility? Irving concludes that Bulwer will be more or less of an indifferent onlooker in the game that is being played. He is to find, however, that the Briton was missing nothing of the drama developing over the marriages of Isabella and her sister.

I N JANUARY the court is thrown into mourning by the sudden death of Doña Luisa Carlota, the clever, restless wife of the Infante Francisco. This morbidly ambitious princess, whose campaigning for the marriage of her son with the young Queen had occasioned so much uneasiness to the Government, had appealed strongly to Irving's imagination. With foreign princes and potentates intriguing to force a foreign prince upon the Queen, with the statesmen of Spain lending ear to these conspirators, this amazing woman, who sought to arouse the Spanish people in favor of her son's aspirations, had resorted to strange devices. She had not hesitated to cultivate the partiality of the people of the streets, and the serenading of her son at Saragossa with songs calling for the marriage had not been without her management. She had diplomatically been ordered from the northern watering-place where she had succeeded with the masses; and so fearful were the statesmen of her intrigues that she had been notified that the winter climate of Madrid was not wholesome for her husband. Her fondest hopes for the time seemed crushed, and Irving reported to Washington:

> The failure of these plans, and the odium, impoverishment, and neglect they had brought upon herself are said to have exasperated her feelings, and to have produced an absolute fever of the mind which immediately preceded her illness and probably contributed to render it fatal. The immediate cause of her death, however, was a simultaneous attack of measles and pneumonia. Her triumph was to come, but she would not be here to enjoy it.[1]

Meanwhile Irving finds the Spanish drama interesting enough. At Alicante a former semi-bandit, and later a commander of carabineers in the service of the revenue, named Colonel Pantaleon Bonet raises the banner of revolt. Jauntily he rides into the town with three or four hundred men of horse and foot, presumably in search of smugglers. At night he surprises and takes the castle, seizes the civil and military leaders, and proclaims himself President, under the 'sovereign people.' The Government at Madrid now strikes with savage severity. The leaders of the progressive party are seized and their houses ransacked throughout the country. The home of Lopez, the former Minister, is searched, and he escapes arrest only because he has been

---

[1] MS. Archives, dispatch, February 6, 1844.

'passing the night with a friend's wife' — or so the gossip ran. Irving is impressed with the short shrift given the progressive leaders who had joined with the old nobility to crush the régime of Espartero, only to be cast aside when they had served their purpose. But the insurrection is put down ruthlessly. Narvaez maintains control with a hand of iron — without velvet glove.

And then Maria Christina rides gaily into Spain from her exile at the Court of France.

IT WAS to be a triumphant entry by slow stages to the capital. Only a little while before, Maria Christina's influence had been pronounced pernicious and her contempt for the Constitution was no secret. She had been driven into exile. Now that the party of the aristocracy was in the saddle and riding hard, she was returning to what seemed from the drums and the trumpets to be a general welcome. Irving, who had admired Espartero, now seemed enthusiastic over the return from exile. He was glad that she was coming back over the same road that she traversed on her way out to 'general execrations.' 'The cities that were almost in arms against her now receive her with fêtes and rejoicing,' he writes before she reaches Madrid. Under triumphal arches she rides into the smallest villages. Te Deums are chanted in the cathedrals. Processions fare forth to meet her on the way. Thus in a continuous triumph she is making a truly royal progress to her capital — for 'her capital' it seemed rather than Isabella's. Even Irving found himself referring to her as 'the Queen.'

He had received official notice of the program. The entire diplomatic corps was to go forth beyond the royal palace at Aranjuez to greet her. All the court and nobility were to attend. It was no easy jaunt in those days to Aranjuez, though the road was rather better than that to Toledo for the accommodation of the court which spent its spring days in the palace. The distance was twenty-seven miles. Instead of the perfect roads of today over which the motorcar may speed with ease in an hour, the journey behind horses or on the backs of horses required time, and a reasonably speedy journey called for relays of horses.

It is six in the morning when Irving in his coach driven by Pedro, his coachman, and with the useful Lorenzo along, drives to the Mexican Legation to pick up Valdivieso, the Minister, and they start for Aranjuez. Many are on the road and they jolt along for almost six hours and reach the village of the palace at eleven-thirty. The meeting of the Queens has been arranged for five in the afternoon at a point in a field beyond Aranjuez on the way to Ocaña. Throughout the afternoon the nobility and the curious among the masses stream into the village, for Irving hears that every vehicle in Madrid has been engaged at high prices, and the facilities for lodgings have been exhausted long before, even to the humblest. At the time the few hotels in the little town were of indifferent quality.

The village of Aranjuez, surrounded by a parched country in the summer, was as an oasis in a desert. It lay in a narrow green valley scooped out, as Irving thought, by the Tagus. Now after almost a century it is not dissimilar to the Aranjuez into which the travel-worn Minister rode ninety-six years ago. The 'large barracks of houses,' somber, uniform, built for the

accommodation of the attendants on the court, still stand,
a little lonely now. In the days of Irving the palace was a
favorite resort of royalty, especially in the spring, and then
these barracks teemed with men in uniform. The palace,
so rich in romance, Irving found 'spacious' without being
'magnificent,' but after a hundred years one may share his
enthusiasm over the 'delicious gardens, with shady walks
and bowers, refreshing fountains, and thousands of nightingales; also noble avenues of trees and fine shady drives.'

The members of the diplomatic corps had joined in
the engagement of a huge house for their accommodation —
a two-story structure enclosing a square court. Here that
day, while awaiting the arrival of Maria Christina, the
diplomats relax and play. Here are the Count and Countess
de Bresson and two young attachés from the French Embassy,
and the Ambassadress in holiday mood and chattering like a
magpie. Albuquerque has arrived with his wife, who is a
New Yorker by birth, if a Brazilian by marriage, and is
quartered in the same great house. The Prince de Carini,
who represented the Sicilies, is also there with the beautiful
and witty Princess, and Ignacio Valdivieso, the Mexican
Minister, who has made the journey with Irving, and the
Count de Marnex, the Belgian Chargé d'Affaires, and
Dal Borgo di Primo, the Chargé for Denmark. Each family,
arriving tired and dusty, retires to its separate apartments,
each with a sitting-room and antechamber, to refresh themselves. And then at noon they gather at the same table for
an excellent dinner, and tongues clack merrily over the
hardships and the mishaps of the journey. In the afternoon
Irving goes to the apartment of his old friends the Albuquerques, where there is a comfortable sofa most enticing to
a gentleman growing old and still not well, and there he
stretches himself luxuriously, and the women of the party

who made the rooms of the Brazilian their lounging-room pet and spoil him. He is fond of the wife of the Brazilian, for not only is she interesting and charming but she brings him a breath of home, and the Countess de Bresson he finds good company, and the Princess de Carini he admires enormously for her beauty and sprightly manner. The Prince, Irving finds, the 'life of the house.' So pass a few hours of release from ceremony.

Then, late in the afternoon, Irving summons Pedro, and with Valdivieso, he drives on the road to Ocaña to the spot selected for the meeting of the Queens. The going is hard, for the road is packed with vehicles and men on prancing horses hastening to the rendezvous. Seated by the roadside all the way are a great number of men, women, and children with flushed, eager faces intent on the spectacle. On reaching the meeting-place Irving and Valdivieso find, a little distance from the highway in an open plain, a large royal tent fluttering with flags and streamers. Close by are three or four smaller tents. Irving is moved by the scene, the mingling of grandees and beggars, the squadrons of cavalry in dress uniform. Some way from the tent Irving and his companion leave the carriage and proceed on foot to join the little Queen in the royal tent.

Within the tent are Isabella and the Princess, surrounded by courtiers and functionaries of the court. In childish eagerness to see their mother, Irving observes, they are unable to remain within the tent. Constantly they are darting out to join a throng of courtiers who from a point commanding the road sloping down to Ocaña can get a first view of the returning Queen's cavalcade. Thus two tiresome hours are passed.

And then a murmur runs through the crowd as the cortège of Maria Christina is seen descending the distant slope.

There is something medieval in the picture, for the royal carriage is accompanied by a squadron of lancers, whose yellow uniforms with the red flag of the lancers fluttering impress Irving as 'a moving mass of fire and flame.'

The cortège draws nearer. The squadron of horse falls back upon the plain. The carriage has reached the point on the road opposite the tent. Isabella and her sister, in feverish impatience, brush all etiquette aside and rush toward their mother, and Irving loses sight of them as they disappear among the courtiers and soldiers.

The vast throng roars an enthusiastic welcome to the woman who a little while before had been followed by their execrations. Irving finds that 'the old nobility, who have long been cast down and dispirited, and surrounded by doubt and danger, look upon the return of the Queen Mother as the triumph of their cause, and the harbinger of happier and more prosperous days.' So ends the first act.

Irving and the diplomatic corps now make all haste to Aranjuez for rest and refreshments before the reception at the royal palace. Not wishing the trouble of donning court dress, Maria Christina, whose daughter, the real Queen, is relegated to the background, receives the corps in plain dress. Repairing to the palace, the corps files into the salon furnished in the classic style in vogue in the days of Napoleon. The palace is brilliantly illuminated. A multitude of commoners stand outside the grounds. At length Maria Christina, preceded by the little Isabella, enters the salon. The corps is drawn up according to precedent and rank, headed by Count de Bresson, with only the Portuguese Minister between the Ambassador and Irving, who is third in line. Count de Bresson makes Maria Christina an address of congratulation on behalf of the corps; the Queen returned from exile reads a brief response. Then the two Queens pass down the line, addressing a few words to each of the diplomats, and with curtsies, pass out of the room.

IRVING and Valdivieso, though weary with the ordeals of the day, drive back to Madrid to be there for the entrance of Maria Christina to the capital. This is announced for between three and four o'clock on the following afternoon. The streets are literally jammed by courtiers and the curious. Horse and foot make a brave showing in parade. From all the balconies and windows hang tapestries. Seated on the left hand of Isabella in an open carriage, Maria Christina makes her bow to the people. But Irving observes that there is not spontaneous enthusiasm among the masses, and concludes that the real rejoicing is confined to the aristocracy. But the grand entrance is followed for days by a succession of civil and religious ceremonies, though Irving's illness prevents his attendance at most. He cannot gracefully absent himself, however, from the *besar los manos* or hand-kissing at the palace—the 'grand act of homage to the sovereign and the royal family.'

It is a brilliant Spanish day, all sunshine, cloudless skies, the air soft and caressing. As Irving drives up to the palace his carriage has to make its way slowly through the spectators in the streets, assembled to see the arrival of the notables. Again the grand staircase and the anterooms are swarming with officers, halberdiers, uniforms 'glittering with gold and embroidery' on every side. Again he passes into the Hall of the Ambassadors. It is already filled with grandees and courtiers and with some of the diplomatic corps. On the throne platform now stand two chairs of state, one on the right for Isabella, and the other for Maria Christina. In front of the throne, and in front of her mother, a chair has been placed for the sister of the Queen.

Despite the colorful nature of the ceremony, Irving foresees a torture. His legs are bad, and no one can sit in the presence of the Queen. Just as he is groaning inwardly over the inevitable delay of the Queen's arrival, the courtly Chevalier de Araña, the Introducer of Ambassadors, observes his distress and, knowing his condition, suggests that he sit on the low pedestal of a statue at the lower end of the hall until Isabella appears. Gladly availing himself of the opportunity, he sits down, and meditates on the changing panorama of human life, recalling the dramas he has here seen enacted, from the days when he was writing his books and attending some of the ceremonies in the court of Ferdinand VII. He observes that with the return of the old nobility the court is resuming something of its ancient splendor. Never, he thinks, has he seen the royal palace 'so brilliantly attended,' and Count de Bresson, who concedes little to the Spanish, admits that he is amazed at the splendor of the court.

Irving's meditations are broken in upon by the announcement of the Queen. The grandees hasten to their places on the right hand of the throne; the diplomats line up in front. Then Isabella appears, followed by her mother and the Princess, and after them a long train of ladies of the highest nobility, magnificently attired. The two Queens and the Princess take their seats; the ladies of the court form a line from the left of the throne to the lower end of the hall. Never has Irving seen more beautiful women, all in court dresses with lappets and trains, a beautiful display of silk and plumes and lace and glistering diamonds. He doubts 'whether even the lilies of the valley, though better arrayed than King Solomon in all his glory, could have stood in comparison with them.'

He notes that Isabella and the Princess wear white satin richly trimmed with lace, with long trains of lilac silk, and with wreaths of diamonds on their heads. Maria Christina, he observes, has a train of azure blue, her favorite color, but he is unable to describe her dress more minutely the next day. He thinks Isabella will soon cease to be 'little,' and indeed he notes that she seems 'rather full and puffy,' but ascribes the impression to her being 'too straitly caparisoned.' The little Princess is pale.

But it is Maria Christina who impresses him now. In 'her best looks,' he thinks her, and after the long and nerve-racking journey she is more cheerful and animated than when he saw her at Aranjuez. She, who had fascinated so many men, casts her spell on Irving, and soon he is writing that 'for queenly grace and dignity, mingled with the most gracious affability, she surpasses any sovereign I have ever seen.' He observes the manner in which she receives those who knelt and kissed her hand and 'the smile with which she sent them on their way rejoicing,' and thinks he has discovered the secret of her popularity among those who had formed her court.

But the ordeal has been trying for Irving, and he retires as soon as possible, going away with Dal Borgo, the veteran Chargé d'Affaires of Denmark, who, thoroughgoing courtier as he is, has actually risen from a sick-bed to witness the homage to the Queens.

A little later there is another kissing of hands at the palace, and Irving is proudly to announce that he has stood through the entire three-hour ceremony 'without flinching.'

T HEREAFTER for a while Irving, recovered both in health and spirits, attacked some stubborn problems at the Foreign Office and gave a number of diplomatic dinners. The political drama diverted him immensely. He was writing Washington that, contrary to expectations, Maria Christina had shown no disposition to force changes in the Cabinet. Indeed, she was expressing her satisfaction with the conduct of the Ministers and her disposition to give them ample time to carry out their policies. Irving could see no occasion in their conduct for her displeasure. With 'unwonted energy and hardihood ... aided by martial law' they were realizing the wishes of the aristocracy, so devoutly wished. The alteration of the law of municipalities that had sent Maria Christina into exile was forced through; the militia was disarmed, the army reorganized, the Guardia Civile was formed, and plans were afoot for the re-creation of a royal bodyguard of the thousand that Espartero had disbanded. And the press was under the most rigid censorship. Politically, on the surface, all was tranquil.

But Irving was amused by the distress of the more aristocratic of the high nobility over the continuance of Gonzalez Bravo, the man of humble origin, as Minister of State. They wished someone of their own order instead, and were willing

to concede Narvaez a place as Minister of War. But Bravo
was in no mood to immolate himself. Irving thought he had
conducted himself in office 'with great spirit and ability.'
He heard that Bravo was trying to organize a party of his
own to be called 'Young Spain,' and to set up General
Concha in opposition to Narvaez. But Narvaez was in high
favor with Maria Christina. And Bravo was being countenanced by her. Irving noticed that he was most assiduous
in his cultivation of the favor of the Queen Mother, and not
without effect. And his position was further strengthened by
the support of Count de Bresson, the French Ambassador,
who was all-powerful in Madrid. Irving informed Washington that Narvaez and Bravo were the master spirits of the
Government and that a schism there might shake the very
foundations of the State. Irving's sympathy clearly was with
Bravo.

BUT Irving was not happy.
Alexander Hamilton was busy packing for his departure.
Brevoort had gone long before, and now the other companion who had accompanied him on his mission was going
too. Irving had found Hamilton most congenial, and had
enjoyed his gossip at the table. Possessing much of the charm
and some of the ability, though none of the genius, of his
great-grandfather, Irving had placed the utmost trust in
him, and found him never wanting. Efficient in business,
he was also 'a sunshiny companion at all times.' Irving felt

that his departure would leave a void among those who had learned to appreciate 'his noble qualities of head and heart.' Irving watched the packing with a heavy heart, and soon he was writing of the 'inexpressible loneliness in my mansion and its great salons empty and silent.' 'I feel my heart choking me as I walk about and miss Hamilton from the places and seats he used to occupy,' he wrote. 'The servants partake in my dreary feelings, and that increases them.' But his health was better and he could resume his walks. May of 1844 found him walking almost daily in the shady green alleys of the Retiro, where he had 'the companionship of nightingales with which the place abounds.'

Chapter 11: FOLLOWING THE COURT

IRVING was not quite tolerant of
the methods of the State Department, and occasionally
complained bitterly of its failure to keep him sufficiently
informed of events in Washington to permit him to appear
intelligent in dealing with the Foreign Office in Madrid.
Because of its insistence on sending dispatches by a roundabout way, it was ninety-four days before he learned of the
tragic death of Upshur, the Secretary of State, and seventy-
two days before he knew that John C. Calhoun had succeeded to the post. He was disgusted that it was eighty-two
days before he received a congratulatory letter to the Queen,
and forty days before he received a letter of condolence to
Isabella on the death of Luisa Carlota. But his frequent
protests found the State Department blissfully impervious to
all impressions.

By the time these letters to Isabella reached Irving, the
Queen and the court had proceeded to Barcelona. Irving
was not eager to follow them. His expense account for the
journey to Aranjuez, not inconsiderable in those days, had
been blithely ignored, and he foresaw a similar indifference
to the personal sacrifices of a mere Minister in going to
Barcelona. He was not a little bitter about it. Now that

the letters had been unreasonably delayed, he would have to make the journey to that city. However, it was eighteen days after their receipt before he was ready for the jaunt. Even so, his naturally happy disposition found compensations. The journey would take him through parts of Spain he had not seen before, and he had never been disappointed in Spanish adventure. Now he would see Aragon.

One late June morning, he took the diligence, accompanied by Albuquerque, his Brazilian friend, and by Dal Borgo di Primo, the Danish Chargé d'Affaires. He was devoted to both, and each was to prove an ideal traveling companion. For three days and a half they jolted along as the drivers applied the persuasive whip to the mules. Only once or twice was there a pause for repose, and then only for six hours, including the time for dinner. Albuquerque's even temper and never-failing good nature were enough to reconcile Irving to the hardships of the journey, but the light-hearted and jovial Dane converted them into a lark. A thorough courtier, he nevertheless was able to mingle on equal terms with all sorts and conditions of men. Indeed, inherently he was kindly toward those in lowly station, and he shared Irving's enthusiasm for the really courtly peasant of the villages. Time and again, tired of the jolting, the three diplomats would leave the diligence at the entrance to a village and stroll through on foot. Dal Borgo would amuse himself and annoy his companions by his insistence on scattering halfpence among the beggars and the children, and invariably before they could join the diligence again they were followed by an impressive concourse of shouting, laughing, vociferous beneficiaries of the Dane's generous bounty. Never did his high spirits fag, even in surrender to the dust and heat.

The travelers went by way of Saragossa, but the pause

there was only long enough to whet Irving's appetite for more. It was in crossing the mountains that he found the excitement not soothing to one whose nerves were fagged. Then as many as eight or ten mules were harnessed to the diligence, two by two. A helper trotted most of the time beside the coach, whacking the mules with a stick and making an outlandish noise as he screamed their names. In time Irving came to find some amusement even in this because of the varying tones and inflections of the indignant helper. On the back of one of the leaders of the team a youth of barely fifteen sat, the better to direct the animals. As mile after mile was passed, and hour after hour was consumed without rest, Irving forgot his tribulations in wonderment over the boy's stamina. But in time he discovered the secret of his perseverance. Time and again he noted that the youth was sound asleep. At first he had an attack of nerves as he observed how the boy slept as the diligence turned the sharp corners of the mountain road along the very verge of precipices of deadly height. But in time he came to place complete reliance on the intelligence and sure-footedness of the mules. Albuquerque was always thoughtful, complacent, gentlemanly, and Dal Borgo light-hearted as a lark and comical as a jester, and in time they reached Barcelona.

IT WAS five in the evening when they rode into the city and took possession of apartments in the leading hotel, happily engaged in advance. Covered with dust and dirt, Irving thought it gracious in the host to admit them. After a bath and dinner, Irving had stretched himself for a nap when he was aroused by a visitor. The greater part of the diplomatic corps had preceded him and were in the full swing of the social activities of the town. Prince de Carini was at the Italian opera, almost across the street from Irving's hotel, when he learned of the latter's arrival. He hurried to the hotel and took the American to his box, where he soon found himself seated by the attractive little Princess, who was his favorite.

The opera house was much more spacious than any in Madrid, and the Italian company was excellent. Looking about, Irving found all his colleagues, who had preceded him, in attendance, and soon he was to learn that the opera was the favorite rendezvous of the court and corps. He found Count de Bresson, the French Ambassador, regally ensconced in an elegant box offered by the municipality. Between the acts he visited his French colleague, and was warmly welcomed by the Countess, whom he found great 'fun.' He was invited to dinner on the following day. Before the evening was over he knew he liked the capital of Catalonia. At least it was a change.

As the days passed, and Irving took time for rambles, his admiration and satisfaction grew. He found the city beautiful and, strangely enough for him, delighted in the new part. He liked the climate, the air 'soft and voluptuous,' the heat tempered by the sea breezes. Between the sea and mountains he found all in Nature that he could wish. On lazy afternoons he drove about into the environs and was charmed by the fertility of the green plains, with the beauty of the mountains, with the villas half-hidden in their groves and gardens. Soon, with his colleagues, he was driving out to these country seats, but two or three miles from the city, and surrounded with groves of oranges, citrons, figs, pome-

a mob. He remembered the conversations of the dinner table, all revolving around the near approach of Maria Christina, the Princess of Naples, en route to her nuptials with Ferdinand. So much water had since passed over the dam! The Princess had been Queen; had been acclaimed; had suffered an eclipse in popularity and had fled the kingdom, followed by the execrations of her enemies; had suffered a long exile, and Irving had joined in her welcome back under the tent near Aranjuez. Then he had missed her; now he would see her almost at the height of her power again. In the midst of his meditations he was ushered into the presence of Isabella, and presented the two letters from President Tyler congratulating her on her accession and sympathizing with her over the death of the aunt who had been so bent on forcing her son into Isabella's nuptial bed.

The Introducer of Ambassadors, the Chevalier de Araña, conducted him to the salon, where he found Isabella in the center of the room, with the beautiful Marchioness of Santa Cruz, first lady-in-waiting, standing just behind her. His heart went out to the young creature forced at her age to play a solo part and to direct the conversation with ambassadors. But again he was impressed by her 'quiet, graceful manner,' her complete self-possession, her perfect poise. In low tones she inquired about his journey. He expressed his gratification in finding that she looked so well, and retired.

Thence he went to Maria Christina, who never failed to kindle his appreciation. In nothing that he wrote in those days will one find a line to show that the wicked stories afloat concerning the Queen Mother had registered in his mind. He wrote Calhoun, then Secretary of State, of 'her characteristic grace and amiability.' It seemed to him that he never had seen such a winning smile, and he ceased to wonder at the tales told of her fascination when a young regal bride. Even now, after all her troubles, he thought her handsome, though he understood that she had moments of deep depression over the perils surrounding the throne of her daughter.

His immediate mission fulfilled, Irving could give himself over to the festivities of the court's sojourn. He delighted in the greater frankness and cordiality of the people of Barcelona. There were dinners and teas in the apartments of de Bresson and Prince de Carini, and drives to the country seats beyond the city, and excursions in the near-by mountains. Even then there was a sincere appreciation of Irving's pronounced partiality for Spain and of his books so vividly painting the bright and heroic pages of her history, and not even the French Ambassador was so popular and in demand so much.

One day he followed the court on a visit to the Fort of Alarazanas. Narvaez attended with Baron de Mar, the Captain-General of the province. Irving followed Isabella through the fort. It amused him to see her careful inspection of the beds and bedding, to hear her inquiring as to comforts and conveniences, and to see her solemnly tasting the food, served with a wooden spoon similar to those used by the soldiers, though made of finer wood and stamped with the arms of Spain. At the conclusion of the ceremony Isabella presented the three spoons used to the three oldest and best-conducted soldiers and raised them all to the rank of corporal. Irving went with the court to other barracks and witnessed the same ceremony.

WₕₕₕHILE Irving was in Barce-
lona he received permission from Washington for a temporary
leave to try the air of France again for his health. The year
before, a Spanish crisis had hastened his return before he had
finished his cure, and he hoped that another sojourn would
make it possible to resume his literary labors in Madrid.
Bidding farewell to his colleagues, Irving embarked on the
Villa de Madrid for Marseilles.

Sailing at seven in the morning, Irving lazily stretched
himself on deck, reveling in the Spanish coastline, moun-
tainous and picturesque, with here and there, upon a rocky
crag, a storied castle now in ruins. He enjoyed the bright
and bustling little towns nestling by the sea and humming
with Catalan industry.

Seating himself on deck to write a letter, he had an
adventure to which he thrilled as though he were not now
sixty. Near-by, sat a beautiful young woman with 'splendid
Spanish eyes,' and, as he scribbled, he was diverted by the
realization that these eyes were frequently flashing curiously
in his direction. They seemed 'to throw a light upon the
paper.' Unable to put her out of his mind, he made a virtue
of necessity and concluded to describe her in his note. She
was about twenty-four and married. He noted that she was
of medium size and beautifully proportioned, with a Grecian
cast of countenance, with skin sallow but aglow with health.
Her hair was raven black, as were her eyes, which were
further softened by unusually long lashes. Her lips, he was

writing, 'are full and rosy yet finely chiseled — her teeth of dazzling whiteness.' He observed that she was dressed in black as though in mourning. Her hand was small, and he looked carefully enough to see that it was 'exquisitely formed, with taper fingers and blue veins.' As she raises her hand to adjust her hair he is sure that he 'never saw female hand more exquisite.' The old romanticist had put the old diplomat in the background, and he was explaining that were he younger he would be unable so calmly to paint the portrait with his pen.

The old bachelor was really engaged in a flirtation, for as he lifted his eyes for details for his portrait, more than once his eye met hers. The lady at least was curious. Finally she took the line.

'Really, señor,' she said with a luminous smile, 'one would think you were a painter taking my likeness.'

Thus challenged, Irving replied: 'Indeed I am taking it. I am writing a friend the other side of the world, discussing things that are passing before me, and I could not help noting down one of the best specimens of the country that I have met with.'

The lady laughed; her husband joined; and there was bantering all around. Taking up his letter and transcribing it into Spanish, he read the description he had written. The lady joined in the merriment and took the compliment in good spirits, though the eye of Irving did not fail to see the blush that mantled her cheek. She thought him a very fanciful portrait-painter, and the husband suggested that were he to stop at San Felieu all the women of the town would flock to have their portraits done. At length the ship stopped in the open sea in front of the little bay of the town, and Irving had the pleasure of assisting the lady to the boat, promising if ever at San Felieu to call upon them. 'The last

I noticed of her,' he wrote, 'was a Spanish farewell wave of her beautiful white hand, and the gleam of her dazzling teeth as she smiled adieu.'

Thus, with a sense of refreshment Irving went forth on his vacation, having caught again for the moment something of the spirit of his youth. That night he stayed on deck most of the night enjoying a gorgeous moonlight that flooded the sea. From Marseilles he went on to Paris. He was not to see Madrid again for three and a half months.

REACHING Paris, Irving put himself in the hands of his physician, and so gratifying was his progress that he lingered longer than he had intended. Hamilton was gone, but Jasper H. Livingston, son of a justice of the United States Supreme Court, who had taken his place, was thoroughly competent and loyal, and Irving had no worries to retard his cure.

But things invariably happened in Spain on his vacations. Narvaez was now in power, head of the Government and Minister of War, and, not content with the discharge of his many onerous duties, he found time for a series of lavish entertainments on a scale of such regal magnificence as to attract the attention of the diplomatic corps. His hospitality in the immense palace on the Calle de la Luna had not been equaled in many generations, for when he entertained, his guests were reminded of what they had read of the splendors of the days when Olivares was favorite and Prime Minister.

Later Irving was to comment upon it and to wonder, confident that vaulting ambition was overleaping itself, and that human vanity was paving the road to ruin.

Scarcely had Irving sailed out of the moonlight into France when rumors were rife in Madrid of a possible insurrection. It was whispered about that the Progresista leaders had been tampering with the army. Again mounted patrols rode up and down the narrow streets and suspiciously surveyed the loungers in the Puerta del Sol and the promenaders in the Alcala and on the Prado. At the principal corners of the town sentinels stood vigilantly on guard. In the barracks the soldiers were under arms ready to respond on an instant's summons. In the homes of the leaders of the opposition, military and civil agents went through drawers and chests and papers. It was observed that these searches were conducted without a warrant. Madrid was under military law and all legal guaranties were brushed aside.

In September came the elections, but Irving, accustomed to the campaigning in the United States and England, would have found them singularly dull. The opposition was silenced, the press was curbed, and all was harmonious and unanimous on the surface. No one doubted the result, for the elections were being personally conducted by the Government, and the Government had a gun. The result was as expected — the party in power swept everything.

In October the Cortes met, and Irving would have enjoyed the spectacle of its opening by young Isabella. Elaborate arrangements had been made to make the event a colorful appeal to the imagination of the people. The streets through which the young Queen would drive were lined with troops in their most brilliant uniforms. The day was clear and sunny, the skies blue as they can be blue in Spain alone. The diplomatic corps was instructed to be on hand at noon, but an hour and a half passed before the sound of trumpets ushered in the Queen. She took her seat on the throne. Narvaez handed her the speech he had prepared, and in distinct and unfaltering tones she read with the poise of a veteran monarch to whom it was an ancient tale. Livingston, who reported, like so many others, marveled at the degree of self-possession in one so young.

With almost a one-party system in the Cortes, the machinery ran smoothly and rapidly. The Constitution was to be so altered as vastly to increase the power of the throne, as Maria Christina and the old nobility had planned. Quite as interesting to some was the alteration which all but deprived the Cortes of any power in the matter of the marriage of the Queen.

When Irving returned, he was to learn that nothing had so occupied the minds of courtiers and statesmen as the marriage. Rumor had it that Maria Christina had engineered a scheme for the marriage of her fourteen-year-old daughter to her uncle, the Count Trapani. It was even said that the importunity and propitiation of the Queen Mother and her supporters had finally brought the Pope to an agreement to disregard the law of consanguinity, but that the Austrian Ambassador had stepped in just in time and 'forbade the bans.' It was whispered around that Narvaez had not given his countenance to the plan and had greatly annoyed the Queen Mother. The gossips had it that Narvaez had a candidate of his own in the Archduke Frederick, a nephew of the Austrian Emperor, and that the youth of twenty-seven was intelligent and manly and had won distinction on the battlefield before Beyrout. Many were watching for the sparks from the clashing blades of France and England, and it was noted that for the moment the French influence had diminished.

But, on the whole, Irving could have found no better time for his vacation. He missed the opening of the Cortes and some of the social functions of Narvaez, he missed the speculations of the gossips, but the Government moved along in a well-oiled groove, Maria Christina intrigued behind her fan in the inner recesses of the palace and captivated the public with her ingratiating smile, and Isabella grew stronger and a wee bit plumper with the passing of the days.

When Irving drove into Madrid the middle of November, he found he barely had missed a grand concert at the palace, but an invitation was waiting to attend the first formal ball for Isabella at the home of Narvaez.

B︎UT back from following the court, Irving was annoyed to find no answer to his note to the State Department setting forth his expenses. He had gone to Aranjuez because, as the representative of his country, he had had to go, and had paid his own expenses. These were light. But when the court moved to Barcelona and all his colleagues followed, and some accompanied the Queen herself, his failure to follow in their wake would have attracted notice. He had sent his expense account to Washington. Apparently the functionaries there had read it, yawning, and tossed it into the basket. To Irving it seemed a scurvy trick, a bit lacking in the dignity of decency, and he made no secret of his feelings. Rather sharply he wrote Calhoun that with the establishment of the Queen upon her throne the old custom of making sojourns during the summer at the rural residences and at Barcelona would be resumed. Should the Minister of the United States follow? Of course the necessity and propriety was not so clear as in the case of other nations having closer and family ties; 'still, it cannot be altogether neglected without an appearance of want of respect for the Royal Personages and the Government.' Would Calhoun give a glance at Irving's expense account?

We may be sure that Calhoun read the letter with a yawn and tossed it into the basket, for two months later Irving wrote again. Isabella was planning another sojourn in Barcelona, the court would go, and the diplomatic corps would follow. Should Irving go along? He had had no answer or even an acknowledgment of his previous letters, but the time had come for an understanding. Other governments met the necessary expenses of their missions, and if the United States preferred to fall back on the charity of its representatives the fact should be proclaimed. Would Calhoun please answer? But Calhoun did not answer. He had other fish to fry, and Irving paid the bills.

Soon there was enough of social activity and gossip on the marriage to divert him from his grievance.

Chapter 12: VANITY FAIR

Never was Irving while in Spain to pass through the hectic life of Vanity Fair as during the season in Madrid which ended the last of May in 1845. The old nobility, plumed and bejeweled, flocked back to court again, for the aristocracy was in the saddle and Maria Christina was in the palace. Unwilling to be outdone in lavish display by the nobility, the great houses of the wealthy flung their doors wide open in genteel competition. Riding in the Prado, Irving observed that 'all Madrid rattles and glitters with new equipages.' It seemed not without resemblance to the Paris of just before the Revolution, since 'one would hardly suspect from the luxury of the capital that the country was so wretchedly impoverished.' Never in Irving's time had the court been so gay and so magnificent. The giddy pace already had been set when Irving returned from his vacation, and the next day he attended a 'kissing of hands' at the palace and a scintillating ball at the home of General Narvaez in honor of the saint's day of Isabella. It was her first big ball, and she was barely fourteen.

Narvaez was living now as though the leaves of the trees were banknotes and he was the owner of boundless woodlands. And he was in fine fettle because for the moment in high favor. Not often did the punctilious Spanish court condescend to attend a ball given by a subject, but the royal family paid Narvaez the rare compliment of their presence. When Irving reached the house of the military chieftain, a mansion of great dimensions built around a court, he found the salons crowded with fifteen hundred guests. He had long concluded that Narvaez had a 'swelling, magnificent spirit' and was indifferent to expense, and nothing had been omitted to make the occasion worthy of a monarch's condescension.

At the far end of the principal salon, in an inner room, he found the Queen, the royal family, the ladies and courtiers, and his colleagues of the diplomatic corps. Slowly, by edging his way through the dense throng, he managed to reach the royal presence.

Isabella had never looked so well as in the simple white dress she wore, with only a necklace of six rows of pearls with a diamond clasp as an adornment. Irving was charmed. He delighted in young girls, and here was one flushed and sparkling from the excitement of her first big ball. For the moment she divested herself of dignity and solemnity that hedges thrones to be a young girl only. She beamed with pleasure.

At length space was cleared in the great salon in front of the room of the dignitaries and a royal quadrille was formed, and Narvaez swept into the dance with Isabella, followed by Count de Bresson, the French Ambassador, with Maria Christina. The Portuguese Minister, Guillermo di Lima, took in the young Princess, and other Ministers had princesses of the blood. But alas, even royalty and courtly dignity tripped on the quadrille and blundered, and Isabella, her eyes sparkling and her cheeks flushed with excitement, laughed loudly in a most uncourtly manner. And when she noticed the queer old-fashioned dancing of the Portuguese

Minister, she did not try to control herself but laughed merrily without restraint. Irving, whose bad ankles excused him from the dance, rejoiced in the robustious merriment of the Queen, who was only a young girl to him, and even when, as was not infrequent that night at Narvaez's, she literally was convulsed with laughter, he was glad. Her risibility permeated and affected all the rest, and nothing less stiff and stately had ever been seen by him before at a royal dance. She passed from partner to partner and danced with all the members of the diplomatic corps but Irving, who was probably her warmest well-wisher among them all, but the fault was his. It was a revelation to him to find there was so much 'fun in her.' The real Isabella was beginning to bud for the blooming.

It was now four in the morning and Maria Christina and the ladies of the court were eager to retire, but Isabella would dance on and on. Would she venture on another dance, she was asked? 'Oh, eight more if necessary,' she answered gaily. It was close to five before Maria Christina could entice her away.

Any curious tourist in search of departed glories may view the scene of Narvaez's folly and the youthful Isabella's first formal dance. The Calle de la Luna has scarcely changed, but as one drives carefully through it, since two cars can barely pass, and notes the garb of the pedestrians on the stone pavements, so narrow that when two pass one must step off the curb, it is evident that he is in the tenement section of the workers. But at Number 29 even the uninformed pauses involuntarily before an immense palace, with a great coat of arms carved in stone above the wide doorway. It is the palace that drove Narvaez to the stock market to meet expenses. Before the numerous windows of the three-story stone structure are iron balconies similar to those at

Irving's palace — all drab enough today. But the night Irving drove into the Calle de la Luna by the light of many torches, music and laughter floated out from six of these on the second floor that looked out from the immense ballroom. But long ago this gaudy stage for Isabella's entrance upon the world of gaiety was partitioned off into many rooms for tenants. The palace was built around a charming patio, but now there is only the ghost of a deserted garden with a solitary tree, and a tradition that in an apartment facing the patio a frail countess, infatuated with a servant, paid the penalty imposed by her outraged lord by seven years of imprisonment in her rooms.

Just History sleeping beneath the concealing dust of generations. But it was gay and grand enough the night Irving arrived by the light of torches, to note with interest the awakening of Isabella to the pleasures of frivolity.

Irving had left at three, fearful lest his long standing at the ceremonies in the afternoon and at the ball would bring another inflammation of his ankles, but happily he awoke on the morrow with no ill effects. He was encouraged. Invitations to functions from the court circle were pouring in and perhaps, he thought, he could outlive the season. Only an insurrection could check the madness of those winter months, and while there were constantly rumors, nothing happened, though one lady preparing for the ball had joyously assured Irving that unquestionably they would all be blown up.

Within a day or so, Pedro drove Irving to the foot of the grand staircase at the palace for the first royal banquet he had attended. As he passed up the broad marble stairs between rows of lackeys in royal livery and halberdiers on every second step, the latter struck the butt ends of their muskets on the marble as a salutation as he passed. More than a hundred of the nobility and court were present, but to curtail the crowd and give no offense, only the ladies of the court and of the diplomatic corps were invited. Protocol, that often stupid jade, had arranged the seating at the table strictly in accordance with precedence. Count de Bresson, as a representative of a king, took in Isabella. Irving was pleased to find that he had been assigned the sprightly Princess Carini, whose keen sense of humor delighted him, but it turned out that an indisposition had kept her in her home, and after much consultation among the masters of protocol, Madame Albuquerque, wife of the Brazilian Minister, of whom he was fond, fell to his lot. On the other side of Irving sat Maria Christina, and he was more than satisfied.

In stately procession the guests passed through numerous rooms to the great Banquet Hall of the Columns. The table was in the form of a circle. The Queen and her mother were separated by about eighty feet. The room was brilliantly lighted by chandeliers and candelabra, the servants were richly uniformed in blue and scarlet, with much lace. In an adjoining room, an orchestra played parts from the most famous operas. Irving thought his position all he could desire, Maria Christina beside him, and directly across the table the Queen and Narvaez, who intrigued him.

Again Irving fell under the spell of Maria Christina's smile and manner. The former he found 'fascinating' and the latter was without the least affectation, being most natural and human. For two mortal hours the dinner moved along, and Irving found himself talking to the former Queen about her daughter who happened to be a monarch. She told an amusing story of the training of the Queen and the Princess to shoot firearms. Isabella had fired without the slightest trepidation, but the Princess was afraid, and cried before she could be persuaded to pull the trigger. Irving concluded that the young girls were thus trained to accustom them to the sound of firearms at military reviews they would have to attend. And he wondered if it was not just as well that princesses should know the use of arms in a land so often then threatened with insurrections.

And then Maria Christina told him how Isabella and her sister had been learning to ride horseback since her return. Irving asked if the Queen had courage. 'Yes; if anything, too much,' replied the mother. Irving had heard that she was a daring rider and usually left the others in the rear.

And then, suddenly, commotion in the banquet hall. Expressions of alarm on many faces. Isabella, feeling ill, had risen and left the table and the room. Narvaez and some of the ladies of the court rose hastily and followed. Maria Christina begged the guests to keep their seats, assuring them it was nothing serious. From time to time messengers hurried in to the mother with explanations that Irving understood. The little lady had been too tightly laced in a desperate endeavor to make her 'a fine figure of a woman.' At length Nature intervened and the uncomfortable young lady had been forced to surrender.

'Well,' said Maria Christina, laughing, 'tell her to leave her dress loose, to put on a shawl and come back.'

And Irving observed that soon she returned, 'not enveloped in a shawl, but free from the miseries of a fine figure.'

AND there was no release for Irving. A few days later, Isabella was to review her troops for the first time. For a full year Narvaez had been persuading her to the ordeal. Irving went forth on foot to see the spectacle and to mingle with the crowds. Soon he met Count de Bresson and the Countess, also walking, and for three hours they tramped, pushing through the congestion of soldiers and citizens, walking the length of the Prado and out into the country beyond the city gates. Irving found the Countess an ideal companion for a trudge. She was a good pedestrian and fearless and lively, and full of amusing observations and suggestions. They finally found their way to the balcony of Bulwer's home at the British Legation, where they would have a clear view of the review.

At length the procession appeared beneath the balcony, the little Queen riding on ahead, with the gallant Narvaez riding by her side. She rode a beautiful, perfectly trained dun-colored horse, and Irving was charmed by her costume — a blue cloth riding habit, a black beaver hat, and on her habit the badge of a captain-general. Behind her rode a cavalcade of officers in dress uniform on prancing, dancing horses. And then came the royal carriage with Maria Christina and the Princess, followed by Don Francisco and his daughters. Irving noticed that Isabella was in a joyous mood and in fine fettle. He thought the whole show splendid.

The de Bressons took him home to the French Embassy for dinner, and he finished the evening at the Teatro de la Cruz, where he heard Moriani sing admirably in the opera of 'Rolla the Artist.' And then, after a full day, to bed.

THE next night found Irving at a great ball at the palace of the Countess of Montijo in the Plaza del Angel — now no longer in existence. When seventeen years before he had passed the day at the country place of her husband, the beautiful mother of the future Empress of the French had been absent, but he had met her during his Malaga and Granada days. He knew her father, the big, bluff Scot who had become a citizen of the United States and had been its Consul at Malaga. When Irving returned to Spain as Minister, and met her at one of her great parties, he had been both delighted and astonished with her manner in meeting him as an old friend. The Count was dead and she had taken a great house in the capital, where her lavish entertainments were adorned by the beauty of the two daughters, one of whom was to ascend an imperial throne and the other soon was to become the bride of the Duke of Alba. Like all other foreigners who met her, Irving was impressed by her kindness and cordiality, her utter lack of affectation, her pleasing conversation, her simple manners.

The baby, known as Eugénie, whom he had trotted on his knee, was now one of the belles of the aristocratic society of the capital, and she was the toast of the town. He heard rhapsodies on her beauty, her charm, her prowess as a horse-woman, her talents, and the gossips had it that she had some eccentricities and was morbidly ambitious, and not likely to be contented with any ordinary fate. Some thought her capricious and a bit spoiled by the adulation of the gallants. Unlike many of the great houses of the nobility that were all but closed to the members of the diplomatic corps, the Countess of Montijo favored them constantly with invita-tions to her balls and receptions, and Irving frequently attended. At this January ball he devoted himself to his 'favorites,' 'the fair Leocadia' and Mrs. O'Shea, and left early.

For Irving, while interested as a spectator in the plumes and peacocks of fashionable society, thought himself 'in the midst of these brilliant throngs the dullest of the dull.' Often among casual acquaintances he found it difficult, and sometimes impossible, to pay the commonplace compli-ments and indulge in the meaningless small talk prescribed by fashion. He wondered if it was because he had grown too old or too wise, and hoped it was the latter. Usually he sought amidst the throng an intimate or so to whom he could attach himself as at the Countess of Montijo's, where the mys-terious Leocadia Zamora and the elusive Mrs. O'Shea had made the evening pleasant.

It was in the drawing-room of the Countess of Montijo that Irving met the gorgeous woman who was to impress him as the most charming and beautiful, and as one of the most accomplished, in Spain. Some time before, a noble and wealthy Cuban family named Zamora had appeared in Madrid and taken up their residence in a great house that later was to be the home of Canovas, the statesman, and to make way for the Via Grande. There were two daughters of rare beauty, and it was in the palace of the mother of the Empress Eugénie that they were formally presented to Madrid society. Their success was instantaneous. Soon one married the Count of Peñalver, whose son was to become one of Madrid's most popular mayors under the monarchy. But we are concerned here solely with the sister, Leocadia Zamora. From the moment her dark, brooding eyes flashed on Madrid's Mayfair she became the darling of the drawing-rooms and the ballrooms and the toast of the beaux.

And yet, alas, so ephemeral is the fame of beauty that for months it was impossible for me to learn more of her than the vague gossip that she had been a favorite of the court and a woman of exquisite beauty. No dictionaries of biography preserved her memory. Members of the highest nobility in Spain had only a shadowy impression handed down from former generations. She was no more than the faint fragrance of a faded flower. Finally, through the courtesy and persistency of the Duke of Alba, I found that a niece was living in Madrid who might have some memories, and that Leocadia had been one of Madrazo's famous gallery of beautiful women. That distinguished portrait-painter stubbornly refused to paint any but the most charming, and his portrait of Leocadia Zamora was said to be the most beautiful of all. I finally found the portrait, and one evening I stood before the masterpiece of Madrazo in a charming old Spanish house.

She had been painted full length in a white ballroom dress. She was not statuesque, but she had a slender, graceful figure, and she clasped a corsage of red flowers in front of her, and a blue wrap hung over her arm. Her coal-black hair was parted in the middle and brought down in graceful curves over her brow. But it was her eyes that explained her fascination. Large, dark, lustrous, beautiful they were, and they spoke eloquently of a keen sense of humor, a love of fun, a joy in living, but in their depths one could not miss a brooding profundity. She was marvelously attractive. Her wealth permitted her to set off her radiant beauty in the most becoming gowns that the artistes of Paris could create.

But it was not alone her beauty that appealed to Irving. Had she been beautiful and dull he could have been content to admire her momentarily from afar. It was her keen intelligence, her sparkling wit, her cleverness in conversation, her playful nature that led him to seek her out in crowded companies as one seeks an oasis in a desert; and she was welcomed warmly in every drawing-room. With a trained musical voice, she sang delightfully, and at the brilliant social gatherings in the drawing-rooms of the Countess of Montijo, in the royal palace, at the Villa Alegri, the country home of Maria Christina, in the palace of the Marques de Badmar, in the house of Madame Calderon, she was always pressed to sing. Not without reason did one of her contemporaries

LEOCADIA ZAMORA
Photograph of the Madrazo painting

describe her as 'chanting and enchanting.' And as she sang, men were entranced. The brusque, stout warrior, Narvaez, was fascinated, and is reputed to have lost both his head and his heart. The General, Ros de Clana, who amused himself with verse, paid poetic tribute to her charm. Even the dignified and staid old statesman, Martinez de la Rosa, would sit like a statue staring through his gold spectacles as one bewitched. She was a magnet that drew all men, and they paid her compliments and made tender speeches; but she gave no heed, and passed them by with a maddening indifference.

Regularly she adorned the drawing-rooms of the Montijos, and invariably she was the soul of the party at the functions of Maria Christina at the Villa Alegri, and she was the friend of Eugénie, destined to an imperial crown, and the young Queen Isabella delighted in her company. 'My favorite,' Irving called her. Never really happy at chit-chat conversation of the wholly frivolous, he came to look for her at crowded parties, for her clever conversation and her wit. In the days of Irving's mission she was as the gayest of the gay.

It was long after Irving left that a change came over the spirit of her dream. She never married. One hears vague stories of a disillusionment in love, but no one really knows. All through the reign of Isabella she maintained her social sway. Frequently she would go to London or to Paris for the shopping. But after Isabella was sent upon her travels, Leocadia was seldom seen in company, and though she made a reappearance after the restoration, it was not for long. She grew more thoughtful. One day she amazed her family by entering the convent for the novitiate, but when she returned her friends knowingly smiled, not surprised that such a woman of the world should have found the seclusion repugnant to her nature. But she entered another convent —

and returned. And then another — and returned. Those who loved her wondered if her mind had been affected. And then she went into the convent of Alba des Tormes, an order of the Carmelites, noted for the severity of its rules — and reappeared.

It was after this that she evidently felt prepared for that which she clearly had in mind in entering the convents. With her own money she went to Oviedo, where she bought a large house and established a Carmelite convent of her own. She entered, never to emerge, and became the Mother Superior.

It was then that she became uneasy about the portrait by Madrazo. The ballroom gown was but modestly décolleté, but now she was the head of a convent, and she wrote a relative in Paris who possessed the picture and asked that it be covered with a nun's habit to the chin. A painter was summoned to the task, and when the work was finished the portrait was sent to Oviedo. There it remained many years, Madrazo's masterpiece forgotten. Long afterward, the Count of Peñalver learned of its existence, and through an arrangement satisfactory to the convent it was restored to the family. An expert at such work was summoned to remove the habit, and once more the portrait stood forth as it had come from the brush of the master.

The reigning belle of the forties grew old at her work. Her retirement from the world was real. The rules of the order were severe and strict. She could talk with relatives only behind barred windows, her charming face covered with a veil. Only once she drew the veil aside. Her eyes were as beautiful as ever, but she showed the effect of the passing years, and thus Leocadia Zamora passed forever from the vision of the world. She grew older in her pious work and in meditation, and died, and there at the convent is buried the 'favorite' of Washington Irving.

The last view we have of Antoinette, his favorite during his first Spanish sojourn, is that of an old woman pottering about the galleries of Florence dressed like a nun; and his favorite during his second sojourn was buried in a cloistered spot in a nun's habit.

B UT Irving was to find no release that winter when the court and nobility, intoxicated by the triumph of the aristocratic party, were indulging in excesses of entertainment. Another day found him ascending the great staircase at the palace for the birthday party for the Infanta. But the brilliant court, the halberdiers on the stairs, had lost their luster for him, and he would have found it dull but for Bulwer, the British Minister, and Prince Carini, who stood on either side of him in the diplomatic line. Bulwer was always amusing with his subtle irony, his cynicism, his genius for caricaturing with a sentence, and Carini was always clever and bubbling over with fun. Irving forgot his ankles and his weariness in listening to the amusing comments of his colleagues on the oddities of some members of the court, and the time passed quickly. But he was to record nothing of these conversations except that with Isabella, who passed along the line. When he congratulated her on her 'first military sally,' she responded with a delighted smile and told him she had 'relished it highly.'

A few days more and he was back at the palace for a

concert in which the ladies of the court were the musicians and the exquisite Leocadia Zamora sang, and 'acquitted themselves in a manner that would have done credit to first-rate artists.' During the first part of the concert, given in a splendid salon, Irving was cooped in with his colleagues immediately behind the royal family, but after they had adjourned to a distant apartment 'fitted up in the style of a grotto' for a cold supper, confectionery and ices served at little tables, he deserted, to wander at will through the brilliantly lighted rooms enjoying the paintings of the masters on the walls, the portraits of dead kings and queens. He was alone but for an occasional domestic in royal livery passing through, or a couple of courtiers who had sought an out-of-the-way place for an exchange of secrets. Soon everyone had crowded back into the concert room to bask in the light of royalty, and Irving was almost as much alone in the palace of the Queen as he had been years before in the palace of the Moorish kings. He unbridled his fancy and let it run at will. These kings and queens, looking down from the walls, who once had played their part upon this royal stage and now had 'gone down to dusty death,' made him pensive. He paused before the portraits of Ferdinand VII, and Amelia, whose death-knell he had heard pealing in the cathedral at Granada as he stood upon the balcony of the Alhambra. The sweet voices of the singers in the concert room came to him from a distance. He wandered on and on, weaving fancies and meditating on the futility of pageantry.

So PASSED the winter, and spring came to Madrid that year with more than its customary splendor. The skies were of a brilliant blue, the air bland, and the sunshine was a glory. More than ever Irving sought the Prado, which was gay with the carriages of the aristocracy, and the walks were thronged with the beauty and fashion of the city. He loved to drive slowly up and down alone with his reflections and his enjoyment of the pleasant scenes. 'I have been for so much of my life a mere looker on in the game of society that it has become habitual to me,' he wrote his sister. For that spring he has left us a record of his routine. He breakfasted alone now, and lazily glanced over his morning papers, and then hurried to his study, where he remained alone until summoned for his drive in the Prado. He lingered on the fashionable drive until time to go home and dress for dinner, which he had with Livingston, with a guest or two occasionally. In the evening he liked to go alone to the opera, where company disturbed his enjoyment of the music. Now and then when he felt the urge for company he would spend the evening with his friends the de Bressons at the French Embassy, or at the home of Mrs. O'Shea. With the recovery of his health he now found it possible to write a bit, for his long exile from his pad and pencil was growing irksome. His sixty-second birthday found him recalling the impressions of his youth that at sixty he would be decrepit, and rejoicing that his health again was good, his sensibilities still fresh, his faculties undiminished in their vigor. One day he found himself bounding up the stairs two steps at a leap, until the astonishment on the face of the porter reminded him that such boyish exuberance was unbecoming in a Minister and a man past sixty.

And then, in early May, when Madrid is at its best in beauty, he was drawn back to the festivities of the court. The birthday of Maria Christina was celebrated with much *éclat* at the palace, and for three torturing hours he had to stand with his colleagues in the presence chamber as all the world, it seemed, trooped by to pay homage to the royal family.

More amusing and charming to him was the continuance of the festivities at the country home of Maria Christina at Villa Alegri, about two miles from Madrid. It was a grand *fête champêtre*. The scene was ideal for the season. The grounds, with their groves, their shrubbery, their canals and walks, were beautiful, and everything conceivable and possible for entertainment was prepared. There were flying horses, and swings, roundabouts and riding at the ring, shooting with crossbows, and gondolas for the canal.

When, at four in the afternoon, Irving arrived, the festivities were at their height, and more than a thousand of the cream of Madrid society were at play. The trees were all in leaf and the lilacs in flower, and the nightingales were singing in the evening. Here and there over the grounds small bands were playing favorite selections from the most popular operas. Beautiful young women were in the swings and trying their hands at shooting with the crossbows. As Irving wandered about the grounds, odorous with the perfume of the lilacs and the fresh foliage, charmed by the smiling faces of beautiful and graceful women, he found much to amuse him. An old courtier caused uproarious laughter when he fell off a wooden horse and almost broke his head. Over the canal in a gondola glided the Countess of Montijo and a group of reigning beauties with whom she invariably surrounded herself. Among them Irving noted his prime favorite, the exquisite Leocadia Zamora. Suddenly the gondola was seen to capsize and its burden of beauty in filmy dresses was thrown into nine feet of water. Gladly men rushed to the rescue and brought the dripping ladies to the shore with difficulty.

The twilight came and darkness, and then the fireworks, and after them under a huge brilliantly lighted tent the company sat down to a repast. Then came the concert, and while some sat in groups and chatted, others, in pairs, sought the wooded walks hung with Chinese lanterns where they could hear the more perfect melody of the nightingales. Never was Irving to attend a garden party so delightful.

The scene of this festivity at Villa Alegri has not greatly changed. After the death of Maria Christina, the property passed into possession of the Marquis of Salamanca, who added to the grounds and spent vast sums on their adornment. Since his death, the property has been dedicated to public purposes, and at the beginning of the Rebellion, within the brick walls that once gave privacy to the frolics of royalty and nobility, were asylums for blind children, for the orphans of officers, and for the very old. The high wall stood, and the grounds still were an oasis in the Castilian desert, with innumerable trees, shrubbery, statuary, and fountains. The old canal, in which the mother of an empress and the beautiful Zamora were capsized into nine feet of water, has disappeared, though the location is clearly indicated. As I wandered over the grounds it was easy to re-create the festive scenes of Irving's time, with the swings, the gondolas, the fountains, the promenading and flirting beneath the shady trees. But there was something sad in the reminder of 'what shadows we are and what shadows we pursue.' Few of the custodians of the place appeared to know that once these gardens had been the playgrounds of a queen. A nun, however, knew the story of Maria Christina's residence there, but a guard at the house, indicated by her as the Queen's, stoutly disclaimed all knowledge. It had been the home of the Marquis of Salamanca, he insisted. Did not a plate on a door indicate the room in which he had died? No doubt it did, but Maria Christina long before had been laid in the magnificent crypt of royalty at the Escorial. Walking about the grounds where children were romping under the trees, and recalling Irving's playful description of the gay scenes of more than ninety years before, it seemed strange that the romantic story of such days had passed so completely from the knowledge of most Madrileños. She who found in it her perfect home, close by the village of Carabanchel, and who once wrote:

> A las Carabancheles se va la Reina,
> que quivere que la llamen Carabanchel.[1]

has been quite forgotten by the multitude, along with the beautiful Zamora, and the gay party that disported itself upon the green to the delectation of Irving. The neighborhood of this villa of the Queen was for more than two years the center of bitter fighting in the recent Rebellion, and I am afraid that not even the house is left.

---

[1] 'To the Carabanchels goes the Queen, and wants them to call her the girl from Carabanchel.'

THEN came the breaking-up of society for the summer, when, toward the last of May, Isabella rode in state to the Cortes, delivered her little speech, and closed the session. Immediately after this ceremony Irving went with his colleagues to the palace to bid farewell to the Queen, the Princess, and Maria Christina, who left immediately for Barcelona. A few days later Narvaez and certain of the Ministers followed in their wake, and the diplomatic corps scattered in all directions.

In the closing session of the Cortes, the reformed Constitution was promulgated, and Irving wrote James Buchanan, now Secretary of State, that from the gossip he had gleaned the impression that no one was satisfied. The absolutists thought it too liberal by far, and the progressives described it as much too autocratic. He thought that 'its very devisors consider it a compromise between their consciences and their interests with which they vainly hope to beguile the people.'

Irving, still out of pocket by paying the bills of the United States before, decided to remain in Madrid through the greater part of the summer, and in the autumn to take a journey to Paris. The heat of a Madrid summer held no terror for him. His house was very large, its walls were very thick, and it was so arranged that pleasant breezes could refresh the lofty rooms. During the heat of the day he could draw the blinds to shut out the sun and the rooms would be 'as cool as vaults.' And in the night he could take his drives or rambles in the Prado, where, toward midnight on a summer's night, he thought the air delightful.

And there was little he could do on his mission. There had been a change in the Administration at Washington, and he assumed that someone would desire his post. He was quite ready if not eager to go home. His mind still was centered on the 'Life of Washington,' which he hoped would be his masterpiece, and he had been bitterly disappointed that his health had restrained him from working on the book. Now, at sixty-two, he had no time to lose, and he was looking forward to undisturbed literary labors in the study at Sunny-side.

Nor could business be transacted with any satisfaction at the Foreign Office now. He wrote Buchanan of the difficulties. Part of the Ministry was in Madrid and part was following the court at Barcelona. The statesmen and the politicians had troubles of their own. The marriage of the Queen was still being managed by cold-blooded intriguers at home and abroad, and with no thought or care about the happiness of Isabella. Don Carlos had 'abdicated,' and his son had issued a manifesto which promised more serious complications involving the throne itself. The funds were fluctuating in most sinister fashion, and there seemed no doubt that some statesmen in authority were gambling desperately for a private fortune. Rumors floated into Madrid day by day of threatened insurrections in the provinces. And all this disturbed the minds of Ministers and rendered them 'heedless of all affairs but such as are immediately important to their political existence.' Many thought Narvaez was slipping. There was nothing to do but wait and watch.

So Irving settled down to weather the shimmering summer in the palace of de Mos with little to do but to observe from his twilight rooms the moves upon the checkerboard of politics, and the sorry maneuvering of the graybeards to marry Isabella to someone or other. He was to find much to write about for Washington. Above the tree-tops he could see the beautiful Guadarrama Mountains in the distance, so often enveloped in a purple haze and crowned with snow.

And in the midst of his ease and pleasure the announcement that the Queen was going to Barcelona awakened him again to the duties of his mission. He too would have to go.

Chapter 13: THE GOSSIP OF THE TIMES

THE summer of 1845 in Madrid, despite the absence of the court and the flight of the diplomatic corps, Irving was to find interesting enough, as his dispatches to Washington imply. Isabella and her mother with the court had gone to Barcelona for the waters and all went smoothly there, until early in July it was announced that before her return to the capital Isabella would make a tour of the Basque provinces, and then the tongues began to clack. The reason given for this change of plans was to give the young Queen the advantage of the sea bathing. But in political circles there was no disposition to accept the explanation as sincere. The Ministry for the most part was bitterly against the journey, and the press almost unanimously, on the ground that there should be a concentration of the Cabinet in Madrid. Irving thought that the suspicions of the public were aroused by Maria Christina's insistence on the tour. He was convinced that the mother's motive was to be found in a real solicitude for the young Queen's health. But, he wrote Buchanan, 'the public considers the Queen Mother a great maneuverer and suspects a covert design in every movement. They consider the projected journey into the Basque provinces as having some connection with her matrimonial schemes for her royal daughters.'

There was just enough of romance and drama in the situation to appeal to Irving's imagination. His ears were open to the gossip, and his pen ran on and on in detailing the rumors and intrigues to Buchanan. He had no doubt himself of the ardent desire of Maria Christina to marry the young Queen to Count de Trapani, her uncle of Naples. The gossips had it that Louis Philippe of France reluctantly had given consent after abandoning all hope of making one of his own sons the husband of a Spanish queen. But, as the story ran, he had bargained before he gave consent and stipulated that the Duke of Montpensier should have the hand of Isabella's sister.

It was in commenting on the motive of the French monarch that Irving proved a wretched prophet. 'The constitutional infirmities of the Queen Isabella make it not unlikely that she will die early, and without progeny; in such case her sister would succeed to the throne,' he wrote Buchanan. In truth, Isabella was to live to a ripe old age and, despite her uncertain health, to produce children in abundance. But the Isabella of 1845 foreshadowed little of the Isabella that was soon to be. Irving was therefore almost persuaded that the projected journey into the Basque provinces had been planned that Isabella might meet the French Prince, then about to visit the Pyrenees. So thought many others.

But there was so much of plot and counterplot and gossip that Irving evidently was afraid to eliminate any of the suggested possibilities. He heard that the court at Naples had abandoned all hope for the Trapani match because of its intense unpopularity in Spain. He wrote Buchanan that a Coburg prince was being urged, and that his friend Bulwer, interested in this project, had journeyed to Paris for a conference with Guizot to smooth the way to its consummation. Would France consent? Irving thought it probable that 'Louis Philippe in his growing spirit of accommodation to the views of England would incline to favor it — provided always that the Duke of Montpensier would have the hand of the Infanta.'

And yet, he continued, another candidate had been brought into the field by Narvaez who might prove popular with the nation. The head of the Government had found in the Infante Don Enrique, Duke of Seville, the second son of the Infante Don Francisco, a proper consort for the Queen. 'He is about twenty years of age,' wrote Irving, 'a captain in the navy, and in command of a brig of war. Report speaks favorably of him; he has acquitted himself well in his studies and duties of his profession, and this implies intelligence and manly qualities.' Irving could clearly see Narvaez's hand in the stage-setting. Had he not arranged that the young Duke should visit Barcelona in his ship of war during the presence of the court in that city? Had he not been received with extraordinary distinction? Narvaez had given one of his elaborate dinners for the youth, and the brilliant Martinez de la Rosa had given him another. The municipal authorities had fêted him, the court itself had dined him, and one day Narvaez arranged a most ceremonial visit of Isabella to her cousin's ship. Irving, who appears sympathetic, was so impressed by the sudden and intensive campaign for the young Duke that he sent his impressions on to Buchanan with much gusto. The ministerial papers were teeming with eulogy. Irving was persuaded that the young man would meet with little opposition, since he was a Spaniard and of the branch of the royal family inclined to liberal principles. 'A newspaper is about to be set up in Madrid under the auspices of the Ministers to enforce his pretensions,' he wrote Buchanan. The family of Don Francisco, which had been neglected and almost snubbed by royalty, was finding itself in high favor and had been invited to repair to San Sebastian during the royal sojourn there. Naturally Don Enrique was included in the invitation.

Irving found the little drama fascinating, for behind Isabella he could see Maria Christina and Narvaez clashing swords. The former, he wrote, 'now finding the Trapani match likely to be entirely defeated, is anxious to postpone the marriage of her daughter until she has arrived at a more mature age, until her health is established and her constitution developed and confirmed.' Irving thought this proper, but doubted if the politicians would be so considerate of the Queen's welfare. He was afraid that 'the poor young Queen may be hurried into an early marriage, which may hurry her into an early grave.' At the moment Narvaez seemed to have an advantage over Maria Christina.

I RVING had admired Espartero, though he had no prejudices against his great protagonist, Narvaez. Both were colorful, admirable soldiers, and loyal according to their lights, but neither was a statesman. Narvaez thought with his sword. He was to pass through various vicissitudes of fortune, but his character as a fighting man never was to change. 'Does Your Excellency forgive all your enemies?' the priest asked him on his death-bed. 'I have no enemies; I had them all shot,' was the proud reply.

In politics he was a reactionary or conservative — which means that he had no patience with the limitations placed by the laws of popular assemblies on the freedom of monarchs. He was willing to go a long way with the absolutists. He had overthrown the far more liberal Espartero through a combination of the absolutists, or reactionaries, and some discontented liberals. By the summer of 1845 he found himself no longer popular with the liberal faction of the old coalition, since his policies had been reactionary.

Irving studied him carefully for his reports to Washington, and found him a man of good intentions, often diverted by his passionate disposition, his morbid ambition to make a great show, his tendency to act on impulse in a temper. Irving wrote Buchanan that Narvaez had fire and force but no bridle or rein for either. Confined by day to the darkened rooms of the thick-walled mansion of de Mos that summer, Irving amused himself by using Narvaez as an involuntary model for portrait-painting. In picturing the impetuosity of his temper Irving used heavy lines, for this temperamental weakness Irving thought explained many of the soldier's despotic acts. He painted in the lines denoting a disposition to domineer with equally bold strokes. And he left nothing out of the portrait that would make his model's vanity stand out like a challenge. On the whole, Irving was convinced that the besetting weaknesses of Narvaez were his violent temper and his inordinate vanity.

It was to the latter that Irving ascribed one of Narvaez's 'acts of sheerest despotism' in a letter to Buchanan. That summer in a fit of temper Narvaez had ordered the arrest of two writers on one of the newspapers. They were denied all the usual guaranties of the law and placed under a military guard, as though they were desperate prisoners guilty of a most sinister crime against the State. They were ordered to

Cadiz, where they were embarked on a boat for the Philippines. When a roar of protest and amazement went up all over the Peninsula, the friends of Narvaez sought to defend the action on the ground that the victims were 'suspected of conspiring against the Government.' But Irving reported that 'the real offense was a wound inflicted upon the General's vanity.' The writers had, it seemed, 'given a burlesque account of his pomp and style on a public occasion, with some ludicrous allusions to his person and his wig'; and this 'was not to be tolerated by a man arrived at a certain age, yet still a general gallant and particularly ambitious of the smiles of the ladies.'

This vanity, Irving thought, overshadowed 'his bolder and better qualities and by its indirect operations has contributed greatly to lessen his stand in public opinion.' Thus his 'prodigal and ostentatious style of living.' Though not a man of great wealth, no sooner had he been elevated to power than he blossomed forth with palaces and magnificent state equipages and began to give princely fêtes and entertainments. Eager for the countenance of royalty, he usually invited the Queen and the Infanta, which enormously increased the cost. Soon the public was commenting that he was living far beyond his ostensible means. True, Maria Christina had rewarded his past services, on the urging of Count de Bresson, the French Ambassador, with a gift of $100,000, but even this could not account for his 'vainglorious prodigality.'

And then, in explanation, the ugly tongue of gossip was busy that summer with insinuations that he was replenishing his coffers by methods not compatible with the dignity of his position. It was whispered about by the promenaders in the Prado and in the cafés that he was gambling in the funds, and had associated himself with some of the principal stock-

brokers in the speculations that had 'shaken society to its
center.' Irving found that 'these gambling operations have
become matters of notoriety and have injured him with the
public.' More dangerous to Narvaez, they had injured him
with the army, since the officers 'detest anything in a commander which may appear sordid and mercenary.' Irving
observed that his enemies in army circles whose ambitions
he had thwarted were trumpeting forth the charges that the
head of the Government was gambling in the funds.

Thus that summer Narvaez felt the need of strengthening
his position.

H IS primary hope was to re-
cover the support of the liberals who had joined the coalition
against Espartero and had been alienated by his disregard
of constitutional limitations. They were in arms against
Maria Christina's plan to marry Isabella to Trapani, and
Irving was sure that Narvaez's espousal of the claims of Don
Enrique was a bid to the liberals, since the young Duke of
Seville belonged to the more liberal branch of the royal
family and was a Spaniard popular with the mass of the
people. Despite her handsome gift to Narvaez, whose triumph
had made possible her return from exile, Maria Christina
had never really cared for the bold and dashing soldier, and
he had found her increasingly difficult. Their attitude had
been that of an armed truce from the moment of her return.
In public they smiled cordially on one another, but the more

observant noticed that the sword of each was out of the scabbard.

Meanwhile, though not popular with the mass of the people, Maria Christina, tireless in intrigue, resourceful, and with powerful backing both at home and abroad, was a formidable opponent. Negotiations with the Vatican had not gone so smoothly as had been hoped, and the gossips had it that this was due to her intermeddling. Narvaez was indignant, and the Cabinet distressed. Irving understood that there were two parties in the Sacred College of Cardinals, 'one called the political, which is disposed to keep peace with the age ... the other the theocratic party, intent on reinstating the Church of Saint Peter in all the sway, religious, political, and fiscal, which it exercised in the days of Gregory VII.' Narvaez was with the political and Maria Christina with the theocratic party, and the former had just suffered a serious loss in the death of Cardinal Cappacini, the head of the political party, and the consequent increase in the power of Cardinal Lambruschini, the leader of the theocracy and Secretary of State.

Nor was Narvaez's position strengthened by the presence in Rome of a goodly number of Carlist partisans under the leadership of the Bishop of Leon, who were representing their country as an ideal theater 'for the great theocratic plan of retrocession.' The Ministry had been unfortunate, Irving thought, in the choice of Castillo y Ayense as their envoy at the Papal Court, since he was known to be secretly subservient to Maria Christina.

Thus financially embarrassed by his extravagance, the victim of gossip on the charge of speculating in the funds, the object of envy and malice among officers of the army, the pet aversion now of Maria Christina, the suspect of the liberals who had once been his friends, Narvaez's position in the summer of 1845 interested Irving enormously. He reported to Buchanan that Narvaez's Government 'occupies a mere isthmus between the Absolutists (including the Carlists) on the one side and the Progresistas on the other,' and that 'this isthmus is continually narrowing.'

And yet Irving had come to admire Narvaez and to sympathize with his trials and tribulations. Though writing with judicial coldness to his Government about him, he had a warmer tone in his personal letters to his family. He wrote to his sister, Mrs. Daniel Paris:

> Narvaez has great faults, but he has, also, great merits. He has risen to the level of his situation, and displays a tact and capacity to the various concerns of government quite beyond what was expected from him. He is extremely vigilant, prompt in action, and possesses the true spirit of command. Altogether he appears to me to be one of the most striking characters, if not the most striking, that has risen to power in Spain during the long course of her convulsions.[1]

For if Narvaez did some gambling on the Madrid stock exchange he was but following the mode at the moment, for a spasm of speculation had swept over the country, and many proud names were numbered among those gambling for more fortune. The frenzy and the tragedy of this saturnalia attracted Irving's attention. He knew something of the market in New York and of the gambling there. But here it was different, and he wrote

[1] Irving *Life*, III, 93.

Buchanan of the difference. Just then he reported that the stock exchange was having 'an immense influence on the morals and the fortunes of society' and that it was 'not governed by the ordinary rules of such institutions.' Political events did not have much influence on its fluctuations. Its patrons were not, as in other countries, holders of stock as a permanent investment, looking for an income from the dividends. 'They are solely and purely gamblers,' he wrote Buchanan; 'they combine among themselves occasionally to play for a rise or a fall, and are pretty sure to effect their purpose.' Indeed, he found that when no such combination was in operation, the funds were stagnant and the exchange dull or the prices low. Sometime a financial tragedy would put an end to such a sorry business, but in the meantime, for a long while, he thought, 'gambling will go on creating and destroying mushroom fortunes.' That summer gambling was the 'mania of the day.' Even Narvaez and a great duke were in the midst of the game.

To this mania of gambling, this speculation in the funds, the intrigues of Maria Christina on the marriage, the spirit of unrest in political and military circles, was added in late July another of Narvaez's acts that many thought despotic. A sweeping decree restraining the freedom of the press was issued, and there was a clamor of protest, with even the ministrial papers joining the opposition press in denunciation of the act. Through those July days when Madrid was simmering in the sun, it was clear to Irving that an undercurrent of unrest was running stronger all the time. Isabella's journey through the Basque country happily had produced no political disturbances, and when the entire Council of Ministers met her at Saragossa and ironed out their differences it seemed that the Government had passed a crisis. But Irving informed Buchanan that 'their common safety would seem to forbid discord or disunion, being assailed from all quarters, even by many of their former adherents.'

And then, in August, Irving found something new in the world with which to entertain himself. The merchants and tradespeople had resented the imposition of certain taxes and had made common cause against them. At first they flooded the Government with memorials. When these were utterly ignored, they all agreed upon a merchants' strike — the closing of the shops.

Keenly interested in this unique venture, Irving went into the streets to observe the effect. The shops for the most part were closed. The curious lounger was making no secret of his amusement. Though the Government had made ample provision against a scarcity of bread and meat, Irving found soldiers patrolling the streets by day and night ready to put down tumult. It seemed clear to him that the strikers had no thought of violence, but some idlers and toughs took advantage of the situation to try to stir up trouble. On the first day of the strike of the merchants, the Government decreed it a penal offense for merchants dealing in necessary articles to close their shops. An attempt at rioting was sternly crushed by military methods and a very few were killed and others wounded. One day a tailor threw a brick at the chief of the municipal authorities, and he was given short shrift by a military tribunal and shot within three days of the offense. Even the intercession of the intended victim of the brick was of no avail, since it was hoped by drastic action to break the spirit of the offending merchants.

Toward the close of the trouble, after the shooting of the tailor, Irving wandered through the streets noting the effect. Most of the shops again were open and business was going on as usual. But he reported to Washington that 'the city is quiet but gloomy and discontented,' since it 'has received a mortifying proof how completely it is under the iron hand of military rule.' He thought a revolutionary scheme all but impossible with the militia disarmed and the Progresistas without a foothold in the municipality.

THUS the summer passed, and Irving, deserted by his colleagues, who had sought the mountains or the seashore, was left very much to his meditations and his own devices. The big thick-walled house on the Calle de las Infantas he had found comfortable enough behind drawn curtains in the sunshine. No courtly ceremonials kept him on his feet three hours at a time. Bulwer had closed the house on the Alcala and was summering in the shades of Aranjuez to the lullaby of the fountains; the Count de Bresson was hovering about the Queen in the country of the Basques; and Prince Carini and his attractive spouse had also left the city. Irving was very much alone with Livingston, with whom he dined, and in the evening, when the refreshing breezes off the Guadarramas fell as a blessing on the parched pavements, he fared forth alone, though sometimes with Lorenzo, for a stroll. Almost invariably this took him up the Alcala to the Prado, past the immense palace of the Duke of Villa Hermosa and the many-balconied palace of the Dukes of Medinaceli (now the site of the Palace Hotel), and out under the trees of the parkway of that impressive promenade. When the moon was bright and mellow he loved to walk alone when the promenaders had deserted and only here and there a pair of lovers were seated beneath the trees. He never was to know anything quite so charming as the Prado at midnight when the moon was at its full.

But earlier in the evening he drove through slowly, enjoying the alleys of stately trees, the fountains and statuary, and most of all the people, the groups of women and men seated together holding their *tertulias* and gossiping far into the night. He had found the Prado to his liking long before, when after hours of application on his biography of Columbus and his 'Conquest of Granada' he would stroll its length alone, finding refreshment for his drooping spirits in the rustling leaves, the murmuring fountains, the loitering lovers, the star-studded sky. So intimately did he identify his Madrid life with the Prado that his spirit seems not remote from it today.

In September, not without regret, he gave up the house of the Marquis of Mos, having no doubt that the new Administration in Washington would want his post for another. He moved such furniture as he possessed with his other belongings to the house occupied by the Brazilian Minister, to spend the remainder of his mission living *en famille* with the Albuquerques. He was assigned a small part of the apartment they occupied. 'The Albuquerques,' he wrote his sister, 'have a commodious, well-furnished house, ready provided for them, at a time when they were at their wits' end to find a habitation.'

Scarcely had he taken possession, however, when he started on what he expected to be a brief visit to Paris. Going by way of Bordeaux, he made a sentimental journey en route to the little town of Tonneins. There he passed Christmas, and four days later he was making his preparations to go to England for a month.

It was from Paris that he sent in his resignation to Buch-

anan. 'The unexpected manner in which I was called to
this high trust from the retirement of private life,' he wrote,
'without reference to any political considerations, and the
cordial manner in which I was welcomed to it by my countrymen of all political creeds, have ever made me regard it as
the crowning honor of my life.' In tendering his resignation
he made it clear that he was not moved by party motives
'nor any indisposition to aid in carrying out the foreign
policy of the present Administration, but solely by my earnest
desire to return to my country and my friends.' He might
have added, had he thought it appropriate, that his eagerness
to finish his biography of Washington and his advancing
years entered largely into his determination.

He passed over the Channel to England on the solicitation
of the American Minister there, who thought his personal
relations with public men in that country might be of service
in the existing crisis of American affairs with Britain. He
was to linger much longer than he thought, and it was almost
spring when, traveling day and night, he returned to Madrid
to greet his successor, who did not arrive until near the first
of August.

Chapter 14: FAREWELL TO SPAIN

IRVING now had but a few months more in Spain, but events moved rapidly and with the flourish of drama. On March 11, immediately after his return to Madrid, we find him writing the Marquis of Miraflores, the Premier, asking for an appointment to pay his respects to the Queen and Maria Christina. Eight days later he was acknowledging the note of the Duke of Valencia announcing his appointment as the successor of Miraflores, and eighteen days after that, he was congratulating Don Xavier Isturiz on his appointment as the successor of Valencia. Narvaez had suffered a momentary eclipse, but Irving wrote Buchanan that the Miraflores Government had 'never had a vigorous existence,' but had been suffered to carry on temporarily while intrigues in the palace and conferences among the politicians arranged matters on a compromise. Then the Miraflores Cabinet 'was suddenly despatched by a kind of *coup d'état.*' Narvaez returned to power with a Ministry of his own choosing, and for the moment he seemed again on the crest of the wave. And Narvaez acted like a dictator.

'The first measures of his government are significant,' Irving wrote Buchanan. 'The sessions of the Cortes are suspended indefinitely. A manifesto has been published by the Cabinet Ministers from which it appears that they intend to carry on the Government by decrees; thus giving, as they say, a "rapid impulse to those public measures which have been impeded for years by the stormy discussions of the legislative chambers." ' The Ministers added that should they 'occasionally transgress the limits of their constitutional faculties' they would finally give an account of their acts to the Cortes and trust their exoneration to the exigencies of circumstances. 'Meanwhile,' they continued, the Ministers would depend on 'a numerous, well-disciplined, and loyal army,' on the good sense and prudence of the nation, and 'on the energy inspired by a generous enterprise, as exciting in its causes as it is holy in its ends.' And with that, the Government, with a heavy hand, broke the back of the freedom of the press.

But Irving had an inspiration that Narvaez would not last. His all but dictatorial power had momentarily 'struck a degree of awe into the community.' The opposition press ceased publication. Meandering through the streets and to the Puerta del Sol, the center of all gossip and much intrigue, Irving listened to the whisperings of the people. He heard some say that the purpose of it all was to force the Trapani marriage on the nation — or Isabella, who scarcely counted. No, said others deep in their throats, the purpose is to put in operation 'the most profligate schemes of finance to retrieve the immense losses which Narvaez and the Duke of Rianzares are said to have sustained in recent gamblings with the funds.' Not at all, interjected another gossip, the whole play is to prepare the way for the final elimination of Narvaez. Had he not lost much of his prestige with the army as well as with the people? Had he not multiplied his enemies, civil and military? Had he not become odious to a great part of the Moderate Party? These, of course, clacked the gossips, would co-operate with the Progresistas in casting him down from his eminence, just as they had toppled Espartero from his seat. Of course, said others, the Trapani marriage would be his Waterloo.

But as Irving snooped about, he heard the explanations of Narvaez's friends. He merely had in mind measures of great public utility and wished to lose no time. He thought Spain behind the age and behind her own institutions, and the faction and corruption in the Cortes made progress impossible. Destroy the Constitution? Not at all — perish the thought! He would merely act 'independently of it' — nothing more. All this gossip Irving sent on to Washington, along with Narvaez's purported statement:

> Give me a few months to carry my plans into effect, unembarrassed by the Cortes and the press, and I will engage to clear away some of the most important evils which are pressing upon my country. I will then report what I have done to the Cortes and will say, 'If I have done wrong, punish me. Order me to the scaffold if you think fit. I will go there.'

In higher circles, Irving heard much speculation as to Narvaez's relations with Maria Christina. The two had never cared for one another, and merely their common benefit had drawn them together. Now that Narvaez knew how odious the Queen Mother had made herself because of her urging of the Trapani marriage, Irving wondered if he might not defy her and take the popular side.

But within three weeks Irving was informing Washington that Narvaez had fallen and had been banished. Irving wrote that he had reasons to believe 'that his fall had for some time been meditated in the secret councils of the palace.' His program did not meet with the approval of Maria Christina, that grand mistress of intrigue. The breach between them widened. Narvaez was defiant, and, to her, offensive. 'His intentions may have been patriotic,' thought Irving, 'but he overrated his means of carrying them into effect, or rather he underrated the influences against him. He was too confident of himself and in that fiery spirit which had borne him on to power.' At one of his first Cabinet councils he had committed the unpardonable sin by saying bluntly that the army would not tolerate the Trapani match.

And then came a violent scene in the Council of Ministers in which Narvaez's position was embarrassing. It grew out of a proposed law regulating the stock exchange and prohibiting speculations in the funds. Many thought the law had been aimed at Narvaez's speculations in the funds and that he would have it rescinded. But his enemies in the Cabinet, who were the partisans of Maria Christina, deliberately forced the fighting by insisting on the law's stringent enforcement. 'The consequence,' Irving heard, 'was violent altercations in which Narvaez gave way to his stormy temper, and at times lost all guard over his language. Some of these took place in the presence of the young Queen, who, it is said, conducted herself on these occasions with a dignity and discretion beyond her years.'

Then Isabella, who hitherto had been grateful for the loyalty of Narvaez to her interests, turned against him. The occasion was the reorganization of a portion of the Ministry. She agreed that some should go. But whoever Narvaez proposed for the succession she promptly vetoed. Urged to give her reasons, Isabella sounded the death-knell of Narvaez in her reply that they were 'enemies of [her] mother.'

Thus, with the realization that Maria Christina was a menace to him in the palace, he made a more serious blunder. In an unguarded or rash moment he proposed to Isabella that it would be excellent for her mother to leave the court and find residence in the provinces. The Queen resented the suggestion and Narvaez's fate was sealed. He tendered his resignation, and, to his surprise, it was accepted. Isturiz hastily formed the rudiments of a Ministry composed of the adherents of Maria Christina, and Narvaez was out.

Then for the moment it was the turn of the palace to tremble. In one of the stormy scenes in the Council Narvaez had referred to the palace intrigues against him, and with Andalusian heat and eloquence had boasted of his popularity with the army and implied that if thrown out he would turn it against the throne. Irving did not take these boasts seriously, but the palace did. It wanted Narvaez not only remote from the capital but from the provinces as well. Military measures instantly were taken to defend the city, and Narvaez unctuously was offered the post of Ambassador in Naples. Proudly he declined.

Meanwhile, the palace heard of mutinous murmurings in the army, and of threats to march upon the royal residence and demand the expulsion of Maria Christina. Panic seized the courtiers about the palace. Isabella by royal command ordered Narvaez to leave Madrid and Spain at once and repair to Naples to await further orders. Then there was turmoil in the town and Irving reported that 'this harsh mandate, equally pusillanimous and impolitic, was regarded with disgust even by the adherents to the court.' Narvaez's popularity revived. He was a political martyr and victim. That day his house was packed by personages of all parties and he was a national hero. Irving thought some of the callers were 'actuated by a generous sympathy, others by the idea that his disgrace might be but temporary, while still others merely wished to express their hostility to the court.' 'Nothing was heard,' reported Irving, 'but exclamations against the royal ingratitude toward so loyal a subject and one who had rendered such vast service to the throne.'

In the midst of the tumult and the shouting Narvaez conducted himself with a quiet dignity as he made his preparations for departure, professing his loyal devotion to the Queen. The popular reaction to the harsh order gave pause to the palace, which now wished to modify its criticized decree. It was much too late. Narvaez was in the act of entering his carriage when a member of the Cabinet appeared unctuously to offer a royal document constituting him Ambassador to Naples. Narvaez returned to his house and sat down at his writing desk to pen a proud reply. Since his presence in Spain was considered detrimental to the country, he had not hesitated a moment in making preparations for departure. But he begged the Queen for permission to decline serving a government which regarded him as an encumbrance. Smilingly offering the letter to the Minister, he entered his carriage and turned toward France.

At Bayonne, he had an amusing encounter. In the last few days of his power his protégé and choice for the hand of Isabella, Don Enrique, the Duke of Seville, was suspected of having plans to place himself at the head of a Galician insurrection at Coruña. Narvaez took military measures to suppress the insurrection, and Isabella ordered the Prince instantly to leave the kingdom for some point in France and not return, else he would be deprived of all the honors and considerations of a royal Prince of Spain. He obeyed at once, and chose Bayonne as his place of residence. Arraying himself in full uniform, Narvaez paid the Prince a call of respect. Madrid smiled at the comedy or tragedy.

Irving was pessimistic over the prospect of an adequate successor to Narvaez. 'The terror of his name and the vigor and promptness of his measures have daunted opposition, kept down insurrection, and contributed to carry on a discordant government for nearly three years,' he wrote. 'In this respect I see no one within the precincts of the court likely to supply his place.'

Never during his tenure was Irving so much engaged in official business of large import as during the brief period between his resignation and the arrival of his successor. In April he was much concerned over a report in the *Heraldo*, a Ministerial paper, concerning the ideas of some prominent Spanish politicians, urged on by France, for concerted action in erecting a monarchy in Mexico with one of the Princes of Spain upon the throne. The throne was to be upheld by the joint action of Spain, France, and England.

Irving would have liked to talk bluntly about it with his friend Valdivieso, the Mexican Minister, with whom he had made the memorable drive to Aranjuez for the meeting of the Queens. But Valdivieso had been almost two years absent from his post. He had gone to Rome and then to Mexico, but for some months he had been dividing his time between Paris and London. Irving wondered if he were engaged in negotiations on this project, and wrote his suspicions to Buchanan.

If Washington knew anything about it, it gave no sign. Indeed, Irving began to feel that his existence had been forgotten. His letter of resignation of December had brought no reply by July 11, when his patience was exhausted. In angry mood, he wrote brusquely to Buchanan. Not only had he been denied the courtesy of a reply to his resignation, but he had not received a line from the State Department for nine months. But for the newspapers he would not have known that his successor had been selected. Assuming that he was not in favor, he wrote modestly enough and yet with some spirit in defense of his mission. He could find no instructions that had been neglected. True, one of the foremost of these had not been carried out. He had secured no commercial treaty. He explained:

> Finding at an early period of my mission that important reforms to the system of trade were in preparation, and that England and Belgium were pressing for commercial treaties with great prospect of success, I thought it a favorable moment to open a negotiation on the subject. Hastily availing myself therefore of such statistics as I could command, relative to our trade with Spain, I addressed a note of some length to the Spanish Government, and at the same time wrote home to my government for further instructions in the matter. A change in the Spanish Cabinet and in the course of Spanish policy destroyed the temporary hope I had conceived; neither did I ever receive from my own government any encouragement to renew the attempt.

From the Spanish Government he had received courteous and friendly treatment, but he noted a growing distrust and uneasiness regarding the movements of the United States in the Gulf of Mexico and our ultimate designs on Cuba. These suspicions had been accentuated by the 'incessant calumnies of the British press.' An ardent friend of England, and numbering Englishmen among his closest, dearest friends, he had been embittered by the British propaganda throughout Europe which was endeavoring to debase the national name. 'I had noticed for some time past slanderous

articles copied from the English journals into the Madrid
Gazette, in which all our acts and intentions in regard to the
Oregon question and the disputes with Mexico were crassly
misrepresented and we were charged with a grasping and
unprincipled avidity of empire.' This had alarmed him,
since the Madrid *Gazette* was 'exclusively a court paper
edited by persons about the Government.' Irving had gone
directly to Isturiz and pointedly asked if these slanders were
'actually believed and countenanced by the Cabinet.' The
Minister had assured him that he had not even noticed the
articles, that the *Gazette* was not used politically by the
Government but merely for the publication of official acts.
However, he would 'take care to have such offensive articles
excluded for the future.'

All this Irving sent to Buchanan, whose silence had become
offensive. Again explaining the reason for his prolonged
sojourn in England and referring to his previous explanation,
to which no reply had been received, he concluded his letter
with a stinger: 'If this silence is meant to intimate that the
explanation has not been satisfactory, I can only say that I
had rather the rebuke had been fully and frankly expressed
than left to mere surmise.'

WITHIN a week, Irving was to
have more occasion for indignation. A dispatch of May 14
announcing the declaration of war against Mexico did not
reach him until July 13. Through the European press, he
had known for some time that a state of war existed and that

the United States had blockaded the Mexican ports. He understood that official notice had been sent American Ministers in other countries for transmission to the governments to which they were accredited. But he had been in darkness all the while. Time and again he had been embarrassed in talking with Isturiz, who spoke of the war and manifested a keen interest. 'I had to confess myself without official instructions,' he wrote indignantly to Buchanan, 'as to the causes which led to it and the temper and spirit with which it would probably be carried on.'

He was saddened by the war and ascribed it to the bad advice given the Mexican Government. Had Slidell been received, Irving had no doubt that an amicable settlement would have been possible. He thought some European powers that had given Mexico the impression they would support her would betray her. And for days he was worried about General Taylor's fate, and lived in dread of some humiliating defeat that would prolong the war by forcing his country to continue the fighting until the disgrace should be wiped out. He wrote:

> When I read therefore the account of the gallant manner in which Taylor and his little army had acquitted themselves, and the generous manner in which they had treated their vanquished enemies, the tears absolutely started into my eyes.... I sincerely hope this brilliant victory will be followed up by magnanimous feeling on the part of our government, and that the war may be brought to a speedy close on fair and honorable terms.[1]

On the receipt of notice, Irving called on Isturiz. The Minister expressed much regret over the war and hoped that an honorable peace could be speedily effected. He assured Irving that Spain would maintain a strict neutrality, and

[1] Irving, *Life*, III, 111.

that he would issue orders to the authorities in Cuba and Puerto Rico to exert their utmost vigilance in preventing any attempts to fit out privateers in the islands against the United States. In reporting the conversation to Buchanan, Irving wrote:

> The opening of this war has been propitious. Should it be carried on in the same spirit and temper in which it has been commenced and brought to a speedy triumphant and magnanimous close, the present year will add a page to our national history of which every American patriot may well be proud.

In compliance with the request of Isturiz that Irving present him with a formal note covering the conversation, he set forth the cause and purpose of the war. Considering the source, this strong statement in justification of the war that still is the subject of controversy deserves more notice than it ever has received. Beginning with an explanation and apology for the delay in communicating such 'important intelligence . . . to Her Majesty's Government,' he launched vigorously into his statement.

'Whatever may be said of the ambitious designs and the aggressive policy of the United States with regard to Mexico,' he said, 'I feel authorized to assure Your Excellency that we have engaged in this war with extreme reluctance. It is our interest and it has ever been our inclination that Mexico should be a powerful republic, and that our relations with her should be of the most friendly character.' But a succession of revolutions, and the character of some of the heads of her government, had 'brought her to the brink of ruin.' The United States had hoped for 'a stable government, sufficiently powerful and pacific to prevent and punish aggressions upon her neighbors.' But for years we had been subjected 'to a series of wrongs and insults.' True, 'she pledged her public faith in solemn treaties to redress, but the treaties have been disregarded and the wrongs complained of have been reiterated.' Our commerce had been all but 'annihilated by the outrages and distortions practiced by her authorities upon our merchants, while all attempts to obtain indemnity have been fruitless.' Despite all this, we had acted with forbearance and patience. 'Ultimately the Mexican Government chose to consider the annexation of Texas ... as a violation of her rights, though that republic was an independent power, owing no allegiance to Mexico, constituting no part of her territory or rightful jurisdiction, and although its independence had been acknowledged by the most powerful and enlightened nations of Europe.'

At length, Irving wrote, Mexico broke off diplomatic relations and announced her determination to wage war. 'As a matter of self-preservation, we prepared to repel the threatened aggression.' Even then efforts were renewed to persuade her to an amicable agreement. 'Having received informal assurances from the Mexican Government that it was willing to renew diplomatic intercourse and would receive a Minister from the United States, we waived all ceremony as to the manner of reviving our relations, assuming the initiative and sending an Envoy Extraordinary and Minister Plenipotentiary to Mexico, clothed with full powers to adjust and definitely settle all pending difficulties between the two countries.' And how was he received? He was courteously welcomed at Vera Cruz, but before he could reach the capital a military revolution took place and General Paredes took possession of the Government by force of arms. 'Our envoy was refused reception and credence, notwithstanding that he came under the plighted faith of the Mexican Government. No attempt was made to ascertain what propositions he was empowered to offer; no propositions were suggested on the part of Mexico. His passports were given him and the door of peace was in a manner shut in his face.'

Thereafter, Irving wrote, nothing but threats of war were heard. Troops were marched in the direction of Texas. Our army was ordered to the frontier but with instructions to 'abstain from all aggressive acts toward Mexico or Mexican citizens.' And the result? 'The public papers have informed Your Excellency of the results. After the armies had remained encamped on the opposite bank of the Rio del Norte, which we claim as the boundary of Texas, the Mexican troops crossed the river, surprised and killed some of our soldiers, and took others prisoners.' Thereupon by practical unanimity Congress declared a state of war.

Such, said Irving, is the story. 'It has been forced upon us by the conduct of Mexico, who has either mistaken our forbearance for pusillanimity or has been urged on by evil counsels to take advantage of a crisis when we appeared to be on the point of hostilities with England on the Oregon question.' Now the war would be prosecuted with vigor both by land and sea, but 'we shall bear the olive branch in one hand and the sword in the other, and whenever she will accept the former the latter will be sheathed.'

With refreshing frankness he passed on to the purpose of the blockade. 'The object is to deprive Mexico of the revenues derived from customs and in the hope of speedily compelling her to offer or accept reasonable terms, and to induce foreign nations, who now enjoy a monopoly on her commerce, to exert their influence with her government in effecting a fair and honorable peace. The liberal mode in which this blockade has hitherto been conducted by the officers of our navy has been acknowledged in the English journals.' Referring to the possible danger of privateers' being fitted out in Cuban and Puerto Rican waters to prey upon the commerce of the United States, Irving asked that instructions be sent to the authorities in both islands. 'I feel confident,' he concluded, 'that the good faith manifested toward us on all other occasions by the Spanish Government will continue throughout the present conflict in which we unwillingly are involved, and that it will discountenance anything calculated to add to the evils of a war which it is the desire of the United States to conduct and terminate with as little injury as possible to the general interest of the civilized world.' [1] Having written this, his final and perhaps his most interesting dispatch, Irving laid his pen aside and turned from his desk.

I RVING'S successor reached Madrid on July 23, and Irving was busy packing. Members of the Ministry and his colleagues of the diplomatic corps were sorry to see him go. During the next few days he was occupied in making his farewell calls: on the de Bressons, within whose Embassy he had passed merry evenings; on Bulwer, whose irony and dry humor and languid manner he would miss; on Prince Carini, whose charming wife he had found so interesting; on the Albuquerques, with whom he had from the beginning enjoyed an intimate friendship. And then he went to the palace for his last audience with the Queen, whose real well-wisher he had been, and whose vicissitudes

[1] MS. Archives, United States Embassy, Madrid, July 17, 1846.

and dangers had often moved him. 'I could not but feel a little sensitive in visiting the royal palace for the last time, and passing through its vast apartments but partially lighted up,' he wrote his sister. He was received in an inner cabinet by Isabella, attended by Isturiz and several ladies- and gentlemen-in-waiting. His speech in taking leave was brief. He said:

> For my own part, I can assure Your Majesty that I shall carry with me into private life the same ardent desire for the welfare of Spain, and the same deep interest in the fortunes and happiness of its youthful sovereign, which have actuated me during my official career; and I now take leave of Your Majesty, wishing you, from the bottom of my heart, a long and happy life and a reign which may form a glorious epoch in the history of this country.

The youthful sovereign, expressing her regret at his departure, also touched the personal note. She replied:

> You may take with you into private life the intimate conviction that your frank and loyal conduct has contributed to draw closer the amicable relations which exist between North America and the Spanish nation, and that your distinguished personal merits have gained in my heart the appreciation which you merit by more than one title.

And for the last time Irving passed from the presence of Isabella, to whom he had presented his credentials in the presence of her nurse.

That evening at six o'clock in the carriage of Weismuller of the House of Rothschild, to whom he had offered the refuge of the Legation on a perilous occasion, Irving drove out from the sunny streets of Madrid en route for France. The middle of August found him in London, and early in September he embarked on the *Cambria* for Boston.

It HAS been written with reason that Spain always calls one back, but Irving was never to see its plains and mountains again. But in the quiet of his closet at Sunnyside on the Hudson he was to remember it with a deep affection to the end of his days. In his meditations he was to revisit it in spirit and to recall his intensive labors in the house of Rich; his joyous hours with the d'Oubrils romping on the floor with the children; chatting with the lively Antoinette; his merry parties with Dal Borgo; his mornings in the studio of Wilkie; his meanderings among the countless treasures of Toledo; his journeys to the Escorial. He was to relive in memory the thrilling days in Seville and the Sunday picnics at Guadalajara; his nocturnal rambles on the Alameda; his dinners at Mrs. Stalker's; his summer with Hall in the walled-in house near the city; his driftings down the river; his countless hours in the cool library of the cathedral; and the festival of Corpus Christi. Never was he to forget his summer in the country on the outskirts of the Port of Saint Mary, and least of all his memorable life at the Alhambra and his friend the Duke of Gor, whose palace always gave him hearty welcome. As history unrolled and clouds descended on the reign of Isabella, he was always to recall her as a winsome, innocent child with preternatural poise, and to hear from afar her merry laughter at her first ball at Narvaez's. When he read the story of an imperial wedding in the Tuileries he was to recall the tiny baby he had danced upon his knee in the castle of the Count of Teba near Granada, and the baby, later a dashing belle who cast a spell on all who saw her at the balls of the Madrid of the forties. Again he was to rise at dawn to jolt over the road to Aranjuez to the meeting of the Queens, and to follow the court to Barcelona and marvel at the lordly manner in which Dal Borgo lavished coins in the villages on the way. And often he ascended in recollection the grand marble staircase to undergo the torture of interminable standing before the throne, and to push through the festive crowds of the capital with the sprightly Countess de Bresson. The Albuquerques, the Carinis, and Bulwer would sit in fancy at his table at Sunnyside. He would review again with Espartero the troops in the Prado, and see Narvaez riding through the city gates to exile.

Never was he to forget or cease to love the expansive plains shut in by mountains in their purple haze, the rugged, awe-inspiring mountain passes, the rich fields of Andalusia, the picturesque age-old villages drowsing in the sun, the witchery of a Spanish night, the geniality of the Spanish people, and the beauty, charm, and glory that is Spain.

THE END

INDEX

INDEX